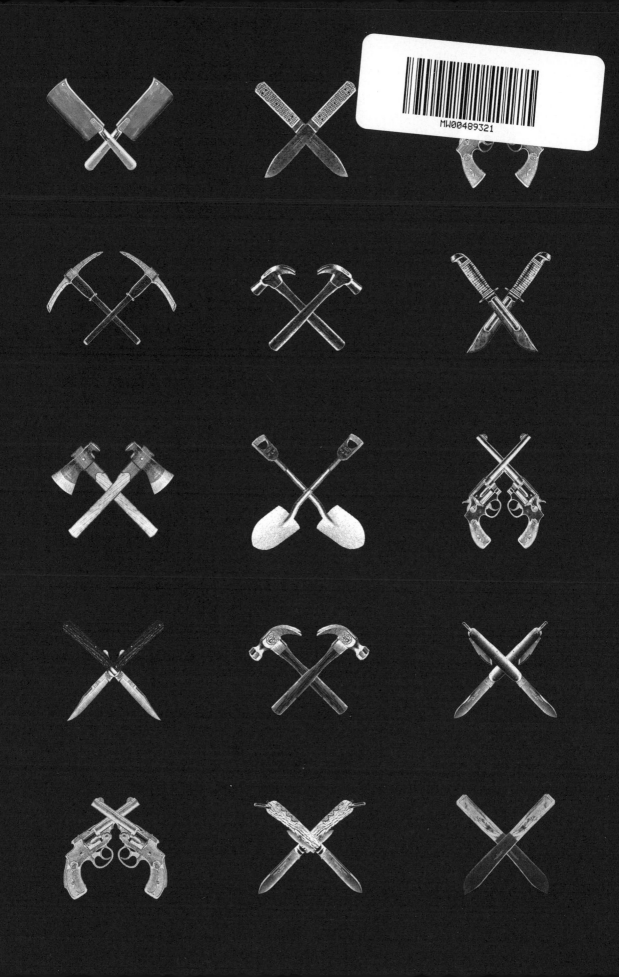

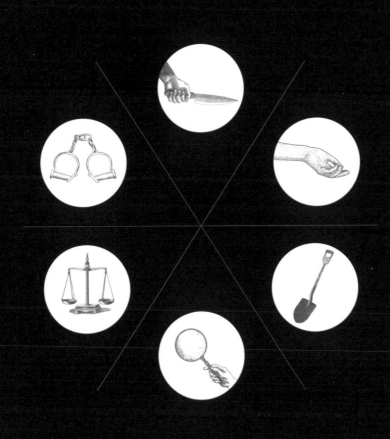

MURDER MAPS.

CRIME SCENES *REVISITED.*

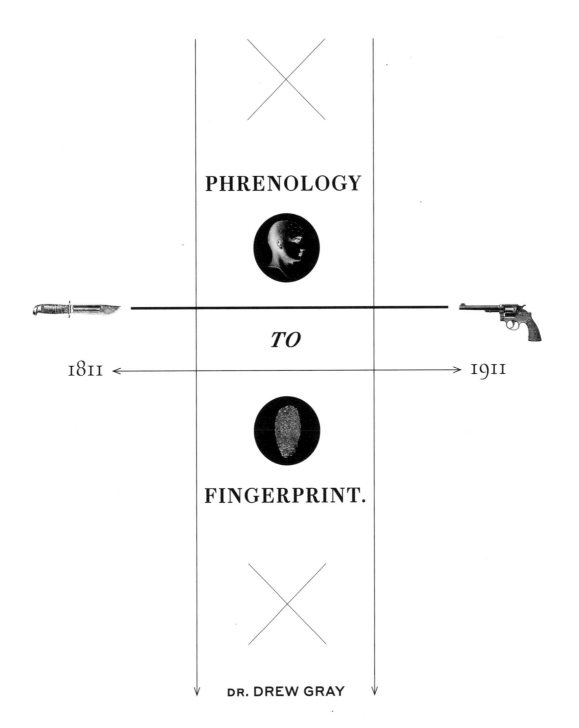

PHRENOLOGY

TO

1811

1911

FINGERPRINT.

DR. DREW GRAY

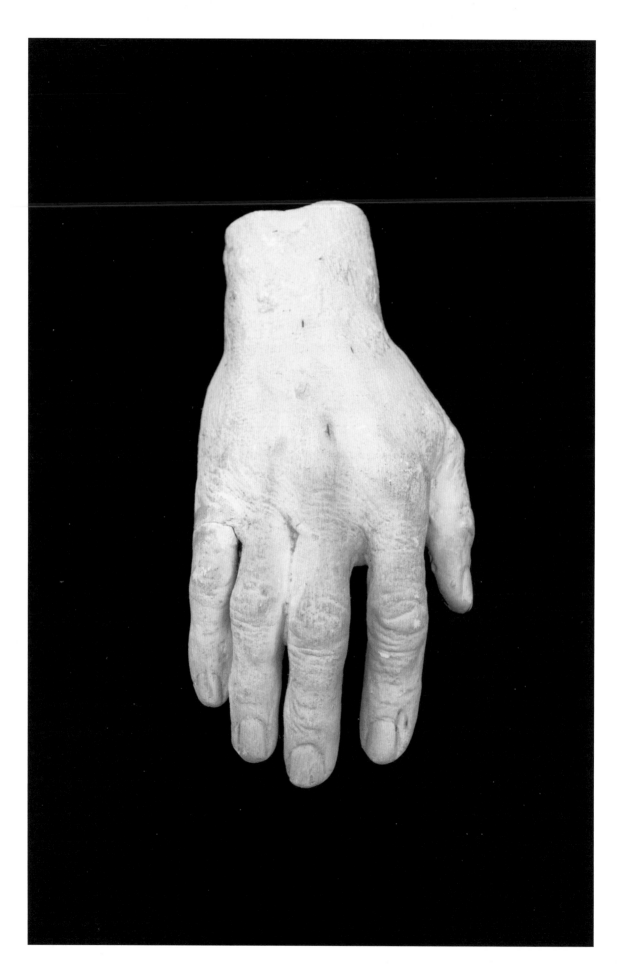

CONTENTS.

6.
INTRODUCTION — SENSATIONALIZED MURDER
& THE RISE OF THE DETECTIVE.

PART ONE.

EUROPE.

20.
ENGLAND — LONDON.

50.
ENGLAND — SUFFOLK.

52.
ENGLAND — LIVERPOOL.

58.
SCOTLAND — GLASGOW.

66.
FRANCE — PARIS.

82.
FRANCE — AUVERGNE.

100.
GERMANY — BAVARIA.

106.
AUSTRIA — VIENNA.

114.
HUNGARY — BUDAPEST.

118.
BOHEMIA — PRAGUE + POLNÁ

120.
ITALY — EMILIA ROMAGNA.

128.
SPAIN — MADRID.

PART TWO.

NORTH AMERICA.

132.
USA — NEW YORK CITY.

146.
USA — MASSACHUSETTS.

150.
USA — INDIANA.

154.
USA — CHICAGO.

174.
USA — KANSAS.

184.
USA — SAN FRANCISCO.

PART THREE.

AUSTRALIA.

196.
AUSTRALIA — NEW SOUTH WALES.

203.
AUSTRALIA — VICTORIA.

214.
A CRIMINOLOGY MATRIX.

220.
FURTHER READING.

221.
SOURCES OF ILLUSTRATIONS.

222.
INDEX.

224.
ACKNOWLEDGMENTS.

This Print is given gratuitous to the purchasers of Weekly Dispatch.

The Head of CORDER as it appeared on the dissecting table.

A correct representation of the Execution of W.m CORDER, the Hangmen is adjusting the rope round the Prisoners neck, while an Assistant is supporting the wretched man M.r Orridge is announcing CORDER's acknowledgement of the justness of his sentence

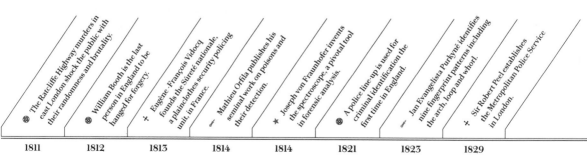

1811	1812	1813	1814	1814	1821	1823	1829
◉ The Ratcliffe Highway murders in east London shock the public with their randomness and brutality.	◉ William Booth is the last person in England to be hanged for forgery.	✛ Eugène-François Vidocq founds the Sûreté nationale, a plainclothes security policing unit, in France.	⚊ Mathieu Orfila publishes his seminal work on poisons and their detection.	★ Joseph von Fraunhofer invents the spectroscope, a pivotal tool in forensic analysis.	◉ A police line-up is used for criminal identification the first time in England.	⚊ Jan Evangelista Purkyně identifies nine fingerprint patterns including the arch, loop and whorl.	✛ Sir Robert Peel establishes the Metropolitan Police Service in London.

INTRODUCTION.

SENSATIONALIZED MURDER &

THE RISE OF THE DETECTIVE.

1811 · to · 1911

Murder has always fascinated us. From Cain to Crippen and from Brutus to Bundy, we want to understand the motivation behind the crime, the manner in which it was carried out and exactly how the perpetrator was tracked down. In the 18th century, our keen interest was exploited by pamphleteers and in the 19th by newspapermen. Up to the mid-1800s, crowds of spectators could watch a murderer hang in front of them and then read the story of their crime reproduced in a cheap 'murder ballad' sold as a souvenir of the grisly occasion. Even after that, when executions were conducted behind closed doors, there was no reduction in appetites to read the stories; in fact, the last quarter of the century saw a growth in 'murder news'.

Taking its lead from the papers of the time, this book revisits murders and serial killings of the 19th century, focusing on murderers whose gruesome crimes shocked their contemporaries. Every murder is plotted on a map of the area to show exactly where it took place. Psychologist David Canter's groundbreaking work in plotting the murders committed by Peter Sutcliffe between 1975 and 1980 in Yorkshire, England, to demonstrate the common behaviours of killers has been applied throughout, including to 1880s Whitechapel where the killer known only as 'Jack the Ripper' first established serial killing in the public consciousness.

Mapping murder allows us to explore homicides on both a micro and macro level. Not only can we map individual and serial murders to discover the connections between them, we can also analyse the distribution of murders to observe links between poverty, wealth, architecture and immigration in the geography of killing. By taking a global perspective, this new study also reflects on the comparative nature and distribution of homicides across the world. Were patterns in London, for example, repeated in Paris or New York, both international cities with diverse populations? To what extent were killings in Australia, the American West or other 'colonial' locations different (or differently detected)?

Opposite. A COMMEMORATIVE PRINT OF THE EXECUTION OF WILLIAM CORDER IN 1828 FOR THE MURDER OF MARIA MARTEN AT THE RED BARN. THE MURDER, AND THEN WILLIAM CORDER'S TRIAL AND SUBSEQUENT HANGING, WAS ONE OF THE MOST SENSATIONAL NEWS STORIES OF THE 19TH CENTURY.

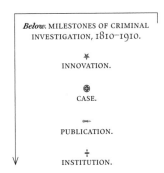

Below. MILESTONES OF CRIMINAL INVESTIGATION, 1810–1910.

✴ INNOVATION.

🌐 CASE.

⌖ PUBLICATION.

† INSTITUTION.

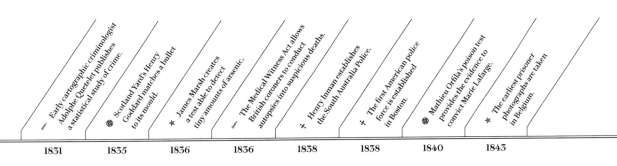

Early cartographic criminologist Adolphe Quetelet publishes a statistical study of crime. — 1831

Scotland Yard's Henry Goddard matches a bullet to its mould. 🌐 1835

James Marsh creates a test able to detect tiny amounts of arsenic. ✴ 1836

The Medical Witness Act allows British coroners to conduct autopsies into suspicious deaths. 1836

Henry Inman establishes the South Australia Police. † 1838

The first American police force is established in Boston. † 1838

Mathieu Orfila's poison test provides the evidence to convict Marie Lafarge. 🌐 1840

The earliest prisoner photographs are taken in Belgium. ✴ 1843

Criminologists and historians of crime have long agreed that there was a long-term overall decline in homicide between the medieval and the modern age. Researchers attempting to plot this decline have suggested that the growth of nation states and the development of a capitalist economy both contributed. As a society, we gradually became more 'civilized' and thus, so the thesis suggests, less likely to resort to violence. Conversely, as we became less physically violent as a society, we grew more fascinated by the violence carried out by the minority. Popular culture sated that interest by offering up images of sadistic killers as examples of the dark side of human nature and presented murderers as representatives of the 'other' at large in modern society.

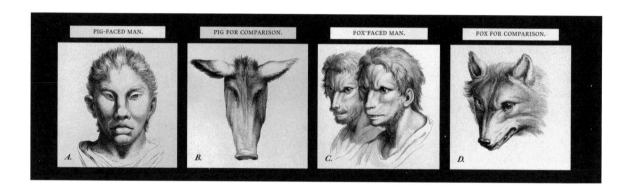

| PIG-FACED MAN. | PIG FOR COMPARISON. | FOX-FACED MAN. | FOX FOR COMPARISON. |

Above. IMAGES FROM CHARLES LE BRUN'S *A SERIES OF LITHOGRAPHIC DRAWINGS ILLUSTRATIVE OF THE RELATIONSHIP BETWEEN THE HUMAN PHYSIOGNOMY AND THAT OF THE BRUTE CREATION* (1671, TRANS. 1827). LE BRUN'S ILLUSTRATIONS ACCOMPANIED A LECTURE IN WHICH HE OUTLINED THE PRINCIPLES OF PHYSIOGNOMY AND ITS STATED ABILITY TO ATTRIBUTE PERSONALITY TRAITS TO PHYSICAL FACIAL CHARACTERISTICS. IT GAVE RISE TO THE NOTION THAT IF YOUR FACE RESEMBLED AN ANIMAL'S, THEN YOUR PERSONALITY MIGHT ALSO BE SIMILAR.

Much of the interest in murder and violent crime was concentrated in the cities of the world. As the Industrial Revolution gained pace during the 19th century, people left the countryside for the crowded metropolises. Such areas became melting pots of multi-culturalism: places where fortunes were made and lost, and where new ideas were formed. Crucially, though, they also became places of social danger, associated with crime, immorality and disease. Anonymity and alienation contributed to the idea that crime and criminals were endemic. By contrast, rural areas were seen to offer an escape to a simpler, safer and more idyllic past. In fact, murders continued to occur in country areas; indeed, the more remote the area, the less likely it was that a murder would be reported, the crime solved and the killer prosecuted. In the cities, sophisticated policing systems developed alongside scientific and technological advances, increasing the detection and prosecution rates there, and forcing murderers to be ever more cunning and resourceful to avoid capture and imprisonment.

Professional policing was still a relatively new innovation in the middle of the 1800s. London's Metropolitan Police Service was only

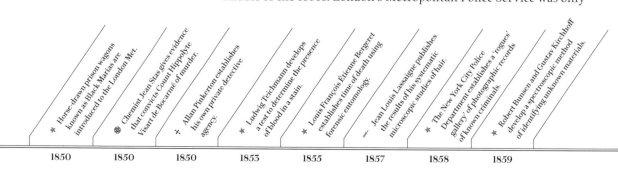

Horse-drawn prison wagons known as Black Marias are introduced to the London Met.

Chemist Jean Stas gives evidence that convicts Count Hippolyte Visart de Bocarmé of murder.

Allan Pinkerton establishes his own private detective agency.

Ludwig Teichmann develops a test to determine the presence of blood in a stain.

Louis François Étienne Bergeret establishes time of death using forensic entomology.

Jean Louis Lassaigne publishes the results of his systematic microscopic studies of hair.

The New York City Police Department establishes a 'rogues' gallery' of photographic records of known criminals.

Robert Bunsen and Gustav Kirchhoff develop a spectroscopic method of identifying unknown materials.

| 1850 | 1850 | 1850 | 1853 | 1855 | 1857 | 1858 | 1859 |

founded in 1829, New York's in 1845, and, although the Paris 'police' had existed since the French Revolution, the police force there did not create a 'detective' branch until the 1830s. France undoubtedly led the way in detection techniques, establishing the first private detective agency at the beginning of the century, led by Eugène-François Vidocq (1775–1857), a former convict and police informer. Vidocq was appointed head of the Bureau de Sûreté in Paris and given the brief to detect crime and catch criminals. In the early years of detection, the idea that it 'took a thief to catch a thief' was dominant, and Vidocq was supported by a squad of ex-convicts and *mouchards* (police informants). This approach persisted until the 1870s when the importance of scientific detection gradually began to be appreciated. London's Detective Department was created

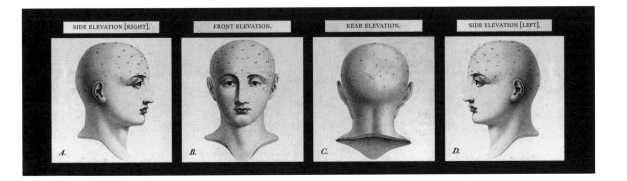

in 1842, following some high-profile failures to solve serious crimes and fears over the growing number of attempts to kill Queen Victoria. The Criminal Investigation Department (CID) – the nerve centre of all detection in modern Britain – was not instituted until 1878 (and only then in the wake of a scandal that had implicated several members of the Detective Department in a betting scam). The city of Boston formed the first US detective agency in 1846, with other US cities following its lead.

The credit for the development of modern forensics must be given to a number of men working in the last quarter of the 19th century and the first decades of the 20th, but one man, Alphonse Bertillon (1853–1914), was the undisputed father of the science. As policing developed, it was quickly recognized that identity was the key to solving crime. The problem was that record keeping was patchy at best and so criminals could evade capture simply by changing their name, moving about the country and altering their appearance. Working in the Prefecture of the Paris Police, Bertillon studied the physical characteristics of people, working on the principle that you could narrow down the number of possible suspects by using data about them. He carefully measured the size of heads, distance between eyes, lengths of fingers and so on.

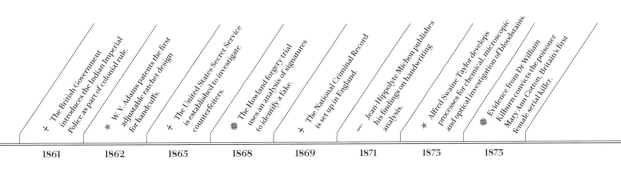

+ The British Government introduces the Indian Imperial Police as part of colonial rule. — **1861**

★ W. V. Adams patents the first adjustable ratchet design for handcuffs. — **1862**

+ The United States Secret Service is established to investigate counterfeiters. — **1865**

⊛ The Howland forgery trial uses an analysis of signatures to identify a fake. — **1868**

+ The National Criminal Record is set up in England. — **1869**

— Jean-Hippolyte Michon publishes his findings on handwriting analysis. — **1871**

★ Alfred Swaine Taylor develops processes for chemical, microscopic and optical investigation of bloodstains. — **1873**

⊛ Evidence from Dr William Kilburn convicts the poisoner Mary Ann Cotton, Britain's first female serial killer. — **1873**

Criminals might colour their hair or shave off their beards, even cover up tattoos, but they could not alter their physical dimensions. Then, using the new technology of photography, he recorded all the data, which were then indexed and cross-referenced to enable suspects to be tracked down and prosecuted successfully. Bertillon also invented the 'mug shot', the quintessential tool of police forces everywhere, although he gave it the more enigmatic title of *portrait parlé*, or 'speaking portrait'. According to an early biographer, 'He was one of the creators of criminal investigation as an applied science, and he was thus one of the architects of the modern concepts of justice.'

Bertillon's work intersected with that of others, including the Italian criminologist Cesare Lombroso (1835–1909). In 1876, Lombroso

 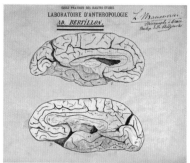

Left. A JAPANESE EXHIBIT AT THE 1904 WORLD'S FAIR IN ST LOUIS, MISSOURI, DISPLAYING CRIMINAL IDENTIFICATION CHARTS BASED ON ALPHONSE BERTILLON'S SYSTEM.

Right. BRAIN SECTIONS DRAWN BY ANTHROPOLOGIST LÉONCE MANOUVRIER, C. 1900.

Opposite. ALPHONSE BERTILLON'S *TABLEAU SYNOPTIC DES TRAITS PHYSIONOMIQUES* (SYNOPTIC TABLE OF PHYSIOGNOMIC FEATURES). IT WAS DESIGNED TO HELP POLICE CLERKS APPLY HIS CLASSIFICATION SYSTEM OF THE HUMAN FACE, KNOWN AS *BERTILLONAGE*.

published his major work – *Criminal Man* – in which he set out the concept of the 'born criminal' and the case for the study of criminal anthropology. Like Bertillon, Lombroso was fascinated by the physicality of the criminals he studied. He recorded the physical features of prisoners and the bodies of executed felons, and allied particular features with specific sorts of criminal activity. He noted that 'habitual murderers have a cold, glassy stare and eyes that are sometimes bloodshot and filmy'. Their noses were 'always large' and their 'beards are scanty'. By contrast, rapists had 'sparkling eyes, delicate features, and swollen lips and eyelids'. He viewed crime as a 'natural' activity (i.e. inevitable for some people) rather than an individual choice. Crime would always exist, he argued, and so evolving better methods of detecting it was paramount. For contemporaries who were familiar with Charles Darwin's (1809–82) theory of evolution, Lombroso's thesis of criminal atavism (that some individuals had not developed as quickly or as far as others) sounded rational. Moreover, Lombroso's scientific approach to criminology chimed with the dominant philosophy of the period, which was scientific positivism.

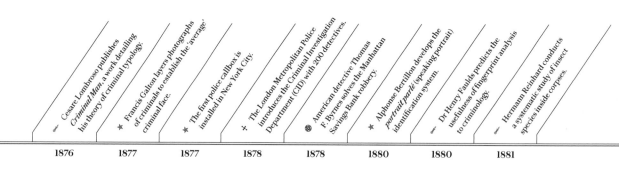

Cesare Lombroso publishes *Criminal Man*, a work detailing his theory of criminal typology.

Francis Galton layers photographs of criminals to establish the 'average' criminal face.

The first police callbox is installed in New York City.

The London Metropolitan Police introduces the Criminal Investigation Department (CID) with 200 detectives.

American detective Thomas F. Byrnes solves the Manhattan Savings Bank robbery.

Alphonse Bertillon develops the *portrait parlé* (speaking portrait) identification system.

Dr Henry Faulds predicts the usefulness of fingerprint analysis to criminology.

Hermann Reinhard conducts a systematic study of insect species inside corpses.

| 1876 | 1877 | 1877 | 1878 | 1878 | 1880 | 1880 | 1881 |

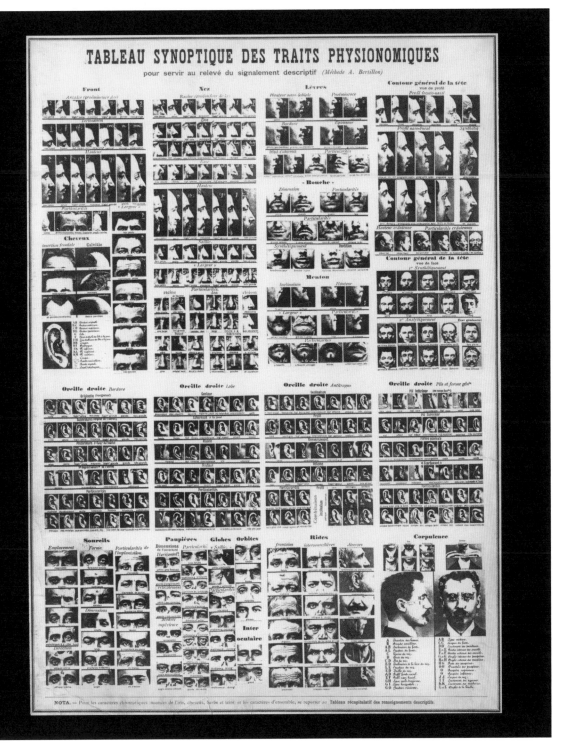

TABLEAU SYNOPTIQUE DES TRAITS PHYSIONOMIQUES

pour servir au relevé du signalement descriptif (Méthode A. Bertillon)

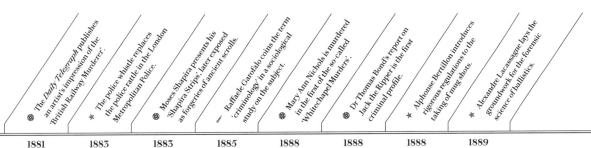

The *Daily Telegraph* publishes an artist's impression of the 'British Railway Murderer'. — 1881

The police whistle replaces the police rattle in the London Metropolitan Police. — 1883

Moses Shapira presents his 'Shapira Strips', later exposed as forgeries of ancient scrolls. — 1883

Raffaele Garofalo coins the term 'criminology' in a sociological study on the subject. — 1885

Mary Ann Nichols is murdered in the first of the so-called 'Whitechapel Murders'. — 1888

Dr Thomas Bond's report on Jack the Ripper is the first criminal profile. — 1888

Alphonse Bertillon introduces rigorous regulations to the taking of mug-shots. — 1888

Alexandre Lacassagne lays the groundwork for the forensic science of ballistics. — 1889

In 1893, an Austrian jurist and magistrate named Hans Gross (1847–1915) published *Criminal Investigation: A Practical Handbook for Magistrates, Police Officers and Lawyers*. One of the founding fathers of criminal profiling, Gross, together with French criminologist Edmond Locard (1877–1966), was a pioneer in crime scene investigation (CSI). Gross set out three essential principles for CSI:

a) The hermetic isolation of the crime scene.
b) Its 'systematic excavation for material evidence'.
c) The establishment of a system for ensuring that all evidence was carefully logged, retained and kept intact on its journey through the criminal justice system.

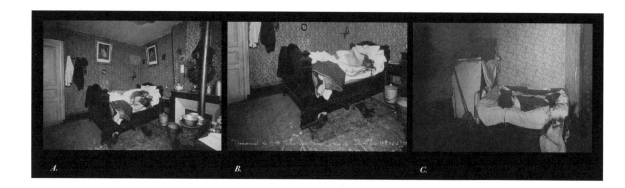

A.   B.   C.

Above. CRIME SCENE PHOTOGRAPHS FROM ALPHONSE BERTILLON'S *ALBUM OF PARIS CRIME SCENES* (1901–08). HAVING DEVELOPED THE USE OF PHOTOGRAPHY TO CAPTURE 'MUG SHOTS' OF CAREER CRIMINALS, BERTILLON LATER USED FORENSIC PHOTOGRAPHY TO PRESERVE THE CRIME SCENE AND THUS AID DETECTION.

Gross was adamant that one person – the investigating officer (IO) – should be in charge of any crime scene and take responsibility for it. He had to be an observant and persistent person. 'He will examine little pieces of paper that have been thrown away,' wrote Gross. 'Everything will afford an opportunity for drawing conclusions and explaining what must have previously taken place.' He warned against holding preconceptions and taking things at face value, which he considered were rooted in human instinct and culture. We tend to see what we expect to see, and a good IO had to acknowledge and transcend this trait to see beyond the obvious. One of Gross's innovations was the use of the microscope, which allowed investigators to examine particles of dust invisible to the naked eye. Locard built on Gross's initial observation that dust retained all manner of information that could help identify criminals and explain exactly what had happened at the scene of the crime. Locard also took inspiration from the greatest fictional detective of the late 19th century, Arthur Conan Doyle's (1859–1930) Sherlock Holmes. The exploits of the Baker Street private detective captivated late Victorian readers and did much to establish a positive image of

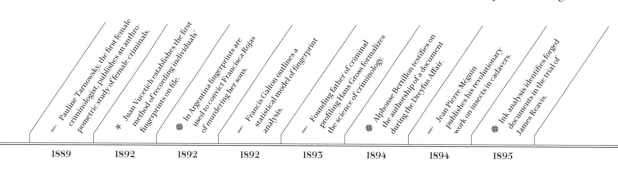

Pauline Tarnowsky: the first female criminologist, publishes an anthropometric study of female criminals.

Juan Vucetich establishes the first method of recording individuals' fingerprints on file.

In Argentina fingerprints are used to convict Francisca Rojas of murdering her sons.

Francis Galton outlines a statistical model of fingerprint analysis.

Founding father of criminal profiling Hans Gross formalizes the science of criminology.

Alphonse Bertillon testifies on the authorship of a document during the Dreyfus Affair.

Jean Pierre Mégnin publishes his revolutionary work on insects in cadavers.

Ink analysis identifies forged documents in the trial of James Reavis.

1889   1892   1892   1892   1893   1894   1894   1895

detection in the minds of the British public, who previously had perceived plain-clothed police as spies.

Locard's work was taken up and developed by French criminologist Dr Jean Alexandre Eugène Lacassagne (1843–1924), head of the Department of Legal Medicine at the University of Lyon, and a close friend of the Parisian forensic specialist. Lacassagne devised a system for matching a bullet found at a crime scene to the gun that fired it, and was able to calculate the length of time a body had been putrefying, enabling detectives to determine time of death more accurately. In 1886, he founded the journal *Archives danthropologie criminelle*, which showcased innovations in criminal investigation from around the world. By dissecting the bodies of victims of murder

D.   E.   F.

and those supposed to have died of 'natural causes', Lacassagne was able to solve a number of murder cases and eventually to enable the conviction of French serial killer Joseph Vacher (1869–98).

Since the 1820s, it had been clear that fingerprints provided a unique reference point of identification. Sir William Herschel (1833–1917), while working as a civil servant in India, started putting fingerprints on contracts in the 1850s to prevent fraud. In the 1870s, while working in a hospital in Japan, Dr Henry Faulds (1843–1930) became convinced that each person's fingerprints were unique and succeeded in exonerating an assumed criminal on the basis that his fingerprints differed from those discovered at the scene of the crime. He contacted Charles Darwin to ask him to help him work on his ideas but Darwin declined, passing his ideas on to Francis Galton (1822–1911). In 1880, Faulds published a paper on fingerprint identification in the magazine *Nature*, and in 1886 offered his ideas to the police in London, who promptly dismissed them. The Met were using Bertillon's system and did not see the need to introduce fingerprinting. In 1888, Galton submitted a Royal Institution paper on fingerprint patterns without crediting Faulds, and in 1892 his book

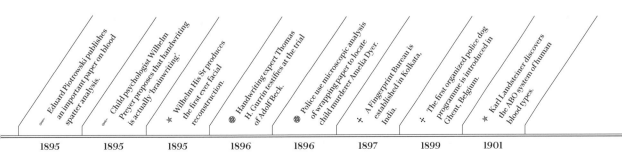

Eduard Piotrowski publishes an important paper on blood spatter analysis.

Child psychologist Wilhelm Preyer proposes that handwriting is actually 'brainwriting'.

Wilhelm His Sr produces the first ever facial reconstruction.

Handwriting expert Thomas H. Gurrin testifies at the trial of Adolf Beck.

Police use microscopic analysis of wrapping paper to locate child murderer Amelia Dyer.

A Fingerprint Bureau is established in Kolkata, India.

The first organized police dog programme is introduced in Ghent, Belgium.

Karl Landsteiner discovers the ABO system of human blood types.

| 1895 | 1895 | 1895 | 1896 | 1896 | 1897 | 1899 | 1901 |

'One can only see what one observes, and one observes
only things which are already in the mind.'

ALPHONSE BERTILLON.

Above. CRIME SCENE PHOTOGRAPH BY ALPHONSE BERTILLON OF AN UNKNOWN
MURDER VICTIM IN PARIS, FRANCE.

'*Justice withers, prison corrupts and society has the criminals it deserves.*'

ALEXANDRE LACASSAGNE.

Above. CRIME SCENE PHOTO BY ALPHONSE BERTILLON OF ELENE POPESCU,
MURDERED AT THE HOTEL REGINA, PARIS, IN OCTOBER 1903.

Finger Prints was published. In it, he demonstrated that the chance of two sets of prints being identical (a 'false positive') was about 1 in 64 billion. In consequence, it was Galton who was given the credit for establishing fingerprinting as a 'major system of identification in forensic terms' (Nigel McCrery, 2013).

The first use of fingerprints to solve a murder in Britain took place in March 1905 in Deptford, London. Mr Farrow and his wife had been attacked and left for dead and the weekly takings had been stolen. Chief Investigator Melville Macnaghten (1853–1921) found a fingerprint on an inside tray of the cash box. Detective Inspector Charles Stockley Collins (dates unknown) examined the print, and established that it did not match the Farrows' prints, nor any of

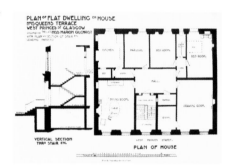

Right. PLAN OF THE HOUSE IN WHICH MARION GILCHRIST WAS MURDERED IN GLASGOW, SCOTLAND, DECEMBER 1908, TOGETHER WITH A PLAN OF THE AREA. HER BODY WAS FOUND IN THE DINING ROOM, WITH HER SKULL SMASHED IN.

Opposite. EXAMPLES OF MUG SHOTS FROM ALPHONSE BERTILLON'S *ALBUM OF PARIS CRIME SCENES* (1901–08). BERTILLON PIONEERED THE USE OF PHOTOGRAPHY AS A TOOL FOR IDENTIFYING CRIMINALS. USING A COMBINATION OF PHYSICAL MEASUREMENTS AND IMAGES HE CREATED A '*PORTRAIT PARLÉ*' ('SPEAKING PORTRAIT') OF OFFENDERS SUCH AS THESE.

those on file (c. 80,000–90,000 at the time). Eventually, a vagabond named Alfred Stratton (1882–1905) was identified as a likely suspect along with his brother Albert (1884–1905). The print matched Alfred's right thumb and he was charged with murder. They were convicted of murder at the Old Bailey and hanged on 23 May 1905.

In the 1800s, it was not scientifically possible to distinguish different blood types, or even whether blood was human or animal. In London in 1888, throughout the Jack the Ripper murders, the killer could have walked around Whitechapel covered in the blood of his victims, safe in the knowledge that it could not be used to convict him. It was not until 1901 that a German scientist named Paul Theodore Uhlenhuth (1870–1957) developed an efficient test to identify human blood, the basis of which is still in use by police today.

This book begins with one of the most celebrated murders of the pre-Victorian age, the Ratcliffe Highway murders of 1811. The slaughter of two families within a week of each other within a small area outraged Londoners and led to early calls for police reform. The period covered by this volume ends in 1910 with the arrest of Hawley Harvey Crippen (1862–1910) for the murder of his wife, Cora – the first arrest to be made through the use of the wireless telegraph. ∎

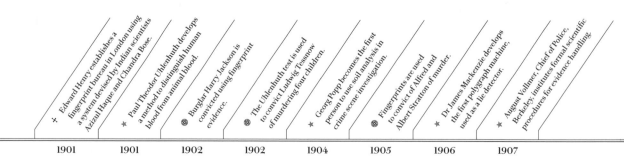

Edward Henry establishes a fingerprint bureau in London using a system devised by Indian scientists Azizul Haque and Chandra Bose.

Paul Theodor Uhlenhuth develops a method to distinguish human blood from animal blood.

Burglar Harry Jackson is convicted using fingerprint evidence.

The Uhlenhuth test is used to convict Ludwig Tessnow of murdering four children.

Georg Popp becomes the first person to use soil analysis in crime-scene investigation.

Fingerprints are used to convict Alfred and Albert Stratton of murder.

Dr James Mackenzie develops the first polygraph machine, used as a lie detector.

August Vollmer, Chief of Police, Berkeley, institutes formal scientific procedures for evidence handling.

| 1901 | 1901 | 1902 | 1902 | 1904 | 1905 | 1906 | 1907 |

A. G. AMIOT.
✕ MME. LUCAS.

B. P. AMIOT.
✕ MME. LUCAS.

C. MME. BERTIN.
✕ MME. LUCAS.

D. CHARLES HUET.
✕ ANDRÉ HAUG.

E. VICTOR BENDER.
✕ ANDRÉ HAUG.

F. M. DEMARCHALIEZ.
✕ MME. LEGRAND.

G. M. LAMOULINE.
✕ MME. LEGRAND.

H. AUGUSTE BONNET.
✕ M. LEGRAND.

I. CHARLES BRESSON.
✕ M. LEGRAND.

J. EUGÈNE SCHULLE.
✕ M. LEGRAND.

K. MARIA BORDEAUX.
✕ MME. MERVELET.

L. EMILE BOUSQUET.
✕ M. MELLEY.

M. MAURICE ASSELIN.
✕ M. MELLEY.

N. GEORGES GOULET.
✕ M. MELLEY.

O. M. FRANCATEL.
✕ M. MELLEY.

P. PAUL JULES MARTIN.
✕ BERTHE BRIENNE.

Q. LAURE GANGES.
✕ JEANNE BEAUGE.

R. BAPTISTE BEAUMONT.
✕ UNKNOWN.

S. VICTORINE GIRIAT.
✕ EUGÉNIE FOUGÈRE.

T. HENRI BASSOT.
✕ EUGÉNIE FOUGÈRE.

+ The Bureau of Investigation (now known as the FBI) is created in the USA. — **1908**

+ Archibald Reiss creates the first academic institute for forensic science in Lausanne, Switzerland. — **1909**

— Albert Osborn publishes his seminal work on the science of questioned document examination. — **1910**

+ Alice Stebbins Wells is the first female police officer hired in the USA. — **1910**

— Frederick Brayley publishes the first American textbook on the use of fingerprinting. — **1910**

+ Edmond Locard establishes the first police laboratory in Lyon, France. — **1910**

⊛ Thomas Jennings's conviction for murder is the first to use fingerprints as evidence in the USA. — **1910**

⊛ Dr Crippen is the first criminal to be arrested with the aid of radiotelegraphy. — **1910**

PART ONE.

JOHN WILLIAMS + FREDERICK MANNING + MARIA MANNING + KATE WEBSTER
PERCY LEFROY MAPLETON + ISRAEL LIPSKI + GEORGE GALLETLY + JACK THE RIPPER
MARY PEARCEY + ANDREA SCOTTI DI CARLO + THOMAS WILLIAM CRIPPS
WILFRED MORITZ FRANKS + ALFRED STRATTON + ALBERT STRATTON
HAWLEY HARVEY CRIPPEN + WILLIAM CORDER + MARGARET HIGGINS
CATHERINE FLANNAGAN + LEWIS PARRY + FLORENCE MAYBRICK
MADELEINE SMITH + EDWARD WILLIAM PRITCHARD + OSCAR SLATER
GABRIELLE BOMPARD + MICHEL EYRAUD + LOUIS ANASTAY + CLAIRE REYMOND
LOUIS COGNEVAUX + KIESGEN + TRUEL + CODEBO + PILLOT
HENRI THIBŒF + MARIE PIETTE + PAUL SCHEFFER + PAUL VAN NOORWEGHE
PAUL JULES MARTIN + FREDERICK GREULING

EUROPE.

CÉLESTIN-NICOLAS PIERSON + JULES MORROT + VICTOR PAGÈS + ANTHELME GAY
JEAN-JACQUES LIABEUF + MARTIN DUMOLLARD + MARIE-ANNE MARTINET
JOSEPH VACHER + VICTOR GRENETIER + LOUIS ALLAIN + FRANÇOIS MARIOTTI
LUIGI GIOVANNI RICHETTO + ANNET GAUMET + EVARISTE NOUGUIER
VICTORINE GIRIAT + HENRI BASSOT + CHAUFFEURS OF DRÔME + FERDINAND GUMP
JOHANN BERCHTOLD + MATHIAS KNEISSL + JAN JIŘÍ GRÁZL + JAKOB FAHDING
IGNAZ STANGEL + HUGO SCHENK + SIMON SCHOSTERITZ + PÁL SPANGA
MIHÁLY OLÁH PITÉLI + JÁNOS BERECZ + BÉLA KISS + OTAKAR DOLEŽAL
FRANTIŠEK DRAGOUN + JOSEF KŘÍŽ + LEOPOLD HILSNER + STEFANO 'IL PASSATORE'
PELLONI + GAETANO 'LO SPIRITO' PROSPERI + PIETRO CENERI + TULLIO MURRI
CLARA MARINA ANTONIO MARINA + HIGINIA DE BALAGUER OSTALÉ + DOLORES ÁVILA

JOHN WILLIAMS.
× 9.

WEAPON.	TYPOLOGY.	POLICING.
MAUL.	RECKLESS ACT.	PARISH WATCH.

29 RATCLIFFE HIGHWAY, WAPPING.
THE KING'S ARMS, 81 NEW GRAVEL LANE, WAPPING.

In December 1811, two brutal sets of murders shook London and prompted calls for a more professional police force. A watchman responding to Margaret Jewell's (dates unknown) cries for help discovered the first. Her master, Timothy Marr (c. 1787–1811), had sent her to fetch some oysters for supper. However, on her return, Margaret found the door locked and received no response to her incessant knocking, prompting the next-door neighbour and a nightwatchman to come to her aid. When they managed to enter through the back of the shop, they found a scene of horror inside. The apprentice, James Gowen (1797–1811), was lying in a pool of blood, his face shattered. Mrs Marr's (1787–1811) body was nearby, blood still oozing from her head. Her husband was found also beaten to death and their baby boy was upstairs in his cot, his throat cut.

The Marrs lived on the Ratcliffe Highway in Wapping, east London, an area notorious for crime, prostitution and poverty. But this crime was

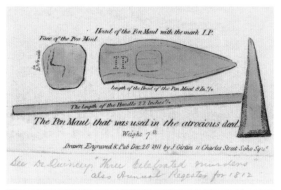

beyond the imagination of even the most hardened denizen of the Highway and it sent shock waves through the capital. When, twelve days later (19 December), another family was massacred, the panic in east London reached unprecedented heights. A crowd outside the King's Arms pub watched as lodger John Turner (dates unknown), clad only in his underclothes, descended a makeshift rope to safety. When the onlookers broke in, they found the landlord, John Williamson (1755–1811), lying dead on the cellar steps. He had been beaten and his throat slashed, and defensive wounds to his arms testified to a forlorn attempt to save himself. His wife, Elizabeth (1751–1811), and the family's maid were found nearby, having suffered a similar fate.

Within days, a man was in custody. John Williams (1784–1811), a 27-year-old sailor and a well-known regular at the King's Arms, was locked up in Coldbath Fields Prison while investigations continued. A bloodied shipwright's hammer, or maul, had been found at the Marrs, which seemed to provide some clues. Williams lodged at another pub, the Pear Tree, sharing rooms with a sailor named John Peterson (dates unknown). Peterson was at sea but a maul he owned was missing. The maul found at the Marrs had the initials 'J. P.' carved on it. It looked bad for Williams. But before the suspect could be brought to trial, he was found hanged, apparently having taken his own life.

Deprived of a trial and public execution, the authorities now engaged in a bizarre ritual. Williams's body was paraded along the Highway on a cart; the maul and a ripping chisel (also suspected of being used in the murders) either side of his head. The cart stopped outside the Marrs' and the Williamsons' homes before proceeding to the crossroads at Cannon Street and Cable Street, where Williams was buried in a narrow grave with a stake driven through his heart. This had been a customary way of dealing with suicides in England since the Early Modern period, but was virtually extinct by 1811. In 1886, the remains were dug up during the routine laying of a gas pipe, reviving interest in a case that the East End had tried very hard to forget. ∎

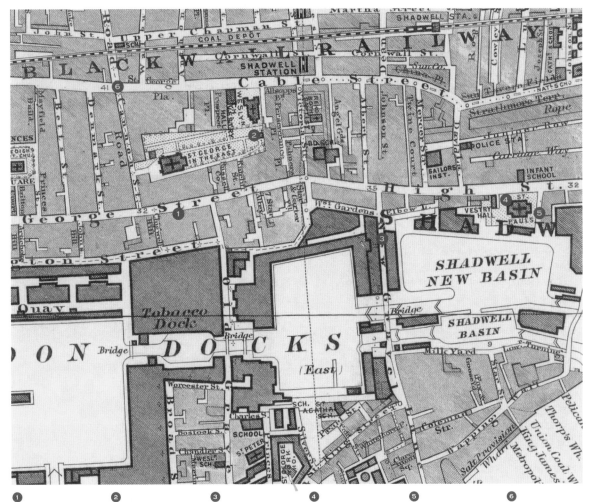

1 29 RATCLIFFE HIGHWAY. THE HOUSE WHERE THE MARRS WERE MURDERED.

2 ST GEORGE IN THE EAST. THE GRAVEYARD WHERE THE MARRS WERE BURIED.

3 THE KING'S ARMS PUB, NEW GRAVEL LANE. THE HOUSE WHERE JOHN AND ELIZABETH WILLIAMSON AND BRIDGET HARRINGTON WERE MURDERED.

4 ST PAUL'S. THE GRAVEYARD WHERE JOHN AND ELIZABETH WILLIAMSON AND BRIDGET HARRINGTON WERE BURIED.

5 PEAR TREE INN. THE INN WHERE JOHN WILLIAMS WAS STAYING.

6 CABLE STREET AND CANNON STREET CROSSROADS. THE CROSSROADS WHERE JOHN WILLIAMS WAS BURIED.

Opposite above. THE MAUL (A SHIPWRIGHT'S HAMMER) FOUND AT THE SCENE OF THE MURDER OF THE MARR FAMILY ON THE RATCLIFFE HIGHWAY, WITH THE INITALS 'J.P.' INSCRIBED.

Opposite below. A CONTEMPORARY ILLUSTRATION OF JOHN WILLIAMS'S BODY BEING PARADED THROUGH THE STREETS OF EAST LONDON, TO BE BURIED AT A CROSSROADS IN A NARROW GRAVE.

Right. A NEWSPAPER ILLUSTRATION OF TIMOTHY MARR'S MERCERY SHOP AT 29 RATCLIFFE HIGHWAY. MARR, HIS WIFE AND BABY BOY, AND THEIR APPRENTICE WERE ALL FOUND DEAD INSIDE.

The Residence of the late
Mr MARR,
RATCLIFFE HIGHWAY,
where he was dreadfully murdered with his Wife, Infant Child, & Apprentice, on the 7th Day of December 1811.

FREDERICK MANNING & MARIA MANNING.
× *Patrick O'Connor.*

WEAPON. PISTOL.	TYPOLOGY. PROPERTY CRIME.	POLICING. N/A.

3 MINIVER PLACE, BERMONDSEY.

FREDERICK MANNING. | MARIA MANNING.

There were few things the Victorian public enjoyed more than a good murder story. From the discovery of a body to the capture, prosecution and execution of the culprits, the newspaper readership of the 1800s was gripped by every twist and turn. In a period that saw the growth of sensational journalism, the revelations that came to light about Frederick (1820–49) and Maria Manning (1821–49) had readers glued to the pages of London's newspapers for weeks.

Maria (or Marie de) Roux had come to England from Switzerland at some point in the late 1830s, or early 1840s, and by 1843 had found work as a lady's maid for the Duchess of Sutherland. It was a prestigious position, and it seems to have entrenched Maria's sense of self-importance. In 1847, she married Frederick Manning and the couple set up home running a pub in Taunton, Somerset. It was not a great success and they were not very happy; Maria probably craved the better things in life. They moved to Bermondsey in south London, taking rooms at 3 Miniver Place. In London, Maria seems to have rekindled a relationship with a former lover named Patrick O'Connor (c. 1796–1849), who had associations with the up-and-coming railway business. For a while, Maria, Fred and Patrick were firm friends and one wonders if Fred turned a blind eye to his wife's infidelity, perhaps fearful of driving her away or simply scared of her temper tantrums.

In the summer of 1849, Maria and Fred hatched a plan to murder O'Connor and steal his railway share certificates. Maria had been shown these in O'Connor's London lodgings and knew how to sell them. On 9 August, O'Connor was invited to dinner (as he often was) and while he washed his hands Maria came up behind him and shot him in the head. This failed to kill him outright, however, so Fred finished the job with a blunt instrument. They buried O'Connor under the flagstones in the kitchen. When O'Connor's friends missed him, the police were alerted and the Mannings' house visited. Spooked by this, the couple split up: Maria headed for Edinburgh, Scotland, to sell the share certificates, while Fred fled to Jersey. The police soon tracked them down and brought them back to London to face trial for murder. In court, each blamed the other and when the jury returned a guilty verdict Maria lost her calm completely and raged at the injustice of it all.

This story had everything: a *ménage à trois*, a foreign female murderess, adultery and greed, an attempted escape and a dramatic trial where the Mannings blamed each other and Maria turned her anger on the court, the judge, the watching public and what she condemned as 'shame, base England'. Thousands turned up to watch them hang outside Surrey's Horsemonger Lane Gaol. The novelists Herman Melville (1819–91) and Charles Dickens (1812–70) were among the onlookers, and Dickens used Maria as the model for his character Hortense, the murderess in *Bleak House* (1853). ∎

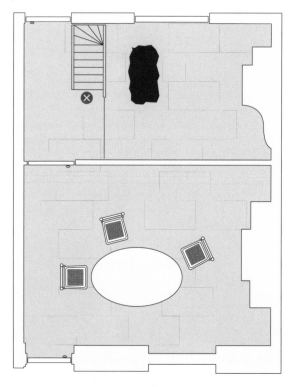

Below. FLOOR PLAN OF THE KITCHEN, HALL AND DINING ROOM, MARKING THE LOCATION AT THE FOOT OF THE STAIRS WHERE PATRICK O'CONNOR WAS SHOT AND INDICATING THE HOLE BENEATH THE KITCHEN FLAGSTONES WHERE HE WAS BURIED.

Above. A MURDER BROADSIDE
DEPICTING THE PUBLIC
HANGING OF THE MANNINGS.
BROADSIDES SUCH AS THIS
WERE SOLD AS SOUVENIRS BY
PEDLARS AT EXECUTIONS.

Below. THREE VIEWS OF MARIA
MANNING'S DEATH MASK,
REFLECTING THE 19TH-
CENTURY INTEREST
IN PHYSIOGNOMY.

LIFE CONFESSION & EXECUTION,
OF MR. & MRS. MANNING, FOR THE MURDER OF
MR. O'CONNER, WITH COPIES OF THE LETTERS.

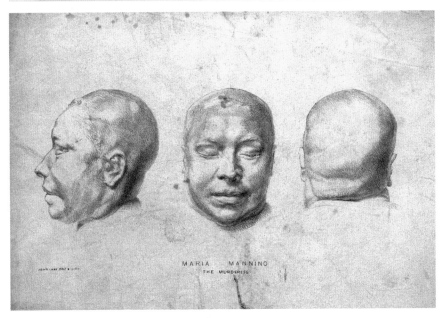

MARIA MANNING
THE MURDERESS.

① THE UNSUSPECTING PATRICK O'CONNOR DINES WITH THE MANNINGS AT MINIVER PLACE.

② MARIA MANNING SHOOTS PATRICK O'CONNOR WITH A PISTOL AS HE WASHES HIS HANDS.

③ MARIA MANNING RAIDS PATRICK O'CONNOR'S LODGINGS, STEALING HIS RAILWAY SHARE CERTIFICATES.

④ THE POLICE DISCOVER PATRICK O'CONNOR'S REMAINS BENEATH THE KITCHEN FLAGSTONES AT MINIVER PLACE.

⑤ MARIA MANNING IS ARRESTED IN EDINBURGH, HAVING TRIED TO SELL THE SHARE CERTIFICATES.

⑥ MARIA MANNING FURIOUSLY ADDRESSES THE COURT DURING HER TRIAL.

KATE WEBSTER.
× *Julia Martha Thomas.*

WEAPON. STRANGULATION.	TYPOLOGY. PROPERTY CRIME.	POLICING. EARLY FORENSICS.

2 MAYFIELD COTTAGES, RICHMOND.

Kate Webster (1849–79) was one of the most notorious murderers in late Victorian Britain. She became a fixture in the Chamber of Horrors at Madame Tussauds and was recognized alongside murderess Sarah Malcolm (1711–33) as emblematic of female malice.

Born in Ireland, Webster found work as a servant to a widow, Julia Martha Thomas (*c.* 1823–79), in Richmond, southwest London, in January 1879. The relationship did not work out: Mrs Thomas was highly critical of Webster's work and they agreed to part company at the end of February. Then, on 2 March, after a public row in church, Webster killed her mistress and dismembered the body. For two weeks, she then pretended to be Mrs Thomas before fleeing back home to Ireland. By 18 March, Mrs Thomas's neighbours had become suspicious and called the police, who searched the house and found multiple bloodstains, as well as bits of finger bone in the fireplace. Webster had left a letter with her Irish address on it, so a wanted notice was issued immediately.

After her arrest, Webster claimed the death was accidental: that Mrs Thomas had fallen and choked as the pair argued. She later admitted cutting up her body and boiling the flesh. She had packed parts of Mrs Thomas's body into a Gladstone bag and a hat box and thrown them into the Thames; they later washed up in Barnes. Furthermore, one foot was dropped into a rubbish tip in Twickenham, and the head was buried under the stables of the Hole in the Wall pub near Mrs Thomas's home. It was claimed that she attempted to sell the fat to neighbours, but this was never proven.

Webster was convicted at the Old Bailey on 30 June. She was revealed as a woman with a string of previous convictions, mostly for theft, but Mrs Thomas had never checked her references. In a last desperate attempt to save herself, Kate 'pleaded the belly', claiming she was pregnant. A jury of matrons rejected this and she was hanged at Wandsworth Prison on 29 July. In a bizarre twist, Mrs Thomas's skull was discovered in 2010 during building work at Sir David Attenborough's Richmond home. ▪

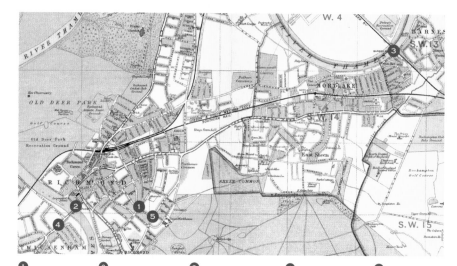

Above. THE STOVE WHERE JULIA THOMAS'S DISMEMBERED BODY WAS BOILED AND JULIA THOMAS'S SKULL, DISCOVERED IN MODERN RENOVATION WORK.

❶ 2 MAYFIELD COTTAGES. THE HOUSE WHERE JULIA THOMAS WAS MURDERED.

❷ RICHMOND BRIDGE. THE BRIDGE WHERE KATE WEBSTER DUMPED THE BODY PARTS.

❸ BARNES BRIDGE. THE BRIDGE WHERE BODY PARTS WERE FOUND IN A TRUNK.

❹ TWICKENHAM (APPROX.) THE AREA WHERE JULIA THOMAS'S FOOT WAS FOUND.

❺ THE HOLE IN THE WALL PUB. THE PUB WHERE JULIA THOMAS'S HEAD WAS FOUND.

PUSHING THE BOX OVER
THE BRIDGE.

PORTER SELLING THE MURDERED
WOMAN'S TEETH.

A SERIES OF IMAGES FROM THE
ILLUSTRATED POLICE NEWS DEPICTING
KATE WEBSTER DISPOSING OF THE
PARTS OF HER MISTRESS'S BODY.

KATE WEBSTER
& HER FRIENDS.

KATE SAID MRS THOMAS
HAD GONE OUT.

THE FLIGHT
OF KATE WEBSTER.

KATE WEBSTER'S ATTEMPTS TO COVER
UP HER CRIME, AS PRESENTED BY
THE *ILLUSTRATED POLICE NEWS.*

A SERIES OF IMAGES FROM
THE *ILLUSTRATED POLICE NEWS*
DEPICTING THE POLICE SEARCHING
FOR EVIDENCE AT MAYFIELD COTTAGES,
AND FINDING BONE FRAGMENTS AND
BLOODSTAINS AT THE SCENE.

THE POLICE FIND HUMAN BONES.

SEARCHING IN MRS THOMAS'S GARDEN.

THE *ILLUSTRATED POLICE NEWS'S*
COVERAGE OF THE DISCOVERY OF
THE BODY PARTS THAT KATE WEBSTER
HAD THROWN INTO THE THAMES.

THE MURDER AT RICHMOND.

RICHMOND BRIDGE.

BARNES BRIDGE.

THE RICHMOND MURDERESS.

KATE WEBSTER DENOUNCING
THE CHURCH.

THE *ILLUSTRATED POLICE NEWS'S*
DEPICTION OF KATE WEBSTER
IN PRISON AND AT HER OLD BAILEY
TRIAL ON 30 JUNE 1879, WHERE
SHE WAS CONVICTED OF MURDER.

IMAGES FROM THE *ILLUSTRATED POLICE
NEWS* OF KATE WEBSTER'S EXECUTION
BEHIND THE WALLS OF WANDSWORTH
PRISON ON 29 JULY 1879, AFTER HER
CLAIM TO BE PREGNANT WAS REJECTED
BY A JURY OF MATRONS.

KATE WEBSTER LEAVING FOR RICHMOND.

THE EXECUTION OF KATE WEBSTER
AT WANDSWORTH JAIL

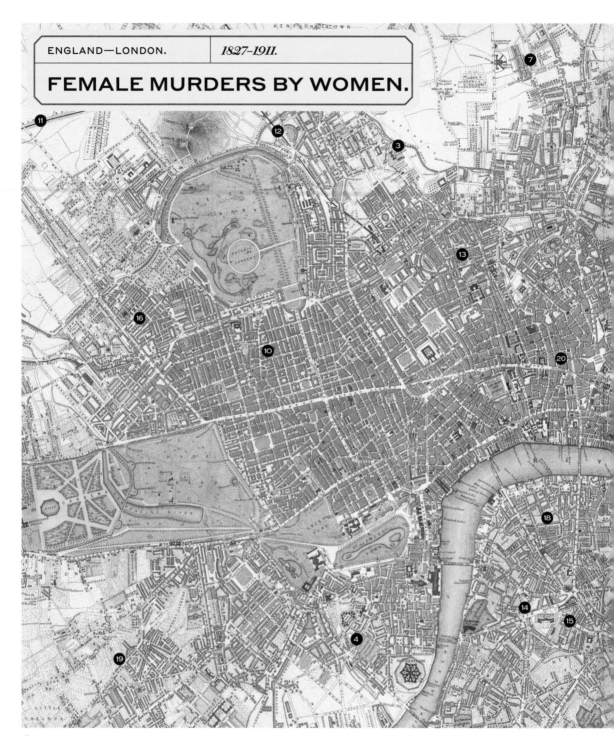

❶ 1827. FEATHERSTONE STREET, ST LUKE'S. **Mary Newdale.** ✕ ELIZABETH DAVIS.

❷ 1828. ROSEMARY LANE, WHITECHAPEL. **Margaret Hartigan.** ✕ MARIA ANN MOORE.

❸ 1842. ST PANCRAS WORKHOUSE, KING'S CROSS. **Sarah Stroud.** ✕ HARRIET STROUD.

❹ 1845. ROCHESTER STREET, WESTMINSTER. **Martha Browning.** ✕ ELIZABETH MUNDELL.

❺ 1848. CUPID'S COURT, ST LUKE'S. **Harriet Parker.** ✕ AMINA BLAKE. ✕ ROBERT HENRY BLAKE.

❻ 1857. 18 LINTON STREET, ISLINGTON. **Celestina Somner.** ✕ CELESTINE CHRISTMAS.

❼ 1872. ROMAN ROAD, BARNSBURY. **Lydia Venables.** ✕ ELIZA VENABLES.

❽ 1875. MUTTON BRIDGE, REGENT'S CANAL, CAMBRIDGE HEATH. **Mary Elizabeth Coward.** ✕ MARY ELIZABETH COWARD.

❾ 1883. LONDON BRIDGE, CITY OF LONDON. **Emily Batt.** ✕ EMILY BATT JR.

❿ 1890. LITTLE MARYLEBONE STREET, MARYLEBONE. **Sarah Hannah Calender.** ✕ FLORENCE ADA BANTON.

⓫ 1890. 2 PRIORY STREET, SWISS COTTAGE. **Mary Pearcey.** ✕ PHOEBE HOGG. ✕ TIGGY HOGG.

⓬ 1891. CHALCOTT CRESCENT, REGENT'S PARK. **Elizabeth Rapley.** ✕ WINIFRED GLADYS RAPLEY.

⓭ 1893. HARRISON STREET, ST PANCRAS. **Julia Attewell.** ✕ JULIA ATTEWELL, JR.

⓮ 1894. 65 KENNINGTON ROAD, KENNINGTON. **Julia Lee.** ✕ FLORENCE LEE.

⓯ 1895. ST GEORGE'S BUILDINGS, SOUTHWARK. **Emma Hayes.** ✕ MARY AMELIA HAYES.

⓰ 1898. CARLISLE STREET, LISSON GROVE. **Dorothy Dickinson.** ✕ JULIA MURPHY.

⓱ 1899. DORSET STREET, SPITALFIELDS. **Kate Marshall.** ✕ ELIZA ROBERTS.

⓲ 1904. PEABODY BUILDINGS, DUCHY STREET, BLACKFRIARS. **Mary Jane Martin.** ✕ ELLEN FRANCES MARTIN.

⓳ 1908. ONSLOW DWELLINGS, CHELSEA. **Alice Jane Money.** ✕ NORAH MONEY.

⓴ 1911. ELY PLACE, HOLBORN. **Margaret Murphy.** ✕ GERTRUDE ELIZABETH MURPHY.

PERCY LEFROY MAPLETON.
✕ *Isaac Frederick Gold.*

WEAPON. PISTOL & KNIFE.	TYPOLOGY. PROPERTY CRIME.	POLICING. COMPOSITE PORTRAIT.

LONDON TO BRIGHTON TRAIN, BALCOMBE TUNNEL.

In June 1881, the stationmaster at Balcombe, Sussex, sent a telegram down the line. It read: 'Man found dead this afternoon in tunnel here. Name on papers "I. Gold". He is now lying here. Reply quick.' The man was Isaac Gold (1817–81) and he had apparently been thrown off the London to Brighton express train.

Earlier that day, a strange man had got off the train at Preston Park station in Brighton, his clothes covered in blood and a gold watch sticking out of his shoe. He claimed he had been robbed and was lucky to escape. His story did not make sense; his wounds were superficial and he seemed keen to get away. Having first been questioned by railway staff, he was then taken to a police station and interrogated. At this stage, the police had not heard about the mysterious body in the tunnel so they assumed the unconvincing story was a cover for an attempt to commit suicide, and let him go. However, once news of Gold's body arrived, the police realized their mistake and put out a description of 21-year-old Percy Lefroy Mapleton (1860–81). It was quite precise, noting: 'very thin, sickly appearance, scratches on throat, wounds on head, probably clean shaved, low felt hat,

black coat, teeth much discoloured'. The wanted poster also featured an artist's impression of the suspect, the first time this was ever used in England.

The inquest into Gold's death recorded a verdict of wilful murder and Mapleton became the number one suspect. On 8 July, detectives tracked him down to a house in Stepney, which he had given his employer as a forwarding address. There, he was arrested by none other than Detective Inspector Donald Swanson (1848–1924), who went on to oversee the police attempt to capture the elusive Whitechapel murderer in 1888. Swanson had more success with the 'railway murder' of 1881. Investigations had discovered that a man fitting the description had recently pawned a pistol and had sold some counterfeit coins. The victim, Gold, had been a coin dealer, and so the police now had a motive for the killing: robbery.

Tried at Maidstone Assizes, Mapleton was convicted of murder and sentenced to death. He denied his crime and told the judge, 'The day will come when you will know that you have murdered me.' William Marwood (1818–83) hanged him on 29 November at Lewes Prison. ∎

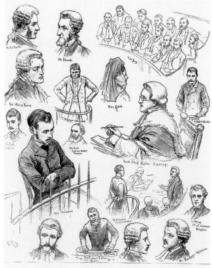

Left. THE WANTED POSTER ISSUED BY THE CID FOLLOWING THE MURDER OF ISAAC GOLD. THIS WAS THE FIRST EVER SUCH POSTER TO INCLUDE A SKETCH OF THE SUSPECT.

Right. A CONTEMPORARY PRESS GALLERY SKETCH OF THE TRIAL OF PERCY LEFROY MAPLETON AT MAIDSTONE ASSIZES, FEATURING ALL THE KEY PROTAGONISTS. MAPLETON WAS CONVICTED OF MURDER.

1

LONDON BRIDGE
STATION.
THE STATION FROM
WHICH THE BRIGHTON
TRAIN DEPARTED.

2

PRESTON PARK
STATION.
THE STATION AT
WHICH PERCY LEFROY
MAPLETON ALIGHTED
FROM THE TRAIN.

3

BALCOMBE TUNNEL.
THE POINT ON THE
RAILWAY WHERE
ISAAC GOLD'S BODY
WAS FOUND.

4

CATHART ROAD,
WALLINGTON.
THE BOARDING HOUSE
WHERE PERCY LEFROY
MAPLETON STAYED
TO EVADE THE POLICE.

5

32 SMITH STREET,
STEPNEY.
THE HOUSE IN WHICH
PERCY LEFROY
MAPLETON WAS
ARRESTED.

6

MAIDSTONE ASSIZES.
THE COURT AT
WHICH PERCY LEFROY
MAPLETON WAS TRIED,
AND SENTENCED,
FOR MURDER.

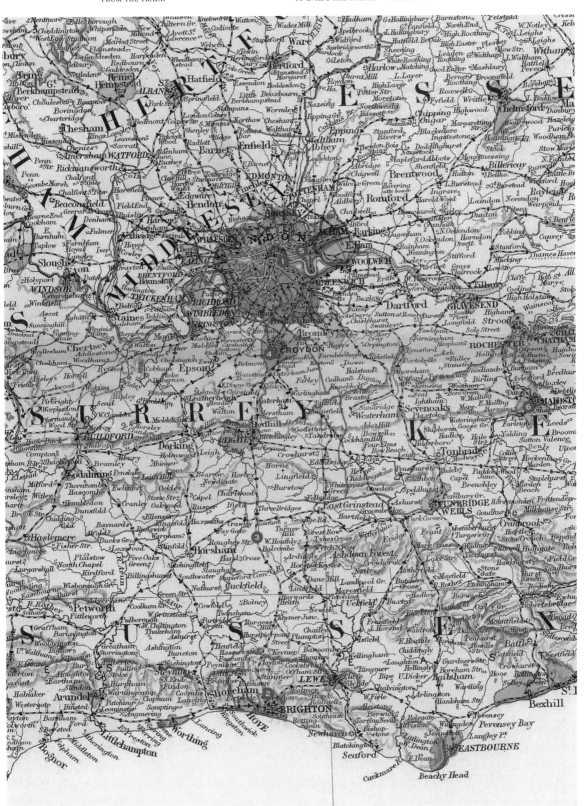

MURDER ON THE BRIGHTON RAILWAY.

LEFROY'S LODGINGS 32 SMITH ST STEPNEY

LEFROY TAKEN TO THE COURT

LEFROY'S BEDROOM

LEFROY IN LEWES GAOL

BEFORE THE MAGISTRATES AT CUCKFIELD

FINDING THE BLOOD-STAINED SHIRT

THE JOURNEY DOWN

PRISONER ALLOWED EVERY INDULGENCE

SEARCHING FOR WATCH
SIFTING THE MOULD

ISRAEL LIPSKI.
✕ *Miriam Angel.*

WEAPON.	TYPOLOGY.	POLICING.
NITRIC ACID.	DOMESTIC.	TOXICOLOGY.

16 BATTY STREET, WHITECHAPEL.

When Miriam Angel (unknown–1887) failed to turn up at her mother-in-law's on 28 June 1887, Mrs Angel went to fetch her from the crowded lodging house on Batty Street where she lived. Here she found Miriam, six months pregnant, lying dead on her bed with traces of nitric acid on her lips. As the police searched for the poison bottle, they discovered a man under the bed, semi-conscious, and with the same telltale signs of nitric acid – burns and yellow stains – around his lips. A locked room with one dead and one semi-conscious, it was a genuine mystery and only the man, a 21-year-old umbrella maker named Israel Lipski (1865–87), could solve it.

When he recovered, he told the police that his two employees had attacked him during an attempted robbery. They had killed Miriam then tried to take his life, too, to cover their tracks. The story was sensational and all too fantastical for the police and the Old Bailey jury that Lipski faced on 25 July. They preferred to believe that he had killed Miriam following a frustrated rape attempt.

Lipski, a Jewish immigrant in London seeking a new life away from the horrors of forced service in the Imperial Russian Army, was badly let down by English 'justice'. A poor defence barrister coupled with what seems like fabricated police evidence resulted in his conviction. Sentenced to death, his young life was about to be brought to an end until William Stead (1849–1912) of *The Pall Mall Gazette* began a vociferous press campaign to save him. In the end, to Stead's annoyance, Lipski confessed. There is still considerable doubt as to whether he simply did so to avoid the life sentence that his rabbi told him was the likely result of a commuted sentence. Having fled forced labour and persecution in Russia, Lipski could not face exchanging that for a loss of freedom in England. He chose to die instead and was hanged at Newgate Prison on 22 August. ∎

Below. ISRAEL LIPSKI'S CLOTHES, THE BOTTLE THAT CONTAINED THE NITRIC ACID USED TO KILL MIRIAM ANGEL AND THE LOCK FROM HER DOOR.

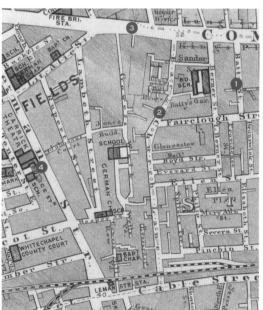

1
16 BATTY STREET.
THE BOARDING HOUSE WHERE MIRIAM ANGEL WAS MURDERED.

2
96 BACKCHURCH LANE.
THE SHOP WHERE CHARLES MOORE CLAIMED TO HAVE SOLD ISRAEL LIPSKI NITRIC ACID.

3
COMMERCIAL STREET.
THE STREET WHERE A DOCTOR'S CAB WAS HAILED.

4
LEMAN STREET POLICE STATION.
THE POLICE STATION WHERE ISRAEL LIPSKI WAS TAKEN BY THE POLICE.

GEORGE GALLETLY.
✕ *Joseph Rumbold*.

WEAPON. KNIFE.	TYPOLOGY. GANG.	POLICING. N/A.

REGENT'S PARK, MARYLEBONE.

Unfortunately for Joseph Rumbold (1865–88), he was in the wrong place at the wrong time and it cost him his life. He was walking out with his sweetheart Elizabeth 'Lizzie' Lee (dates unknown) in Regent's Park in May 1888. The couple were 'double dating' with her sister Emily (dates unknown) and her young man, Alonzo Byrnes (dates unknown). The four were loosely connected to a local youth gang, the 'Lisson Grove Lads'. Like several other big cities in the 1880s, London had a well-publicized 'gang' problem. These gangs (usually termed 'roughs' in the media, then later 'hooligans') laid claims to territory, dressed in a distinctive group style and sometimes armed themselves with weapons and studded leather belts. Anti-social behaviour, petty crime and violence were commonplace, but deaths were rare.

The previous evening two members of a rival gang (known as the 'Tottenham Court Road Lads') were attacked near Madame Tussauds. Beaten and bloodied, but mostly affronted, they demanded immediate revenge. In the late evening of 24 May, several lads chased Rumbold out of the park to York Gate, where he was stabbed to death.

The Old Bailey dock was packed as ten young men faced trial for the killing. They were a mixture of working-class youths, but none fitted the media depiction of them as unemployed wastrels. In the end, only one was convicted: George 'Garry' Galletly (1871–unknown). Galletly had publicly boasted that he would 'do for them', borrowing a knife from another boy as they gathered to settle their score with their rivals. As the youngest member of the gang, he may have felt obliged to prove his mettle. His death sentence was eventually commuted to life imprisonment on account of his age. ∎

Below. THE PENNY ILLUSTRATED PAPER, 2 JUNE 1888. GEORGE GALLETLY IN THE DOCK AT THE OLD BAILEY WITH HIS FELLOW GANG MEMBERS.

① BRIDPORT STREET.
THE STREET WHERE JOSEPH RUMBOLD LIVED.

② MARYLEBONE LANE.
THE LANE WHERE JOSEPH RUMBOLD AND ALONZO BYRNES WORKED.

③ BARRETT'S COURT.
THE COURT WHERE LIZZIE AND EMILY LEE LIVED.

④ CORNWALL TERRACE.
THE ROAD WHERE THE GANG ATTACKED JOSEPH RUMBOLD.

⑤ YORK GATE.
THE PLACE WHERE JOSEPH RUMBOLD COLLAPSED.

① *31 August 1888.*
BUCK'S ROW,
WHITECHAPEL.

② *8 September 1888.*
29 HANBURY STREET,
SPITALFIELDS.

③ *30 September 1888.*
DUTFIELD'S YARD,
BERNER STREET,
WHITECHAPEL.

④ *30 September 1888.*
MITRE SQUARE, MITRE
STREET, ALDGATE.

⑤ *9 November 1888.*
MILLER'S COURT,
DORSET STREET,
SPITALFIELDS.

ENGLAND—LONDON. | *1888–91.*

JACK THE RIPPER.
×5. +

WEAPON. KNIFE.	TYPOLOGY. SEXUAL.	POLICING. CRIMINAL PROFILING.

WHITECHAPEL & SPITALFIELDS.

In 1888, London was shocked by a series of brutal murders that left the police baffled and East Enders terrified. No one was ever successfully caught and convicted of the so-called 'Whitechapel Murders', allowing historians and amateur sleuths to speculate on the true identity of the killer known as 'Jack the Ripper' ever since.

Most researchers agree that 'Jack' killed five women between August and November 1888. Others argue that there could be as many as eight or nine murders committed by the same killer. What is not in dispute is the brutality of these killings, which were out of the ordinary and well beyond the usual domestic homicides that blighted life in this desperately poor community. All the murders took place in a geographically small area: Whitechapel and Spitalfields were home to tens of thousands of Queen Victoria's poorest subjects, many crammed into dingy lodging houses where rooms could be rented for a few pennies a night. Prostitution was rife in the East End and most researchers believe that the women the 'Ripper' targeted were selling sex in order to find the money they needed to put a roof over their heads.

The first of the 'canonical five' victims was Mary Ann 'Polly' Nichols (1845–88), whose dead body was found by two workmen, Charles Cross (1849–1920) and Robert Paul (dates unknown), on their daily commute at just after 3:30 a.m. on 31 August. Cross had seen what he thought to be a tarpaulin lying close to the gates of a stable yard on Buck's Row. Examining the bundle, he soon realized it was a body and called Paul over. While the pair went off in search of a policeman, the local beat bobby, Police Constable 97J John Neil (1850–unknown), arrived and blew his whistle for help. Polly had

① ✕ *Mary Ann Nichols.*
Throat twice-cut,
abdomen mutilated.
Aged 43.

② ✕ *Annie Chapman.*
Throat cut, body mutilated,
disembowelled, uterus
partially removed.
Aged c. 47.

③ ✕ *Elizabeth Stride.*
Throat cut.
Aged 44.

④ ✕ *Catherine Eddowes.*
Throat cut, tip of nose
cut off, uterus and one
kidney removed.
Aged 46.

⑤ ✕ *Mary Jane Kelly.*
Throat cut, skinned (abdomen
& thighs), disembowelled, face
mutilated, breasts removed.
Aged 25.

Ⓐ
3/4 April 1888.
OSBORN STREET,
WHITECHAPEL.

Ⓑ
7 August 1888.
GEORGE YARD
WHITECHAPEL.

Ⓒ
17 July 1889.
CASTLE ALLEY,
WHITECHAPEL.

Ⓓ
10 September 1889.
PINCHIN STREET,
WHITECHAPEL.

Ⓔ
13 February 1891.
SWALLOW GARDENS,
WHITECHAPEL.

been murdered: her throat cut and (although this only became apparent when she was removed to the workhouse mortuary) her abdomen opened up. Earlier that month, Martha Tabram's (1849–88) body had been found in nearby George Yard with forty-nine stab wounds, all but one targeting her abdomen and genitals: could this be the same killer? In April, a street prostitute named Emma Smith (1843–88) had been beaten and left for dead, with a blunt instrument shoved up into her vagina, and it seemed (to the press and public at least) as if someone was making war on the local sex workers.

The killer struck again on 8 September in Hanbury Street, just a short walk from Buck's Row. John Davis (dates unknown), a resident of a shared lodging house, found the dead body of 'Dark' Annie Chapman (1840–88) at 5:45 in the morning. As the police inspected the scene, they found that, like Polly Nichols, Annie had had her carotid artery cut, but so deeply that the wound had almost severed her head from her body. She was left with her legs up, in a horrific caricature of a surgical operation.

Her intestines had been draped over one shoulder and part of her stomach over the other; the killer had removed Annie's uterus before making his escape into the early autumn morning. To some, it seemed as if a ritualistic killer was on the loose, a monster born of the slums that one contemporary writer termed 'the Abyss'.

As Whitechapel digested this latest horror, the press seized on the story and turned it into a national and international sensation. This was fuelled by a letter that was supposedly sent to the papers by the killer himself. In this missive, dated 25 September but stamped on 27 September, the mysterious author claimed his knife was 'very sharp' and signed himself 'Jack the Ripper'. It was almost certainly a hoax, created by the media to keep interest in the case at a heightened state. They probably did not need such artifice. In the morning of 30 September, two murders took place within an hour and a mile of each other. First, Elizabeth 'Long Liz' Stride's (1843–88) body was found in Berner Street by a Jewish trader returning home from

Ⓐ
× *Emma Elizabeth Smith.*
Peritoneum ruptured by blunt object inserted into vagina; died of peritonitis the morning after the attack. Aged 45.

Ⓑ
× *Martha Tabram.*
Multiple stab wounds to the chest area.
Aged 39.

Ⓒ
× *Alice McKenzie.*
Carotid artery severed; multiple stab wounds to the abdomen area.
Aged 40.

Ⓓ
× *'Pinchin Street Torso'.*
Unidentified torso found; no other body parts uncovered.
Aged 30–40.

Ⓔ
× *Frances Coles.*
Throat twice-cut.
Aged 25.

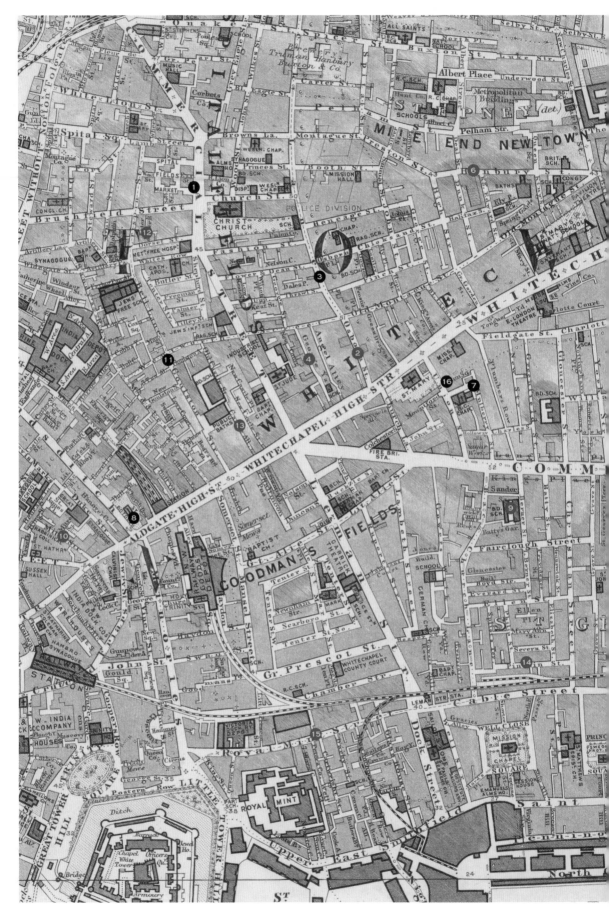

❶
1888.
THE TEN BELLS PUB,
84 COMMERCIAL
STREET,
SPITALFIELDS.
ALL CANONICAL
VICTIMS WERE KNOWN
CUSTOMERS HERE.

❷
3 APRIL 1888.
OSBORN STREET,
WHITECHAPEL.
× EMMA ELIZABETH
SMITH.

❸
1 AUGUST 1888.
FRYING PAN PUBLIC
HOUSE, 13 BRICK
LANE, SPITALFIELDS.
MARY NICHOLS WAS
LAST SEEN HERE.

❹
7 AUGUST 1888.
GEORGE YARD,
WHITECHAPEL.
× MARTHA TABRAM.

❺
31 AUGUST 1888.
BUCK'S ROW,
WHITECHAPEL.
× MARY ANN NICHOLS.

❻
31 AUGUST 1888.
29 HANBURY STREET,
SPITALFIELDS.
× ANNIE CHAPMAN.

❼
1888.
22 MULBERRY STREET,
WHITECHAPEL
HOME OF POLISH-
JEWISH BOOTMAKER
JOHN PIZER, AKA
'LEATHER APRON',
THE FIRST KEY SUSPECT.

❽
30 SEPTEMBER 1888.
ST BOLTOPH
WITHOUT ALDGATE
CHURCH, ALDGATE
HIGH STREET.
CATHERINE EDDOWES
WAS LAST SEEN HERE.

❾
30 SEPTEMBER 1888.
DUTFIELD'S YARD,
BERNER STREET,
WHITECHAPEL.
× ELIZABETH STRIDE.

❿
30 SEPTEMBER 1888.
MITRE SQUARE,
MITRE STREET,
ALDGATE.
× CATHERINE EDDOWES.

⓫
30 SEPTEMBER 1888.
40–41 WENTWORTH
MODEL DWELLINGS,
GOULSTON STREET,
SPITALFIELDS.
A FRAGMENT OF
CATHERINE EDDOWES'S
APRON AND CHALKED
GRAFITTI WERE
FOUND HERE.

⓬
9 NOVEMBER 1888.
13 MILLER'S COURT,
DORSET STREET,
SPITALFIELDS.
× MARY JANE KELLY.

⓭
17 JULY 1889.
CASTLE ALLEY,
WHITECHAPEL.
× ALICE MCKENZIE.

⓮
10 SEPTEMBER 1889.
PINCHIN STREET,
WHITECHAPEL.
× UNIDENTIFIED TORSO.

⓯
13 FEBRUARY 1891.
SWALLOW GARDENS,
WHITECHAPEL.
× FRANCES COLES.

⓰
1894.
3 SION SQUARE,
WHITECHAPEL.
THE HOME OF POLISH-
JEWISH BARBER
AARON KOSMINSKI,
THE SECOND KEY
SUSPECT.

market. Her throat had been cut but the killer had been disturbed and fled before he could mutilate her. Since that was his intention, he struck again, this time in the City of London at Mitre Square. Catherine 'Kate' Eddowes's (1842–88) body was horribly brutalized: her uterus and left kidney removed, and her face cut up. Three men leaving a Jewish club near Mitre Square that night had seen Kate talking to a man. Descriptions were given and hundreds of potential suspects interviewed, but no arrests were made. More letters arrived on the detectives' desks and one, sent to the chair of the local Whitechapel Vigilance Committee, George Lusk (1839–1919), came accompanied by a portion of human kidney that the anonymous sender claimed he had cut from Eddowes's dead body.

For a while, the murders ceased, possibly because the killer was aware that the police were closing in, or perhaps because he was sated by the 'double event' that raised the levels of terror in the capital. Then, in the early hours before the Lord Mayor's Show, he struck again. His final

canonical victim was Mary Jane Kelly (1863–88), whose eviscerated body was found on 9 November at her digs in Miller's Court, Dorset Street. So terrible were her injuries that her lover was only able to identify her by her 'eyes and ears'. At least two other women may have met their end at the hands of Jack: Alice McKenzie (1849–89) killed in Castle Alley in July 1889 and Frances Coles (1859–91) murdered in Chamber Street in February 1891.

The investigation into the killings was conducted by the Criminal Investigation Department that had been setup just ten years previously. However, due to both internal incompetencies and external complications, they were never able to get one step ahead of the killer. The practice of crime scene investigation was still in its infancy, and for the early murders there was virtually no attempt at a systematic, detailed analysis of where the bodies were discovered. The possibility of achieving this was undoubtedly undermined by the press, who trampled all over the crime scenes and interviewed witnesses with

Above. *ILLUSTRATED POLICE NEWS,* 15 SEPTEMBER 1888, COVERAGE OF THE MURDER OF ANNIE CHAPMAN IN HANBURY STREET, OFF BRICK LANE, AND THE LINK BETWEEN THIS CASE AND MARY ANN NICHOLS'S KILLING EIGHT DAYS EARLIER.

Above. *ILLUSTRATED POLICE NEWS,* 22 SEPTEMBER 1888, COVERAGE OF ANNIE CHAPMAN'S MURDER AND THE HEIGHTENED TENSION THE 'RIPPER' MURDERS WERE CAUSING IN THE EAST END OF LONDON IN 1888.

no regard for future trials. However, by the time of Mary Jane Kelly's murder, the police had adopted the method suggested by pioneering French police officer Alphonse Bertillon (1853–1914), and sent a photographer to Miller's Court to capture one of the very first 'crime scene' images for possible use in any court trial. The investigation was also groundbreaking for its use of criminal profiling. In October 1888, Dr Thomas Bond (1841–1901) was asked to review the evidence and speculate on what kind of person the killer might be. He hypothesized that the Ripper was likely 'solitary and eccentric', 'respectably' dressed and susceptible to 'homicidal and erotic mania'. Despite these advances, the police were plagued by setbacks, all of which were voraciously covered by the highly critical press.

Jack the Ripper's identity remains a mystery; the real murderer has largely vanished as attempts to point the finger of blame at a mad doctor, a crazed immigrant or a dissolute aristocrat have created a myth from the tragic deaths of several poor East End women. ∎

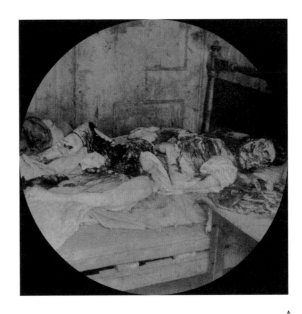

Above. THE CRIME SCENE PHOTOGRAPH TAKEN AT MILLER'S COURT, DORSET STREET, AFTER MARY JANE KELLY'S EVISCERATED BODY WAS DISCOVERED BY THOMAS BOWYER AND JOHN MCCARTHY.

Above. ILLUSTRATED POLICE NEWS, 6 OCTOBER 1888, COVERAGE OF THE SO-CALLED 'DOUBLE EVENT': THE MURDERS OF LIZ STRIDE AND THEN, AN HOUR LATER, CATHERINE EDDOWES, WHICH CAUSED WIDESPREAD PANIC IN THE CAPITAL.

Above. ILLUSTRATED POLICE NEWS, 13 OCTOBER 1888, COVERAGE OF THE MURDER IN MITRE SQUARE AND THE THAMES TORSO MURDERS. IN 1888 HUMAN BODY PARTS WERE WASHED UP IN VARIOUS LOCATIONS IN THE CAPITAL.

MARY PEARCEY.
× *Phoebe Hogg.* × *Tiggy Hogg.*

WEAPON.	TYPOLOGY.	POLICING.
POKER & CARVING KNIFE.	JEALOUSY.	FORENSICS.

2 PRIORY STREET, SWISS COTTAGE.

Mary Pearcey (1866–90) was executed on 23 December 1890 for killing her lover's wife and daughter. She was unfortunate: female killers were rare in the late 1800s and only a handful went to the gallows for their crimes. However, Pearcey excited public opinion because of the nature of her crime. Its brutality, her attempt to conceal it, her apparent indifference and the fact that she had murdered an infant child all counted against her.

A few years earlier, Pearcey had begun a relationship with Frank Hogg (dates unknown) and lived with him in Kentish Town, northwest London. Hogg was a womanizer, but when he got another lover, Phoebe Styles (1858–90), pregnant he married her. Unwilling to give him up, Pearcey persuaded Hogg to continue seeing her. Mary also became friends with Phoebe, so much so that Mrs Hogg often visited Mary, accompanied by her baby girl, Tiggy. It was a misjudgment of character that was to prove fatal. On the evening of 24 October, a body was found in Hampstead, the head crushed and throat savagely cut. A mile farther away was

a black pram, and then, in Finchley, a dead baby girl. Phoebe's sister-in-law Clara was worried when she could not find her, and went to the police after the papers reported the discovery of an unidentified body (with the initials 'P. H.' stitched onto the clothes). Mary went with her. Something must have raised police suspicions, because they escorted Mary home and found evidence of the crime there. Her room was splattered with blood (which she declared was the result of her 'killing mice') and bloodied curtains were discovered in the washhouse. The forensics were mounting up: a button from Phoebe's coat was fished out of Mary's kitchen grate, and a screw from the pram was found near Phoebe's dead body. Witnesses reported having seen Mary pushing a pram piled high with what they assumed was laundry, but turned out to have been the bodies of her victims. Mary's trial was prejudiced by a biased judge, and the evidence presented was largely circumstantial, but she had no defence to speak of. She told the hangman: 'My sentence is a just one, but a good deal of the evidence against me was false.' ∎

Below. ILLUSTRATED POLICE NEWS, 15 NOVEMBER 1890. MARY PEARCEY IN THE DOCK AT THE OLD BAILEY FOR THE MURDER OF PHOEBE HOGG AND HER DAUGHTER.

Below. ILLUSTRATED POLICE NEWS, 29 NOVEMBER 1890 (TOP) & 1 NOVEMBER 1890 (BOTTOM). MARY PEARCEY AWAITING TRIAL IN HOLLOWAY PRISON AND THE DETAILS OF HER ALLEGED CRIME.

Below. ILLUSTRATED POLICE NEWS, 13 DECEMBER 1890. SENSATIONAL PRESS COVERAGE OF THE CASE, TAKEN FROM EVIDENCE HEARD AT MARY PEARCEY'S TRIAL.

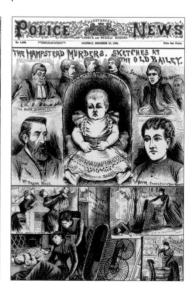

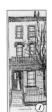

Above. PRESS ILLUSTRATIONS OF THE KEY
SCENES IN THE MURDER OF PHOEBE
AND TIGGY HOGG BY MARY PEARCEY.

THE NUMBERS ON THESE ILLUSTRATIONS
CORRESPOND TO THE LOCATIONS
PLOTTED ONTO THE MAP BELOW.

1 141 PRINCE OF
WALES ROAD.
THE HOUSE WHERE
PHOEBE HOGG LIVED.

2 CROSSFIELD ROAD.
THE ROAD WHERE
THE BODY OF PHOEBE
HOGG WAS DISCOVERED.

3 HAMILTON TERRACE.
THE LOCATION OF THE
PRAM USED TO TRANSPORT
THE DEAD BODIES.

4 FINCHLEY ROAD.
THE ROAD WHERE
TIGGY HOGG'S BODY
WAS FOUND.

5 2 PRIORY STREET.
MARY PEARCEY'S
HOME, WHERE BLOOD
STAINS WERE FOUND.

ENGLAND—LONDON. | *25 June 1893.*

ANDREA SCOTTI DI CARLO.
✕ *Jane Thompson.*

WEAPON.	TYPOLOGY.	POLICING.
KNIFE.	RECKLESS ACT.	N/A.

51 SILVERLOCK STREET, ROTHERHITHE.

When a prostitute was found dead, her throat horribly cut, it revived memories of the Jack the Ripper murders five years earlier. The victim was Jane Thompson (unknown–1893), also known as Jenny Hinks. Witnesses told police they had seen Jane drinking earlier that evening with a man whose appearance suggested he might be a sailor, so detectives targeted their inquiries to the local Surrey Commercial Docks. Two sailors were arrested: Paolo Cammarola (dates unknown) and Andrea Scotti Di Carlo (1873–unknown). Cammarola had an alibi but Di Carlo did not. He was convicted at the Old Bailey and sentenced to death, but reprieved and imprisoned for life. ∎

Above. ILLUSTRATED POLICE NEWS, 8 JULY 1893. POLICE DISCOVER THE BODY OF PROSTITUTE JANE THOMPSON IN ROTHERHITHE, WHOSE THROAT HAD BEEN CUT.

ENGLAND—LONDON. | *30 January 1896.*

THOMAS WILLIAM CRIPPS.
✕ *Elizabeth Biles.*

WEAPON.	TYPOLOGY.	POLICING.
KNIFE.	DOMESTIC.	N/A.

WILLIAM STREET, NOTTING HILL.

Domestic murder was all too common in late 19th-century London. Thomas Cripps (1867–unknown) and his common-law wife Elizabeth Biles (unknown–1896) quarrelled all the time according to neighbours. So when one argument ended tragically, with Biles lying outside her door with blood draining from a wound in her throat, the police knew where to look. Cripps had been fined for hitting her previously and was quick to confess. 'I done it,' he told police, 'I'll take a bit of rope for her.' He was spared that fate because an Old Bailey jury only found him guilty of manslaughter, not murder. He got seven years. ∎

Above. ILLUSTRATED POLICE NEWS, 8 FEBRUARY 1896. A HEAVILY STYLIZED PRESS RECREATION OF THE DISCOVERY OF ELIZABETH BILES'S BODY BY NEIGHBOURS IN NOTTING HILL.

ENGLAND—LONDON.	*10 August 1896.*

WILFRED MORITZ FRANKS.
✗ *Temple Edgecumbe Crozier.*

WEAPON. DAGGER.	TYPOLOGY. ACCIDENT.	POLICING. N/A.

NOVELTY THEATRE, GREAT QUEEN STREET, HOLBORN.

In August 1896, a tragedy on the London stage briefly made Temple Edgecumbe Crozier (dates unknown) a household name. Crozier was playing the villain in a popular melodrama – *The Sins of the Night* – opposite his theatrical chum Wilfred Moritz Franks (dates unknown). At the height of the drama, Franks lunged forwards to stab his fellow actor with a fake dagger. For some reason, however, the dummy knife was real and pierced Crozier's chest, inflicting a fatal wound. As the audience departed, Crozier literally died on stage. Franks was arrested for manslaughter, but a magistrate dismissed the charge on the grounds no jury would convict him. ∎

Above. ILLUSTRATED POLICE NEWS, 22 AUGUST 1896. WILFRED MORITZ FRANKS STABS HIS CO-STAR, UNAWARE THAT HIS THEATRICAL PROP IS IN FACT A REAL WEAPON.

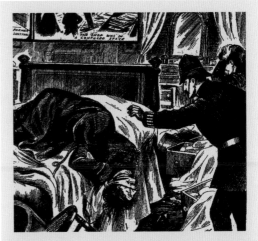

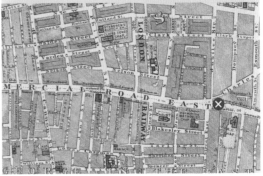

ENGLAND—LONDON.	*12 October 1904.*

UNKNOWN.
✗ *Harriet Farmer.*

WEAPON. SUFFOCATION.	TYPOLOGY. PROPERTY CRIME.	POLICING. N/A.

478 COMMERCIAL ROAD, WHITECHAPEL.

Even in a district where violence was depressingly familiar, the callous murder of an elderly shopkeeper still had the power to shock. Harriet Farmer (dates unknown) was found, bound and gagged, with rags stuffed in her mouth at her newsagent's shop in the East End of London. Local gossip rumoured that Miss Farmer was 'worth thousands', yet despite being attacked previously, she lived alone. This had all the hallmarks of a robbery gone wrong. Thieves had slipped in when she opened the shop, overpowering her as she tried to escape upstairs, and suffocating her in the process of keeping her quiet. No one was ever caught. ∎

Above. ILLUSTRATED POLICE NEWS, 22 OCTOBER 1904. HARRIET FARMER'S DEAD BODY IS FOUND, GAGGED AND BOUND, BY POLICE ON THE COMMERCIAL ROAD.

ALFRED STRATTON & ALBERT STRATTON.
× *Thomas Farrow.* × *Ann Farrow.*

WEAPON.	TYPOLOGY.	POLICING.
KNIFE.	PROPERTY CRIME.	FINGERPRINTING.

CHAPMAN'S OIL AND COLOUR SHOP, HIGH STREET, DEPTFORD.

| ALFRED STRATTON. | ALBERT STRATTON. |

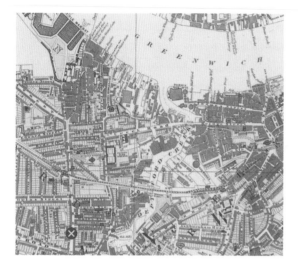

Below. CHAPMAN'S OIL AND COLOUR SHOP IN DEPTFORD, WHERE THE SHOPKEEPER THOMAS FARROW WAS BEATEN TO DEATH BY ROBBERS.

Bottom. THE CASH BOX, ON WHICH MACNAGHTEN DISCOVERED ALFRED STRATTON'S FINGERPRINT.

In March 1905, when Melville Macnaghten (1853–1921), head of the London Criminal Investigation Department, found a smudge on a cash box, he seized the opportunity to put a new forensic technology to the test. The box was found at Chapman's Oil and Colour Shop in Deptford, southeast London, where the body of the shop's owner, Thomas Farrow (1834–1905), lay dead. The 71-year-old had been beaten to death and his wife, Ann (1840–1905), had been similarly attacked and later died in hospital. The newly established Fingerprint Bureau quickly determined that the smudge was a thumbprint, probably from a right hand. Prints were taken from the shop employees, which allowed them to be eliminated as suspects.

Witnesses reported seeing two men leave the shop in the early hours on the morning of the attack, and more than one witness positively identified one of them as Alfred Stratton (1882–1905). Alfred and his brother Albert (1884–1905) were arrested and their prints taken – Alfred's right thumb exactly matched the one Macnaghten had found. The pair stood trial on 5 May, where the defence case rested on rubbishing fingerprinting as a forensic tool. This failed and the brothers were hanged eighteen days later, the first killers to be condemned in Britain by their fingerprints. ∎

Above. MAP SHOWING WHERE THOMAS AND ANN FARROW WERE MURDERED BY THE STRATTON BROTHERS.

Opposite. CRUDE MASKS MADE BY THE ROBBERS ALFRED AND ALBERT STRATTON FROM A PAIR OF STOCKINGS.

Below. ALFRED STRATTON'S FINGERPRINT (RIGHT), A PERFECT MATCH FOR THAT FOUND ON THE CASH BOX (LEFT).

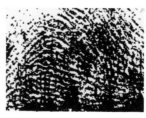

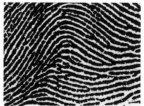

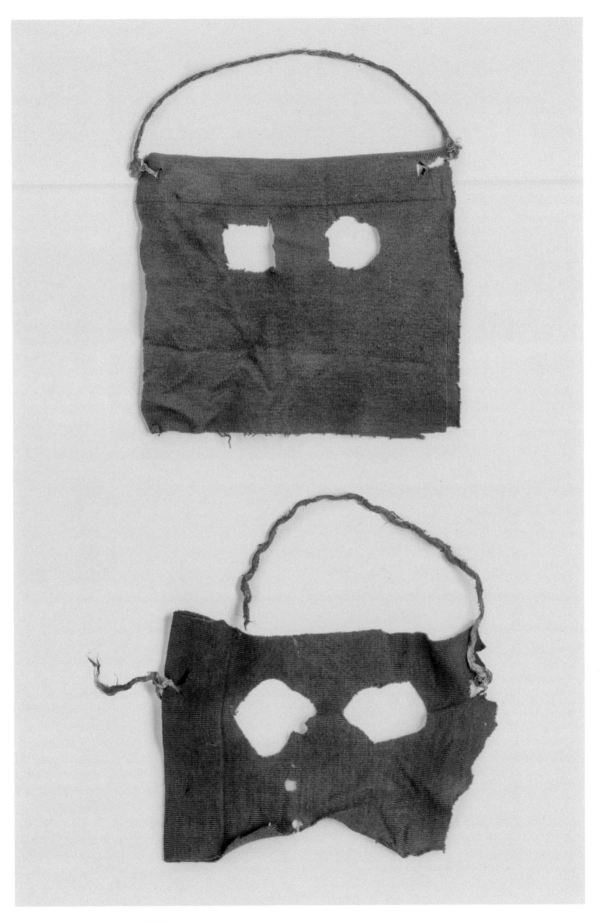

❶ COLDWATER, MICHIGAN. THE CITY IN WHICH HAWLEY HARVEY CRIPPEN WAS BORN.

❷ 39 HILLDROP CRESCENT, LONDON. THE HOUSE WHERE CORA CRIPPEN WAS MURDERED.

① ⟶
HAWLEY CRIPPEN RETURNS TO ENGLAND ABOARD THE *SS MEGANTIC*.

② ⟶
CROWDS WAIT ON THE HARBOURSIDE FOR THE RETURN OF THE MURDERER.

③ ⟶
HAWLEY CRIPPEN WALKS DOWN THE GANGPLANK OF THE *SS MEGANTIC*.

④ ⟶
HAWLEY CRIPPEN ACCOMPANIED BY A POLICEMAN.

ENGLAND—LONDON.	*January 1910.*

HAWLEY HARVEY CRIPPEN.
× *Cora Crippen.*

WEAPON. POISON.	TYPOLOGY. DOMESTIC.	POLICING. RADIOTELEGRAPHY.

39 HILLDROP CRESCENT, ISLINGTON.

Dr Hawley Harvey Crippen (1862–1910) was an unlikely murderer. Quiet and mild-mannered, he was 'a most pleasant fellow' according to his executioner. Despite this, he is credited with perhaps the most celebrated murder of the early 20th century, a murder that garnered almost as many newspaper columns as Jack the Ripper. The man who 'caught' Crippen – Chief Inspector Walter Dew (1863–1947) – retired soon afterwards, this case bookending a career that had begun in 1888 in Whitechapel and ended in 1910 in north London.

In July 1910, Dew called at the Crippen house at 39 Hilldrop Crescent, Islington, north London, to enquire after Cora Crippen (1872–1910), who had disappeared. Cora (also known by her stage name Belle Elmore) was a colourful character and her marriage to Hawley was far from perfect. She was a dominating personality and Hawley sought love

in the company of his demure secretary Ethel Le Neve (1883–1967). In January 1910, the morning after a dinner party with friends, Mrs Crippen vanished. Hawley said she had gone abroad, and then reported she had died of an illness. Her friends' suspicions were raised when Ethel was seen out wearing Cora's jewelry. Dew interviewed Crippen, who admitted his relationship with Ethel and said he had made up the story about Cora's death to avoid the shame of her leaving him. Dew found him plausible but had doubts, and when he visited him a few days later 39 Hilldrop Crescent was deserted: Crippen and Le Neve had fled. By running away, Crippen seemed to be implicating himself in his wife's disappearance, but since there was no body and nothing to tie Crippen to any harm that might have befallen Cora all he could do was issue a description of Cora and hope she turned up.

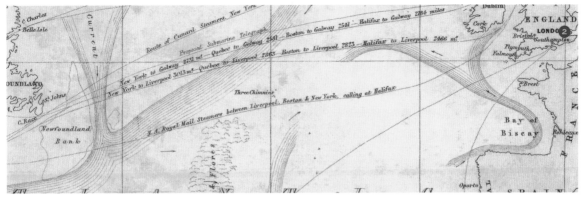

③ QUEBEC. THE CITY FROM WHICH CHIEF INSPECTOR WALTER DEW CONTACTED THE CANADIAN AUTHORITIES.

④ ST LAWRENCE RIVER. THE LOCATION OF THE *SS MONTROSE* WHEN CHIEF INSPECTOR WALTER DEW ARRESTED HAWLEY CRIPPEN.

⑤ ⟶
ETHEL LE NEVE ARRIVING AT HOLLOWAY PRISON FOLLOWING HER ARREST AS AN ACCOMPLICE.

⑥ ⟶
CROWDS OUTSIDE THE BOW STREET MAGISTRATES' COURT DURING THE TRIAL.

⑦ ⟶
HAWLEY CRIPPEN AND ETHEL LE NEVE IN THE DOCK AT THEIR TRIAL.

⑧ ⟶
NEWSPAPERS PUBLICIZING THE DETAILS OF THE CASE.

A discovery in the cellar of Crippen's home changed everything. A police search unearthed what appeared to be human remains, wrapped in cloth, under the flagstones. 'We found only masses of human flesh,' Dew wrote in his memoirs. 'The head was missing. No bones were ever discovered. Identification seemed impossible.' An unrivalled team now investigated the find; the pathologist, Augustus Joseph Pepper (1849–1935), and Bernard Spilsbury (1877–1947), his junior, were assisted by two toxicologists: William Willcox (1870–1941) and Arthur P. Luff (1855–1938). A scar on the abdomen was assumed to be evidence of a miscarriage Cora had suffered and a pyjama top found in the house matched the cloth found wrapped around the body in the cellar grave.

The forensics experts were sure that this was Cora's mutilated body; they now had to determine the cause of death. A chemical test for alkaloids revealed the presence of the poison hyoscine, which was far from a common means of killing. Crippen was an expert in drugs, having trained in medicine in the United States (where he was born) and in London. He sold remedies by post, and a pharmacist testified that Crippen had purchased 5 grams (⅕ oz) of hyoscine hydrobromide on 19 January 1910. The evidence was stacking up, but the police still did not have a suspect in custody because Crippen had vanished.

Then Dew got the breakthrough he needed. The captain of the *Montrose*, a passenger ship bound for Montreal, Canada, who had seen the press reports of Crippen's flight sent a 'marconigram' (radio telegram) to his employers. The message, passed on to Dew, relayed that the captain believed he had the fugitives on board under false names, with Ethel (disguised as a boy) travelling as Crippen's son. This was to result in Crippen becoming the first criminal to be caught with the aid of wireless telegraphy. Dew boarded a faster vessel – the *Laurentic* – and arrived in Quebec, Canada, on 30 July, at Farther Point, where the *Montrose* docked a day later. Dew went aboard disguised as a ship's pilot and arrested Crippen, who made no attempt to escape. 'I won't [jump],' he told Dew, 'I am more than satisfied because the anxiety has been too awful.'

Crippen's trial began on 18 October amid huge public interest. It lasted five days and the jury took just twenty-seven minutes to convict him. Ethel was acquitted of being an accessory, and sold her story to a newspaper. After an appeal failed, John Ellis (1874–1932) hanged Crippen at Pentonville Prison on 23 November 1910. 39 Hilldrop Crescent was bombed during the Second World War. Cora's head and limbs have never been found, leaving the remote possibility that the remains belonged to someone else. Crippen killed for love and he maintained Ethel's innocence to his last breath. ∎

'Thank God it's over. The suspense has been too great.
I couldn't stand it any longer.'

HAWLEY CRIPPEN TO WALTER DEW AT HIS ARREST.

Above. SCENES FROM THE CRIPPEN HOUSE INVESTIGATION, AND THE
LOCATION IN THE CELLAR WHERE THE BODY WAS DISCOVERED.

THE
LONDON MURDER
MYSTERY.

Mutilated Body found in a Cellar

Arrest of Crippen & Le Neve On board S.S. Montrose

THE NAUGHTY DOCTOR
The Crippen Diary.

'You must entertain no expectation or hope that you will escape the consequences of your crime.'

LORD ALVERSTONE BEFORE SENTENCING HAWLEY CRIPPEN.

Above. BILL POSTER FROM CONTEMPORARY PRESS COVERAGE
OF THE CRIPPEN MURDER MYSTERY.

WILLIAM CORDER.
✕ *Maria Marten.*

WEAPON.	TYPOLOGY.	POLICING.
PISTOL.	DOMESTIC.	BOW STREET RUNNERS.

THE RED BARN, POLSTEAD.

In May 1827, Maria Marten (unknown–1827) disappeared. She was last seen heading off to marry her latest beau, William Corder (1803–28), a local tenant farmer who owned a barn at Polstead, Suffolk. Maria was no virgin bride; she had already had two illegitimate children by two different lovers and she had given birth to Corder's child earlier that year. However, the subsequent discovery of her dead body, buried in Corder's red-painted barn, allowed her less than respectable past to be airbrushed for a very public refashioning of her life story.

Corder almost certainly killed Maria and then fled, claiming he and his bride had moved to the Isle of Wight. Maria's father found her body, supposedly after Maria's ghost had appeared to her stepmother in a dream. More plausibly, Mr Marten (dates unknown) grew suspicious after he received a letter from Corder saying all was well but that his new wife had injured her hand and was unable to write herself. The local magistracy commissioned a Bow Street Runner from London to hunt down the farmer and Corder was caught and put on trial for murder. Even if he had been innocent, he would have stood no chance of being acquitted. The press had already condemned him, painting Maria as the melodramatic victim of an evil seducer intent, without any foundation in truth it seems, on getting his hands on her property. It was claimed that Corder had tricked her into marriage, that he had tried this several times with other women and that he had even attempted to poison Maria's two older children by secreting pills inside pears. None of this was true, but that hardly mattered to a reading public who were becoming increasingly fascinated by each and every twist of the 'red barn' murder case.

A play was made about Maria's murder and was performed while Corder was awaiting trial; there was even a report of a magic lantern show in the local church hall that presented Corder as Maria's killer. His defence team did what they could to complain but it made little difference. Corder was convicted, having cut a pathetic and unconvincing figure in the dock. He was hanged in August 1828 and died slowly, taking eight minutes to expire as the hangman pulled on his legs. His dissected body was flayed and the skin tanned and used to bind a printed account of the murder; the rope was sold off at a guinea an inch, and pottery miniatures of Corder, Maria and the red barn at Polstead were bought by curious middle-class collectors.

Corder was an ordinary murderer, Maria's death a fairly ordinary murder, but the press and the emerging 'murder industry' turned an otherwise squalid, if tragic, killing into the leading sensation story of its day. In several respects, the red barn murder was the birth of 'true crime' in 'modern' Britain and it set the model for the exploitative presentation of murder news that developed across the next century or more. ∎

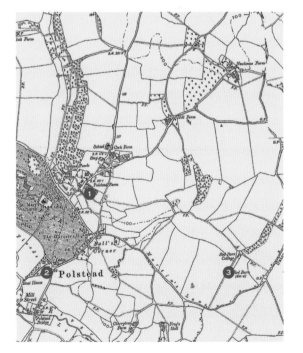

❶
WILLIAM CORDER'S HOUSE.
THE FARMHOUSE INHABITED BY WILLIAM CORDER.

❷
MARIA MARTEN'S HOUSE.
THE COTTAGE IN WHICH MARIA MARTEN LIVED.

❸
THE RED BARN.
THE BARN IN WHICH MARIA MARTEN WAS MURDERED BY WILLIAM CORDER.

Right. THE VILLAGE OF POLSTEAD IN SUFFOLK VIEWED FROM BELL HILL: AN IMAGE OF BUCOLIC TRANQUILLITY THAT WAS SOON TO BE DISRUPTED BY THE MURDER OF MARIA MARTEN.

Right. THE MARTENS'S PICTURESQUE COTTAGE IN POLSTEAD. MARIA MARTEN GREW UP IN POLSTEAD AND HAD HAD SEVERAL LOVERS BEFORE WILLIAM CORDER.

Right. THE EXTERIOR OF WILLIAM CORDER'S RED BARN; AN IMAGE THAT WOULD BE REPRODUCED ENDLESSLY IN THE LATE 1820S AND 1830S.

Right. MARIA MARTEN'S BODY WAS DISCOVERED LONG AFTER WILLIAM CORDER HAD LEFT POLSTEAD, SUPPOSEDLY AFTER MARIA APPEARED TO HER STEPMOTHER IN A DREAM.

Right. WILLIAM CORDER WAS EXECUTED FOR MARIA MARTEN'S MURDER OUTSIDE THE PRISON AT BURY ST EDMUNDS. HIS CORPSE WAS THEN GIVEN TO THE SURGEONS FOR ANATOMIZATION.

MARGARET HIGGINS & CATHERINE FLANNAGAN.
× *Thomas Higgins.*

WEAPON.	TYPOLOGY.	POLICING.
ARSENIC.	PROPERTY CRIME.	TOXICOLOGY.

27 ASCOT STREET, VAUXHALL.

MARGARET HIGGINS. CATHERINE FLANNAGAN.

In 1883, a series of deaths from 'natural causes' raised suspicions that occupants of one Liverpool house were being systematically murdered. The death of Thomas Higgins (1838–83) triggered an investigation. Thomas had been insured by five different burial societies and his widow, Margaret (1843–84), received a payout of £100. A post-mortem revealed that Thomas had been killed by arsenic poisoning, traced to flypaper. This discovery led the authorities to investigate other 'natural' deaths and the exhumed bodies of John Flannagan (1858–80), Mary Higgins (1874–82) and Margaret Jennings (1864–83) all tested positive for arsenic.

Two sisters, Margaret Higgins and Catherine Flannagan (1829–84), were arrested and charged with Thomas's murder. There was not sufficient evidence to press charges for the other deaths, but it was widely believed that the pair had killed them. The motive was the profit to be made from burial insurance, something many working-class families paid into in order to avoid a pauper funeral. A wider conspiracy, involving a mysterious woman named Bridget Stanton (dates unknown), was suspected but not proved. Higgins and Flannagan were hanged at Kirkdale Prison on 3 March 1884. ∎

① SKIRVING STREET. MARGARET HIGGINS AND CATHERINE FLANNAGAN'S FIRST LODGING HOUSE, WHERE THREE PEOPLE DIED.

② 105 LATIMER STREET. MARGARET HIGGINS AND CATHERINE FLANNAGAN'S SECOND LODGING HOUSE.

③ 27 ASCOT STREET. MARGARET HIGGINS AND CATHERINE FLANNAGAN'S THIRD LODGING HOUSE. THOMAS HIGGINS DIED HERE.

④ LYDIA ANN STREET. A STREET WHERE CATHERINE FLANNAGAN HID FROM THE POLICE.

⑤ MOUNT VERNON STREET. THE STREET WHERE CATHERINE FLANNAGAN WAS ARRESTED.

Right. ILLUSTRATED POLICE NEWS, 1 MARCH 1884. EXTRACTS FROM THE PRESS REPORTAGE OF THE CYNICAL MURDERS COMMITTED BY CATHERINE FLANNAGAN AND HER SISTER, MARY HIGGINS. THE PAIR KILLED TO CASH IN ON INSURANCE CLAIMS.

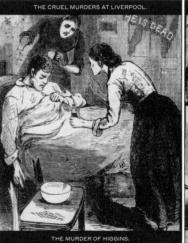

LEWIS PARRY.
× *Susannah Hutton.*

WEAPON.	TYPOLOGY.	POLICING.
BEATING.	DOMESTIC.	N/A.

LEEDS & LIVERPOOL CANAL, VAUXHALL.

| LEWIS PARRY. | SUSANNAH HUTTON. |

On the surface, it seemed as if Lewis Parry's (dates unknown) marriage to his wife, Mary (dates unknown), was a happy one. At some point, his wife had taken on a younger woman, 18-year old Susannah Hutton (1865–83), to help her with piecework as a seamstress, and this fatally undermined their relationship. Lewis and Susannah became lovers, and on 13 October 1883 witnesses noticed them in the 'snug' of a pub in Liverpool's dock quarter on Summer Seat. The pair drank quite a lot and left.

Parry would later argue that they parted company at that point, but soon afterwards a man and woman were heard quarrelling in a nearby stone yard. Screams shattered the peace of the night and a woman's body was later dragged from the Leeds & Liverpool canal. Despite the head being smashed in and 'horribly mutilated', Susannah's mother was able to identify her daughter's body. Parry was arrested, tried at Liverpool Assizes and convicted. There were, however, doubts as to whether he had killed his lover and this fuelled successful attempts to have his death sentence commuted to life imprisonment. ∎

❶ PUBLIC HOUSE, 13 SUMMER SEAT. THE PUB WHERE LEWIS PARRY MET WITH SUSANNAH HUTTON.

❷ LEEDS STREET [1]. THE FIRST STREET IN THE ROUTE TAKEN BY LEWIS PARRY AND SUSANNAH HUTTON.

❸ PLUMBE STREET. THE SECOND STREET IN THE ROUTE TAKEN BY LEWIS PARRY AND SUSANNAH HUTTON.

❹ YARD BETWEEN CANAL BRANCHES. THE PLACE WHERE SUSANNAH HUTTON WAS MURDERED.

❺ LEEDS STREET [2]. THE STREET THROUGH WHICH LEWIS PARRY MADE HIS ESCAPE.

❻ PRUSSIA STREET. THE STREET WHERE LEWIS PARRY WAS CAUGHT BY WALTER STEBBING AND PHILIP MCGARRY.

Right. ILLUSTRATED POLICE NEWS, 3 NOVEMBER 1883. SCENES FROM PRESS COVERAGE OF THE SO-CALLED 'CANAL TRAGEDY'. SUSANNAH HUTTON'S BODY WAS FOUND IN THE LEEDS & LIVERPOOL CANAL AFTER SHE HAD BEEN KILLED BY HER LOVER FOLLOWING AN ARGUMENT.

FLORENCE MAYBRICK.
× *James Maybrick.*

WEAPON.	TYPOLOGY.	POLICING.
ARSENIC.	DOMESTIC.	TOXICOLOGY.

BATTLECREASE HOUSE, RIVERSDALE ROAD, AIGBURTH.

| FLORENCE MAYBRICK. | JAMES MAYBRICK. |

The trial of Florence Maybrick (1862–1941) for the murder of her husband, the Liverpool businessman James Maybrick (1838–89), was one of the most sensational of the 1800s. It was also an example of a miscarriage of justice that condemned a woman on the grounds of character, rather than any evidence that she had committed a crime.

US-born Florence Chandler had married James Maybrick in 1881 and the couple settled in Liverpool's Aigburth suburb. When James became ill in April 1889, suspicions fell on Florence. She was known to have purchased flypaper and to have extracted arsenic from it, which she claimed she used as a cosmetic for her skin. When James died, Florence was accused of poisoning him. The forensic case assembled by her defence team was solid: James had been self-medicating with a cocktail of drugs for years and there was ample evidence that he had stocks of arsenic and other poisons in the house. His death was put down to gastroenteritis, but the judge – Justice James Fitzjames Stephen (1829–94) – misled the jury to find Florence responsible. The underlying motive was unclear, as both parties had engaged in extramarital affairs and James had cut his wife out of his will so she had little to gain, financially at least, from his death. The slight evidence presented against her was circumstantial at best, but she came across in court as a 'vivacious and headstrong' woman, which alienated the judge and the all-male jury. Florence was convicted of murder and sentenced to hang. A huge public outcry and a petition containing half a million signatures saved her life and she spent the next fourteen years in jail, returning to the United States in 1904.

In 1992, a diary surfaced that purported to have been written in 1888 by none other than Jack the Ripper. While it did not name him directly, the diary was alleged to have been penned by James Maybrick, who had visited London at the time of the Whitechapel Murders. Was Maybrick the Ripper, and was this why Florence killed him? It seems unlikely, and more realistic to view Florence as a woman badly let down by British 'justice'. ▪

BATTLECREASE HOUSE, RIVERSDALE ROAD.
THE HOUSE WHERE THE MAYBRICKS LIVED.

THOMAS SYMINGTON WOKES, CHEMIST, AIGBURTH ROAD.
A CHEMIST WHERE FLORENCE MAYBRICK PURCHASED FLYPAPERS.

CHRISTOPHER HANSON, CHEMIST, AIGBURTH ROAD.
A CHEMIST WHERE FLORENCE MAYBRICK PURCHASED FLYPAPERS.

Right. ILLUSTRATED POLICE NEWS, 22 JUNE 1889. IMAGES OF FLORENCE AND JAMES MAYBRICK. THE PRESS DUBBED THE CASE THE 'LIVERPOOL POISONING MYSTERY'.

Right. ILLUSTRATED POLICE NEWS, 31 AUGUST 1889. THERE WAS CONSIDERABLE PUBLIC SYMPATHY FOR FLORENCE MAYBRICK, EVEN IF THIS WAS NOT SHARED BY THE JUDGE AND JURY THAT TRIED HER.

Right. ILLUSTRATED POLICE NEWS, 9 JULY 1889. A PETITION TO SAVE FLORENCE MAYBRICK'S LIFE WAS SUCCESSFUL BUT SHE STILL SPENT FOURTEEN YEARS IN PRISON FOR A MURDER SHE ALMOST CERTAINLY DID NOT COMMIT.

Right. ILLUSTRATED POLICE NEWS, 10 AUGUST 1889. SIR JAMES FITZJAMES STEPHEN, JUDGE AT FLORENCE MAYBRICK'S TRIAL, WAS ACCUSED OF DIRECTING THE JURY TO CONVICT FLORENCE DESPITE A LACK OF EVIDENCE OF HER GUILT.

MURDER IN VAUXHALL.

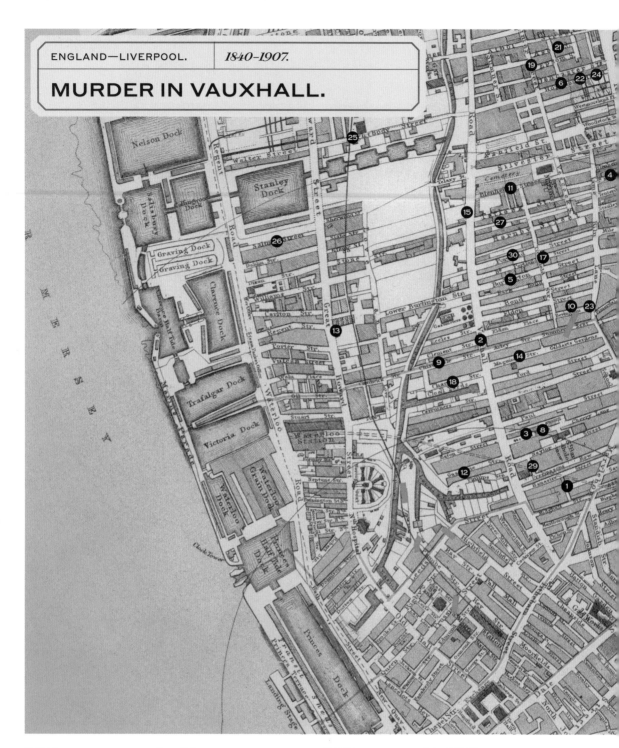

1840. STOCKDALE STREET. Owen Kehoe. × ANN KEHOE.

1846. PAINE'S PUBLIC HOUSE, VAUXHALL ROAD. John Frost. × JOHN DAVIES.

1849. ORIEL STREET. Patrick Culkin. × JAMES CULKIN. × CATHERINE CULKIN.

1850. ST MARTIN STREET. Michael Callaghan. × PATRICK CAFFRAY.

1852. BURLINGTON STREET. William Sanderson. × GEORGE SPRATT.

1855. HOPWOOD STREET. Thomas Cavanagh. × FRANCIS BEAGAN.

1855. NORRIS STREET, BEVINGTON HILL. Jane Clayton. × INFANT.

1855. ORIEL STREET. John O'Neill. × THOMAS CAHILL.

1856. CHISENHALE STREET. Philip Wall & James Carr. × JAMES HOUSE.

1858. BEVINGTON STREET. Jacob Wilhem. × CAROLINE JAGER.

1859. BLENHEIM STREET. Alice Mcallister. × SARAH EVANS.

1865. GASCOYNE STREET. Alice Vallally. × JANE GOODIER.

1867. GREAT HOWARD STREET. Robert Porter. × THOMAS COUNSEL.

1867. MAGUIRE STREET. James Hobin. × ELIZA HOBIN.

1869. 249 VAUXHALL ROAD. Stephen Brennan. × MARY WHITE.

1871. GROSVENOR STREET. Maria McHale. × PATRICK HOGAN.

17 1874. TITCHFIELD STREET. Sarah Mccarthy. × CATHERINE RICE.

18 1876. CHARTERS STREET. Ellen Carson. × ABIGAIL CARSON.

19 1877. LATIMER STREET. Patrick Mcgovern. × JOHN CAMPBELL.

20 1882. MR GRACE'S PUBLIC HOUSE, SCOTLAND ROAD.
Edward McGuiness. × PHILIP CLARKE.

21 1883. 27 ASCOT STREET. Margaret Higgins & Catherine
Flannagan. × THOMAS HIGGINS.

22 1887. HOPWOOD STREET. Catherine Chapman. × ANN DOYLE.

23 1892. BEVINGTON STREET. Thomas Heeney.
× THOMAS MANNING.

24 1892. HOPWOOD STREET. Unknown. × ANN CONCANNON.

25 1892. LIGHTBODY STREET. Walter Peloe, John Leicester,
Joseph Wilson & Thomas Davies. × JOHN SWINDELLS.

26 1897. SALTNEY STREET. Thomas Lynch. × MARGARET LYNCH.

27 1900. RAYMOND STREET. James Maloney.
× MARGARET ROXBURGH.

28 1901. CORNER OF SPRINGFIELD STREET AND CHRISTIAN
STREET. Thomas McAllister. × CATHERINE MCALLISTER.

29 1902. GLADSTONE STREET. Francis Burke. × CATHERINE DALY.

30 1907. PORTLAND STREET. Thomas Nolan. × MRS NOLAN.

MADELEINE SMITH.
× *Pierre Emile L'Angelier.*

WEAPON. ARSENIC.	TYPOLOGY. DOMESTIC.	POLICING. TOXICOLOGY.

BLYTHSWOOD SQUARE, BLYTHSWOOD HILL.

Left. A NEWSPAPER PORTRAIT OF MADELEINE SMITH IN COURT.

Right. THE HOUSE ON BLYTHSWOOD SQUARE.

Pierre Emile L'Angelier (unknown–1857) had come to Glasgow, Scotland, from his Jersey home to prepare for a life in business. Swapping the Channel Islands for 1850s Glasgow was not successful, however, and Emile had to settle for work as a shipping clerk. Somehow, he met an attractive young woman, Madeleine Smith (1835–1928), who was the daughter of a successful architect. The couple began a relationship, platonic at first but sexual after 1856, and exchanged hundreds of letters. When Madeleine's family got wind of an affair with someone so unsuitable, they set about finding a better match.

Madeleine became engaged to William Minnoch (dates unknown), a wealthy merchant. She broke off the affair with Emile, who reacted badly and threatened to expose their relationship. Madeleine played Emile along for a while and then bought arsenic and, possibly inspired by a performance of the opera *Lucrezia Borgia*, she poisoned his drinks on three occasions. Emile died on 23 March 1857. A post-mortem revealed that he had consumed 85 grams (3 oz) of arsenic, a huge amount and more than sufficient to kill him. A police search of the clerk's room uncovered more than 200 letters from Madeleine and led to her arrest and trial. Smith's defence team suggested that Emile might have poisoned himself by accident, pointing to a history of gastric problems that might have caused him to self-medicate. Yet while the jury accepted the cause of death, they were not convinced by the prosecution's accusation that Madeleine was involved. In court, Emile's reputation was trashed: he was a foreigner who had taken advantage of a defenceless girl. Scottish law allows a verdict of 'not proven' and so she escaped the immediate consequences of her actions. This did have some repercussions, though: the scandal spooked her fiancé who broke off the engagement. Madeleine moved to London and, four years later, married an artist. When he died (of natural causes; no suspicions were raised this time), she emigrated to the United States, where she died in 1928. ■

① ⟶ EMILE L'ANGELIER AND MADELEINE SMITH'S RELATIONSHIP IS PLATONIC TO BEGIN WITH.

② ⟶ BUT IT SOON PROGRESSES INTO A SEXUAL RELATIONSHIP.

③ ⟶ MADELEINE SMITH CHOOSES TO MARRY A WEALTHY MERCHANT AND REJECTS EMILE L'ANGELIER.

④ ⟶ MADELEINE SMITH POISONS EMILE L'ANGELIER WHEN HE THREATENS TO EXPOSE THEIR RELATIONSHIP.

⑤ ⟶ EMILE L'ANGELIER LIES ON HIS DEATH BED, POISONED WITH ARSENIC.

⑥ MADELEINE SMITH APPEARS BEFORE A JURY IN GLASGOW, BUT THE CASE IS 'NOT PROVEN'.

1 BEDROOM.
THE ROOM WHERE
MADELEINE'S
PARENTS SLEPT.

2 BEDROOM.
THE ROOM WHERE
MADELEINE'S
SISTER SLEPT.

3 BEDROOM.
THE ROOM WHERE
MADELEINE'S
BROTHER SLEPT.

4 PANTRY.
A ROOM WHERE
THE SMITH FAMILY
STORED FOOD.

5 DINING ROOM.
THE ROOM WHERE
THE SMITH
FAMILY DINED.

6 DRAWING ROOM.
THE ROOM WHERE
MADELEINE SMITH
RECEIVED EMILE
L'ANGELIER.

7 BEDROOM.
A SPARE BEDROOM
IN THE SMITH
HOUSE.

8 PANTRY.
A ROOM WHERE
THE SMITH FAMILY
STORED FOOD.

9 BEDROOM.
THE ROOM WHERE
MADELEINE
SMITH SLEPT.

10 WINDOW.
THE WINDOW
THROUGH WHICH
MADELEINE SMITH
PASSED LETTERS TO
EMILE L'ANGELIER.

11 BEDROOM.
A SPARE BEDROOM
IN THE SMITH
HOUSE.

12 KITCHEN.
WHERE MADELEINE
SMITH PREPARED
THE DRINK LACED
WITH ARSENIC.

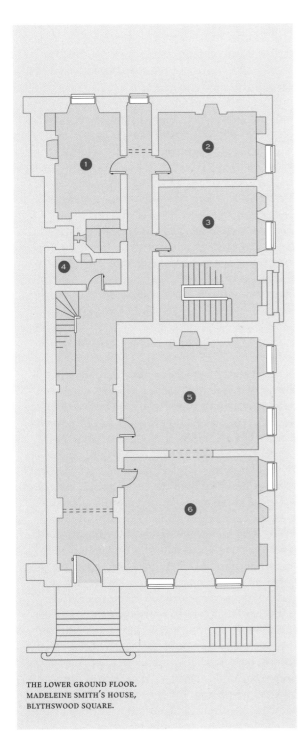

THE LOWER GROUND FLOOR.
MADELEINE SMITH'S HOUSE,
BLYTHSWOOD SQUARE.

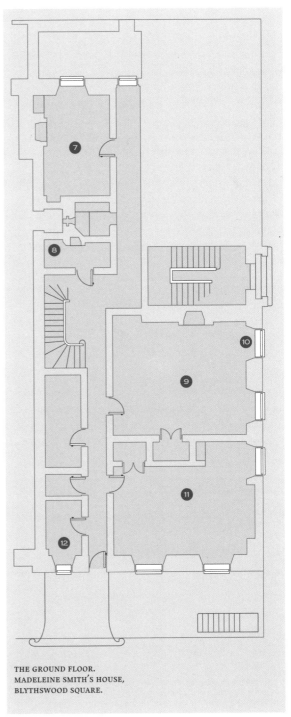

THE GROUND FLOOR.
MADELEINE SMITH'S HOUSE,
BLYTHSWOOD SQUARE.

EDWARD WILLIAM PRITCHARD.
× *Jane Taylor.* × *Mary Jane Pritchard.*

WEAPON. ANTIMONY.	TYPOLOGY. PROPERTY CRIME.	POLICING. TOXICOLOGY.

131 SAUCHIEHALL STREET, CENTRAL GLASGOW.

Dr Edward William Pritchard (1825–65) managed to achieve the dubious distinction in Scottish history of being the last man to be publicly executed. For a man who seemed to crave the attention of others, it was perhaps fitting that 100,000 Glaswegians watched him die on 28 July 1865. Dr Pritchard was a shameless self-publicist, much better at talking up his exploits than practising medicine. He was also a man who had a taste for young women and this, ultimately, was to be his undoing.

After an unsuccessful career in the Royal Navy and a period of general practice in Yorkshire, Pritchard and his wife Mary (1827–65) settled in Glasgow. In May 1863, a fire broke out at their home. It was spotted by a passing policeman who raised the alarm. The fire killed one of the Pritchards' servants, Elizabeth McGrain (1838–63). Her death was thought to be suspicious, because she seemed to have become trapped in her room and possibly drugged, but nothing pointed directly to Pritchard as a killer. What was not known at the time was that Pritchard had been sleeping with the girl's predecessor and may well have got her pregnant before turning his attentions to McGrain.

After moving house, Pritchard started an affair with another servant, Mary McLeod (dates unknown), whom he also managed to get pregnant. This time, his wife found out, McLeod had an abortion, and Pritchard was forgiven. Unbeknoto Mary Pritchard, her husband had not only impregnated their domestic, he had also made promises of marriage. He told McLeod that should his wife die she would be next in line to become mistress of the house. So, it was no surprise when Mary Pritchard fell ill. At first, Pritchard treated his wife, resisting her calls for him to get in an independent doctor. Everything he tried failed or made her worse. Mary Pritchard begged her husband to send for her brother, himself a doctor, but Pritchard fobbed her off, bringing in a succession of physicians whom he misled. As Mary deteriorated, her brother arrived, but Pritchard continued to interfere to cloud his diagnosis. All the time, he was poisoning her with antimony. When Mary's mother, Jane Taylor (1795–1865), came to nurse her, Pritchard started to poison her as well, using a cocktail of opium, aconite and antimony.

Mary's mother died on 28 February, followed by her daughter on 18 March. Dr Pritchard shed 'crocodile tears' as his wife's coffin was sealed for burial. His charade might have succeeded had the police not received an anonymous tip-off. Mother and daughter were exhumed and tested. While it was hard to determine poisoning conclusively, the presence of orange stains led to a conclusion that antimony potassium tartrate had been used. Dr Pritchard had bought unusual quantities of the drug from local chemists, which helped convict him. Before he went to his execution, Pritchard admitted his crimes and exonerated his maidservant. It was the only decent thing he did. ∎

Fig 1.

Under influence of genuine Battley's Solution of Opium

Fig 2.

Above. ILLUSTRATIONS DEMONSTRATING THE EFFECTS OF MEDICINAL OPIUM (TOP) COMPARED TO THE POISONOUS SOLUTION USED BY DR EDWARD WILLIAM PRITCHARD (BOTTOM).

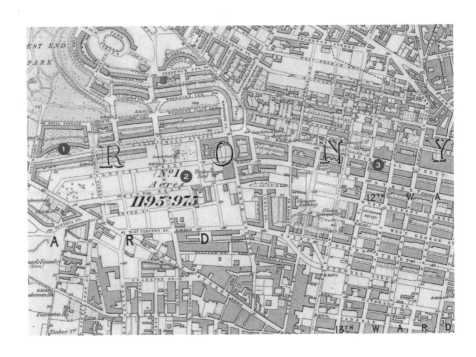

1
22 ROYAL CRESCENT.
THE HOUSE IN WHICH DR PRITCHARD
RESIDED 1863–64.

2
11 BERKELEY TERRACE.
THE HOUSE WHERE THE FIRE
TOOK PLACE ON 5 MAY 1863.

3
249 (FORMERLY 131)
SAUCHIEHALL STREET.
THE HOUSE WHERE
JANE TAYLOR AND MARY
JANE PRITCHARD WERE
MURDERED BY EDWARD
WILLIAM PRITCHARD.

MARY MCLEOD & DAUGHTER.

MARY JANE PRITCHARD.

JANE TAYLOR.

OSCAR SLATER.
✕ *Marion Gilchrist.*

WEAPON.	TYPOLOGY.	POLICING.
HAMMER.	PROPERTY CRIME.	IDENTITY PARADE.

15 QUEEN'S TERRACE, WEST PRINCES STREET, WOODLANDS.

OSCAR SLATER. | MARION GILCHRIST.

Marion Gilchrist (1825–1908) was murdered by someone, but not by the person who was eventually convicted of doing so. On the evening of 21 December 1908, the Adams family who lived below Miss Gilchrist in a flat on Queen's Terrace, Glasgow, heard a thud above them, and three 'distinct knocks'. The elderly and wealthy Miss Gilchrist was terrified of being robbed in her own home and had primed her neighbours for just such an alarm signal. They hurried upstairs to see if she was safe. Minutes later, her maid Nellie (dates unknown) arrived and opened the door. As she did so, a smartly dressed man pushed past her down the stairs. Miss Gilchrist's dead body was in front of the fireplace, a rug covering her smashed head. The motive was suspected to be robbery, as one of the lady's brooches was missing. The police arrived and quickly discovered a new clue; a 14-year-old girl named Mary Barrowman (c. 1894–unknown) claimed to have seen the man running from the house. Her description was so wildly different from that given by Nellie and the Adams family, however, that detectives believed two men were involved. They then got a tip-off that a German Jew, Oscar Slater (1872–1948), had tried to pawn a brooch that matched the one missing. Before they could interview him, he took a ship from Liverpool to the United States, where he was arrested in January.

The police sent Mr Adams, Nellie and Mary to New York to identify him, but the identity parade was a farce because Slater was put up against several off-duty policemen. The prosecution case was weak. Slater had booked his ticket to the United States a month earlier, there was no evidence that he had pawned a brooch, and he also had an alibi. However, the outrage at the killing of an octogenarian and the lack of other suspects led a Glasgow jury to convict Slater, who was sentenced to hang. A well-orchestrated campaign led 20,000 people to sign a petition and this (coupled with underlying doubts about the safety of the conviction) saved his life. Nevertheless, Slater spent nineteen years in jail for a murder he did not commit.

A year after the trial, his case became the subject of a book by William Roughland (dates unknown), an early example of a modern 'true crime' investigation that exposed the inconsistencies in the evidence presented at the trial. This reignited calls for the verdict to be overturned and for Slater to be released. In 1914, the Secretary of State for Scotland, Thomas McKinnon Wood (1855–1927) ordered a review, but this failed to quash the conviction. Then another book, in 1927, finally convinced the authorities that Slater had been wrongly convicted of Marion Gilchrist's murder. In 1928, his conviction was quashed, and he was paid £6,000 in compensation. ∎

❶
15 QUEEN'S TERRACE.
THE FLAT WHERE MARION GILCHRIST LIVED AND WAS MURDERED.

❷
46 WEST PRINCES STREET.
THE HOUSE FROM WHICH A WITNESS CLAIMED TO HAVE SEEN OSCAR SLATER.

❸
CORNER OF QUEEN'S CRESCENT.
THE PLACE FROM WHICH A WITNESS CLAIMED TO HAVE SEEN OSCAR SLATER.

❹
14 QUEEN'S TERRACE.
THE FLAT WHERE THE ADAMS FAMILY LIVED.

❺
ST GEORGE'S ROAD.
THE ROAD ON WHICH OSCAR SLATER LIVED.

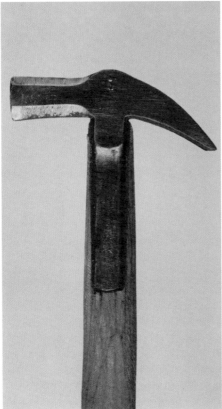

Top. A VIEW FROM THE CORNER OF QUEEN'S TERRACE.

Above left. A HAMMER FOUND IN OSCAR SLATER'S LUGGAGE.
THE PROSECUTION'S MEDICAL EXPERT, PROFESSOR GLAISTER,
BELIEVED IT COULD HAVE BEEN THE MURDER WEAPON.

Above right. OSCAR SLATER'S TRIAL. XENOPHOBIC PREJUDICE
AND HORROR AT THE MURDER SECURED HIS CONVICTION.

Below right. A FRONT VIEW OF THE FLATS AT 14 AND 15
QUEEN'S TERRACE.

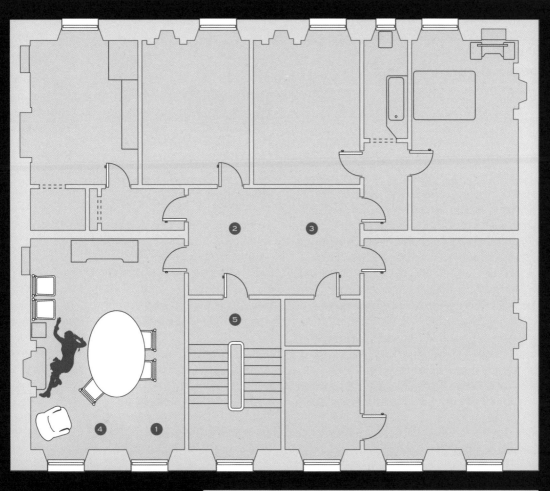

① **DINING ROOM (VIEW I).**
THE ROOM IN WHICH MARION
GILCHRIST'S BODY WAS FOUND.

② **HALLWAY (VIEW I).**
FACING THE ENTRANCE TO
THE DINING ROOM IN WHICH
MARION GILCHRIST'S BODY
WAS FOUND AND A DOOR
OPENING TO A LOBBY.

③ **HALLWAY (VIEW II).**
FACING THE DOOR TO A LOBBY
AND THE ENTRANCE TO A
DRAWING ROOM.

④ **DINING ROOM (VIEW II).**
SHOWING THE SPACE BETWEEN
THE FIREPLACE AND THE
DINING TABLE WHERE MARION
GILCHRIST'S BODY WAS FOUND.

⑤ **STAIRWAY AND LANDING.**
THE STAIRS DOWN WHICH
THE MURDERER FLED.

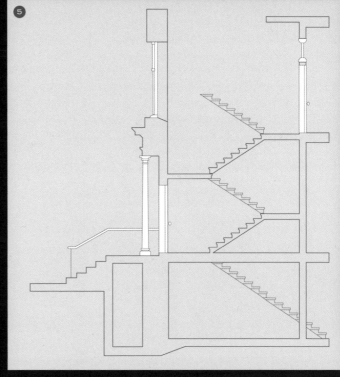

GABRIELLE BOMPARD & MICHEL EYRAUD.
✕ *Toussaint-Augustin Gouffé.*

WEAPON. PULLEY.	TYPOLOGY. PROPERTY CRIME.	POLICING. PATHOLOGY.

RUE TRONSON-DU-COUDRAY, 8E ARRONDISSEMENT.

GABRIELLE BOMPARD.	MICHEL EYRAUD.	TOUSSAINT-AUGUSTIN GOUFFÉ.

Without Dr Alexandre Lacassagne (1843–1924), the killers of Toussaint-Augustin Gouffé (unknown–1889) may well have got away with murder. Gouffé, a Parisian bailiff, vanished in July 1889 and his worried brother alerted the police. Marie-François Goron (1847–1933) of the Paris Sûreté took the case and his dogged determination eventually brought the culprits to justice.

A body was discovered at Millery, southeast France, wrapped in an oilskin cloth bag and close to the broken fragments of a trunk. Experts examined the decomposing cadaver, but Gouffé's brother was unable to identify it. Undeterred, Commissioner Goron continued his investigation and was rewarded with a breakthrough. Gouffé had been seen, just before his disappearance, with a known fraudster named Michel Eyraud (1843–91) and a young woman.

Gouffé had a reputation as a womanizer and Eyraud had teamed up with Gabrielle Bompard (1868–c. 1920) to exploit this. Bompard lured Gouffé to her Paris apartment, where Eyraud had concocted an elaborate plan to kill and rob him. Having steered him onto a chaise longue Gabrielle was supposed to playfully place a silk cord around his neck, as a precursor to sex. The cord was attached to a pulley fixed to a crossbeam and Eyraud was concealed behind a curtain waiting to pull it tight and strangle the couple's victim. It seems Bompard lost her nerve and her partner in crime had to intervene, violently despatching Gouffé as he struggled for life. Unfortunately for the thieves, their wealthy victim had not brought any money with him and so all they achieved was a corpse to dispose of. They shoved him in a trunk, dumped him near a river and fled to Lyon.

Armed with his tip-off, Goron called in the renowned pathologist Lacassagne from Lyon and had the body exhumed. Despite the cadaver being four months in the ground, Lacassagne was able, using both pathology and anthropometrics (developed by his student Étienne Rollet [1862–1937]), to establish Gouffé's identity beyond doubt. He used a sample of hair from a comb the dead man was known to have used and medical records that showed he had once sustained a serious back injury. Eyraud and Bompard were hunted across the Americas, captured in Havana and Vancouver, respectively, and brought back to Paris to face trial.

Bompard's lawyer claimed that his client's actions were involuntary as she had been hypnotized by the older Eyraud. It may not have saved her from conviction, but it probably seeded enough doubt in the minds of the authorities to ensure she did not lose her head. The Paris jury convicted both defendants of the murder of Gouffé. Bompard got twenty years while Eyraud went to the guillotine on 3 February 1891 in front of a huge crowd. The 'bloody trunk' case is an important milestone in forensic history, marking one of the first occasions when a post-mortem, now routine, established clues to a victim's identity. ∎

Above. CONTEMPORARY RECONSTRUCTION OF THE ARREST OF MICHEL EYRAUD BY POLICE IN HAVANA, CUBA, IN 1889.

Above. STAGED PHOTOGRAPH OF FRENCH POLICE EXAMINING A BODY (POSSIBLY THAT OF TOUSSAINT-AUGUSTIN GOUFFÉ).

Above. STAGED RECONSTRUCTION FROM THE GOUFFÉ CASE, PRESUMABLY MADE TO AID THE INVESTIGATION.

1

RUE TRONSON-DU-COUDRAY, PARIS.
THE LOCATION OF THE APARTMENT WHERE GABRIELLE BOMPARD AND MICHEL EYRAUD MURDERED TOUSSAINT-AUGUSTIN GOUFFÉ.

2

MILLERY, RHÔNE.
THE VILLAGE WHERE THE BODY OF TOUSSAINT-AUGUSTIN GOUFFÉ WAS FOUND UNDER A BUSH IN AN OILSKIN BAG.

3

SAINT-GENIS-LAVAL, RHÔNE.
THE VILLAGE WHERE THE ABANDONED TRUNK USED TO TRANSPORT TOUSSAINT-AUGUSTIN GOUFFÉ'S BODY WAS FOUND.

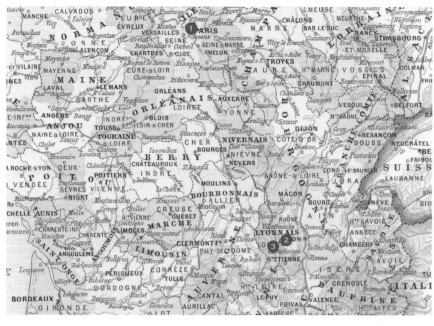

Left. MICHEL EYRAUD STRANGLED TOUSSAINT-AUGUSTIN GOUFFÉ FROM BEHIND ONCE GABRIELLE BOMPARD HAD LURED HIM TO THE CHAISE LONGUE.

Right. THE MURDERERS STUFFED THEIR VICTIM'S LIFELESS BODY INTO AN OILSKIN BAG.

Left. HAVING TRANSPORTED TOUSSAINT-AUGUSTIN GOUFFÉ OUT OF THE CAPITAL IN A TRUNK, THE MURDERERS DUMPED HIS BODY NEAR A RIVER BANK.

Right. WHEN QUESTIONED, GABRIELLE BOMPARD DENIED HER GUILT, AND CLAIMED SHE HAD BEEN COERCED INTO HELPING MICHEL EYRAUD.

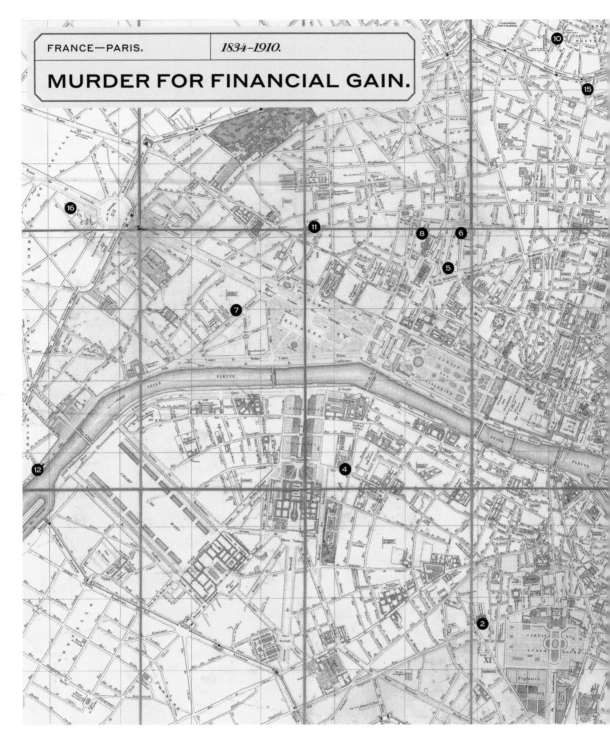

MURDER FOR FINANCIAL GAIN.

❶ 1834. PASSAGE DU CHEVAL ROUGE, 3E ARRONDISSEMENT. Pierre François Lacernaire. ✕ M. CHARDON. ✕ MME. CHARDON.

❷ 1874. 242 RUE DE VAUGIRARD, 15E ARRONDISSEMENT. Paul Thauvin, Blaise Georges & Adolphe Maillot. ✕ MME. ROUGIER.

❸ 1878. 11 RUE D'HAUTEVILLE, 10E ARRONDISSEMENT. Aimé Barré & Paul Lebiez Barré. ✕ MME. BERTHE LIBERRE-LIMOUSE.

❹ 1884. 145 RUE DE GRENELLE, 7E ARRONDISSEMENT. Adolphe Tiburce Gamahut. ✕ MME. BALLERICH.

❺ 1885. RUE DE SÈZE, 1E ARRONDISSEMENT. Charles Marchandon. ✕ MLLE. CORNET.

❻ 1886. RUE CAUMARTIN, 9E ARRONDISSEMENT. Luis Federico Stanislas Prado Linska y Castillon. ✕ MARIE AGUETANT.

❼ 1887. RUE MONTAIGNE, 8E ARRONDISSEMENT. Henri Pranzini. ✕ CLAUDINE-MARIE REGNAULT. ✕ ANNETTE GRÉMERET. ✕ MARIE-LOUISE GRÉMERET.

❽ 1890. 3 RUE TRONSON-DU-COUDRAY, 8E ARRONDISSEMENT. Gabrielle Bompard & Michel Eyraud. ✕ TOUSSAINT-AUGUSTIN GOUFFÉ.

❾ 1891. 2 BOULEVARD DU TEMPLE, 11E ARRONDISSEMENT. Louis Anastay. ✕ BARONESS DELLARD.

❿ 1893. 38 RUE BERTHE, 18E ARRONDISSEMENT. Pierre Kutz. ✕ ANGÉLIQUE FALQUIE.

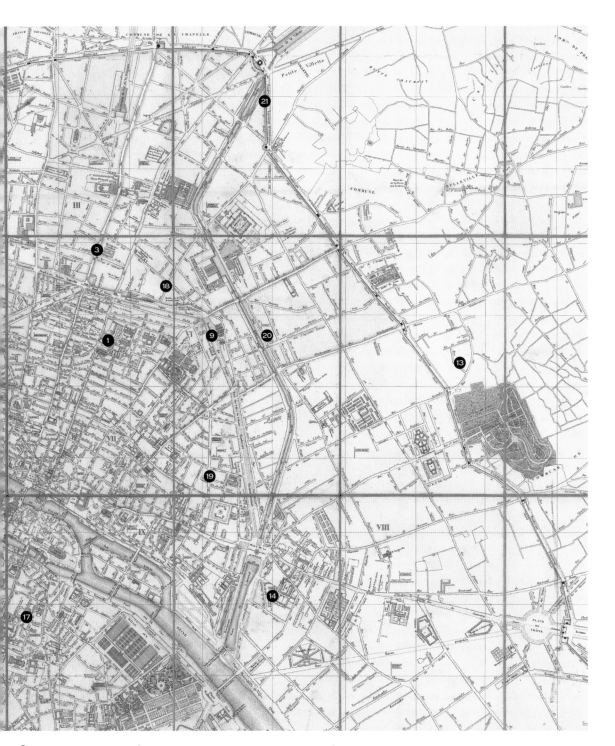

11 1896. 26 RUE DE PENTHIÈVRE, 8E ARRONDISSEMENT. **Kiesgen & Truel.** ✕ BARONESS HERMINIE DE VALLEY.

12 1896. AVENUE DE VERSAILLES, 16E ARRONDISSEMENT. **M. Aubert.** ✕ M. DELAHAEFF.

13 1897. RUE ÉTIENNE-DOLET, 20E ARRONDISSEMENT. **Xavier-Ange Carrara.** ✕ AUGUSTIN-FRÉDERIC LAMARRE.

14 1901. RUE MOREAU, 12E ARRONDISSEMENT. **Codebo & Pillot.** ✕ UNKNOWN WOMAN.

15 1902. 74 RUE DE MARTYRS, 18E ARRONDISSEMENT. **Unknown.** ✕ MME. LECOMTE.

16 1903. 9 RUE CHALGRIN, 16E ARRONDISSEMENT. **Paul Jules Martin.** ✕ BERTHE DE BRIENNE.

17 1903. 7 RUE LANNEAU, 5E ARRONDISSEMENT. **Unknown.** ✕ M. BONNOMEU.

18 1904. RUE DE LANCRY, 10E ARRONDISSEMENT. **Victor Bender & Charles Huet.** ✕ ANDRÉ HAUG.

19 1904. 32 RUE DE TURENNE, 3E ARRONDISSEMENT. **Célestin-Nicolas Pierson, Jules Morrot, Victor Pagès & Anthelme Gay.** ✕ MME. BAL.

20 1906. 101 RUE FOLIE MÉRICOURT, 11E ARRONDISSEMENT. **Georges-Frédéric Amiot.** ✕ MME. LUCAS.

21 1910. BOULEVARD DE LA VILLETTE, 10E ARRONDISSEMENT. **Georges Tissier & Paul Demarest.** ✕ JEAN-ÉMILE ANDRÉ.

LE CRIME DU BOULEVARD DU TEMPLE

LE DRAME DE LA RUE DU ROCHER
Une Femme tuant la Maîtresse de son Mari

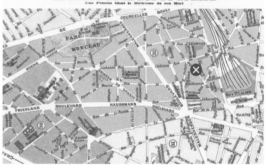

FRANCE—PARIS.	*November 1891.*

LOUIS ANASTAY.
✕ *Baroness Dellard.* ✕ *1.*

WEAPON. KNIFE.	TYPOLOGY. PROPERTY CRIME.	POLICING. N/A.

2 BOULEVARD DU TEMPLE, 11E ARRONDISSEMENT.

Down on his luck and desperate for money, Louis Anastay (1866–92) resorted to robbery and murder. He knew that the elderly Baroness Dellard (unknown–1891) was wealthy, and so broke into her home in November 1891. He seized the baroness and cut her throat, and when her maid (unknown–1891) found him ransacking the house he stabbed her to death as well. He later confessed to both murders and was sentenced to death in February 1892. Having previously lost his position in the army through misconduct, he now lost his head to Madame Guillotine. ∎

Above. LE PROGRÈS ILLUSTRÉ, 13 DECEMBER 1891.
THE MURDER AT BOULEVARD DU TEMPLE.

FRANCE—PARIS.	*June 1892.*

CLAIRE REYMOND.
✕ *Yvonne Lassimonne.*

WEAPON. KNIFE.	TYPOLOGY. JEALOUSY.	POLICING. N/A.

33 RUE DU ROCHER, 8E ARRONDISSEMENT.

When Claire Reymond (dates unknown) discovered that her husband was having an extramarital affair with her long-time friend Yvonne Lassimonne (unknown–1892), she was determined to put an end to it. She found the apartment her husband had rented for the purpose and forced her way in. She confronted her rival and shot her in the stomach with a revolver, before stabbing her repeatedly as she lay on the floor. Pleading temporary insanity, Madame Reymond was acquitted of the murder, to applause from several women in the court's public gallery. ∎

Above. LE PETIT PARISIEN, 5 JUNE 1892.
MADAME REYMOND SHOOTS HER RIVAL.

LE DRAME DE LA RUE VANEAU

LA BARONNE DE VALLEY ÉTRANGLÉE

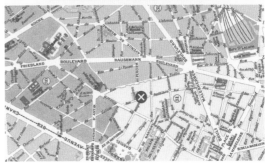

FRANCE—PARIS.	23 August 1892.

LOUIS COGNEVAUX.
✕ *Marie Ruppert.*

WEAPON. KNIFE.	TYPOLOGY. JEALOUSY.	POLICING. N/A.

HOTEL DE NORMANDIE, 84 RUE VANEAU, 7E ARRONDISSEMENT.

One of the most abiding motives for murder is jealousy, particularly when relationships fall apart. This is what happened when Marie Ruppert (unknown–1892) ended her relationship with Louis Cogneveaux (unknown–1892). She had lived with the shoemaker for thirteen years but left him and took rooms with her son by a previous marriage. Cogneveaux tried to coax her back with a mixture of promises and threats but she resisted. Enraged, he lay in wait in the hotel's courtyard and stabbed her to death. As he tried to shoot himself, Marie's son rushed out and killed him where he stood. ∎

FRANCE—PARIS.	1896.

KIESGEN & TRUEL.
✕ *Baroness Herminie de Valley.*

WEAPON. KNIFE.	TYPOLOGY. PROPERTY CRIME.	POLICING. N/A.

26 RUE DE PENTHIÈVRE, 8E ARRONDISSEMENT.

In 1896, four young men went before the Court of Assizes charged with the murder of a wealthy widow in her home. Baroness Herminie de Valley (1814–96) was 82 and possessed a large fortune from her property investments. Fernard Lagneny (dates unknown) knew this as he had previously worked for the baroness and he persuaded three others to conspire to kill her. She was tied up and strangled to death, but the quartet were arrested and tried. The killers, Kiesgen (dates unknown) and Truel (dates unknown), got life; Lagneny, as the instigator, received ten years and the gang's lookout received five. ∎

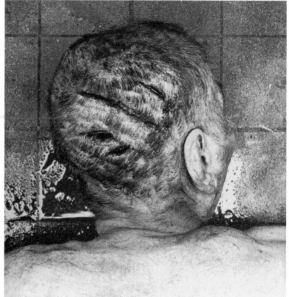

CODEBO.

PILLOT.

FRANCE—PARIS.	*1901.*

CODEBO & PILLOT.
✕ *Unknown woman.*

WEAPON. BLOWS.	TYPOLOGY. PROPERTY CRIME.	POLICING. BERTILLONAGE.

RUE MOREAU, 12E ARRONDISSEMENT.

The faces of two young killers stare out from Alphonse Bertillon's (1853–1914) enigmatic *portraits parlés* (or mug shot). The lads were named Codebo (dates unknown) and Pillot (dates unknown) and they were accused of killing an unnamed female shopkeeper on the Rue Moreau in Paris's 12e arrondissement. The woman was killed by several heavy blows to the back of her head and lay stretched out on the floor of the grocer's store. Bertillon captured the entire crime scene precisely, before photographing the dead body as it lay in the morgue. He even took the step of shaving the victim's head so as to better capture the six deep gashes to her skull. The killing took place in 1901 when the penalty for murder in France was death by guillotine. Whether or not Codebo and Pillot suffered such a death or were spared and sent into enforced exile for their crime is unknown. Without Bertillon's careful and meticulous recording of the event, it would almost certainly have remained as unknown today as the name of their victim. ∎

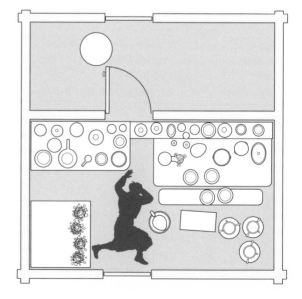

Below. VICTOIRE TUSSEAU'S BODY AS IT WAS DISCOVERED IN HER APARTMENT, PHOTOGRAPHED BY ALPHONSE BERTILLON.

Below. ALPHONSE BERTILLON'S MORTUARY PHOTOGRAPH OF VICTOIRE TUSSEAU, SHOWING A DEEP WOUND TO HER NECK.

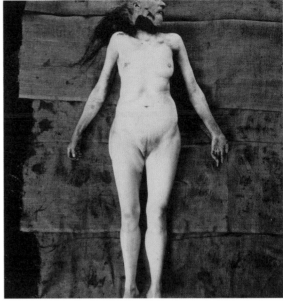

HENRI THIBŒF.

MARIE PIETTE.

FRANCE—PARIS. | *1902.*

HENRI THIBŒF & MARIE PIETTE.
✕ *Victoire Tusseau.*

WEAPON.	TYPOLOGY.	POLICING.
HUNTING KNIFE.	PROPERTY CRIME.	BERTILLONAGE.

GROUND FLOOR APARTMENT, 5 RUE MARIE LAURE, BOIS-COLOMBES, ÎLE-DE-FRANCE.

Victoire Tusseau (1828–1902), a 74-year-old widow, lived alone on the ground floor at 5 Rue Marie Laure, Bois-Colombes, just northwest of Paris. In autumn 1902, two prospective tenants were being shown around upstairs, and a neighbour noticed a dark-haired woman who appeared to be watching the building. Two days later, Madame Tusseau was discovered dead in her hallway. The flat had been ransacked and the police concluded that while the landlord was showing one of the men around the second floor the other had slipped off to plunder the widow's rooms for money, jewelry and other valuables. Surprised, he killed Victoire with a hunting knife. The robbers went to ground and were only captured after a long search. Marie Piette (dates unknown), the watcher in the street, and Henri Thibœuf (dates unknown) were arrested in New York, having sailed from Le Havre using assumed names. Piette was subsequently acquitted but Thibœuf received a life sentence; the other robber escaped entirely. ∎

Below. FLOOR PLAN OF THE CORRIDOR IN WHICH THE BODY OF VICTOIRE TUSSEAU WAS DISCOVERED.

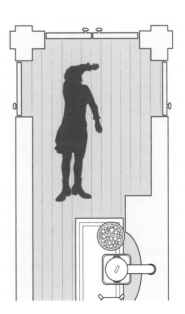

UNKNOWN.
✕ *Hélène Mercier.*

WEAPON. STRANGULATION.	TYPOLOGY. PROPERTY CRIME.	POLICING. BERTILLONAGE.

RUE DE L'YVETTE, BOURG-LA-REINE.

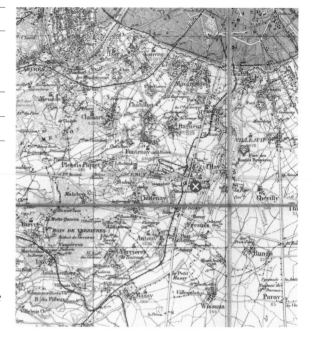

After her husband's death, Hélène Mercier (unknown–1902) lived quietly with her four children on his army pension at a smart villa in Bourg-la-Reine, a southern suburb of Paris. Then, suddenly and dramatically, the widow was found dead in the street outside her home in October 1902. Alphonse Bertillon (1853–1914) took a series of photographs of the crime scene to help the police investigation, but no one was ever successfully prosecuted for the widow's death. The police put out a description of a watch they believed had been stolen in the hope that anyone offered it for sale would report it. Hélène was known to help passing vagrants, giving them food and sometimes shelter, and it was thought that perhaps one of these had robbed and killed her. At the time, the police were on the lookout for a roving serial rapist who had attacked at least ten women in the area. Was he the murderer? Sadly, despite the use of photography to preserve the scene, the French authorities were unable to solve this callous act of violence. ∎

Above. MAP SHOWING THE LOCATION OF THE VILLA WHERE HÉLÈNE MERCIER LIVED IN BOURG-LA-REINE.

Above left. HÉLÈNE MERCIER'S HOME IN A QUIET PARISIAN SUBURB.

Above right. ALPHONSE BERTILLON'S CRIME SCENE PHOTOGRAPH SHOWING HÉLÈNE MERCIER'S DEAD BODY *IN SITU.*

Below left. AFTER THE BODY WAS REMOVED MARKERS WERE PLACED TO HELP THE POLICE INVESTIGATION.

Below right. A FOOTPRINT FOUND CLOSE TO THE SCENE OF THE MURDER.

PAUL SCHEFFER & PAUL VAN NOORWEGHE.
× *Madame Guérin.*

WEAPON. STRANGULATION.	TYPOLOGY. PROPERTY CRIME.	POLICING. BERTILLONAGE.

RUE LAMBRECHTS, COURBEVOIE.

When Madame Lebassac (dates unknown) visited Madame Guérin's (1833–1903) cabin, she had a terrible shock: 71-year-old Madame Guérin was lying dead, having been strangled. A police search of the area around Rue Lambrechts in Courbevoie, a suburb of Paris, was ordered and four 'usual suspects' quickly picked up. Paul Scheffer (1885–unknown) was a painter from Geneva, Paul Van Noorweghe (1885–unknown) was a homeless locksmith, Albert Meignen (dates unknown) had no trade at all, while a M. Denis (dates unknown) was known to be a dangerous 'prowler'. They all had stories to link them to each other and provide alibis, but they were so contradictory that they confirmed police suspicions. The motive was thought to be theft, as Madame Guérin was widely rumoured to have savings hidden in her shop. Since both Scheffer and Van Noorweghe were associated with 'a house of ill-fame' (a contemporary euphemism for a brothel), it was these two who were eventually held accountable for the murder. ∎

Above. MAP SHOWING THE LOCATION OF THE CABIN WHERE MADAME GUÉRIN LIVED AND WAS MURDERED IN COURBEVOIE.

Above left. RUE LAMBRECHTS, COURBEVOIE, WHERE MADAME GUÉRIN WAS FOUND MURDERED.

Above right. VIEW I OF MADAME GUÉRIN'S CABIN, WHERE THE MURDER TOOK PLACE.

Below left. VIEW II OF MADAME GUÉRIN'S CABIN.

Below right. INTERIOR OF THE CABIN WHERE MADAME GUÉRIN WAS FOUND STRANGLED. THE THIEVES ALSO RANSACKED THE ROOM.

PAUL JULES MARTIN.
✕ *Berthe de Brienne.*

WEAPON. STRANGULATION.	TYPOLOGY. PROPERTY CRIME.	POLICING. BERTILLONAGE.

9 RUE CHALGRIN, 16E ARRONDISSEMENT.

PAUL JULES MARTIN.   BERTHE DE BRIENNE.

In May 1903, a man appeared at London's Bow Street Magistrate's Court charged with the murder of a wealthy Parisienne. Madame Berthe de Brienne (unknown–1903) had been found strangled to death in her apartment on the Rue Chalgrin earlier that month. The police suspected robbery as a number of items of jewelry were missing: jewelry that was later found on Paul Jules Martin (dates unknown) when he was tracked down and arrested in Glasgow, Scotland. Martin, a French national, claimed he had been inveigled into a conspiracy to rob Madame de Brienne. He described meeting a man who he had asked to lend him money. Instead of doing so, the unnamed stranger suggested that if Martin could somehow get himself inside the lady's flat and then leave the door open, he would effect a burglary. So, according to Martin's version of events, having dined with Berthe at the Café Américain, he went back to her rooms and stayed the night. As she slept, the other man crept into the flat and stole her jewelry, giving some of it to Martin before disappearing. Martin denied having any part in her murder. A French jury disagreed, and in January 1904 he was sentenced to penal servitude for life. ∎

Above. ALPHONSE BERTILLON'S CRIME SCENE PHOTOGRAPH OF BERTHE DE BRIENNE'S LIFELESS BODY IN HER PARIS APARTMENT.

Below. FLOOR PLAN SHOWING THE BEDROOM IN WHICH BERTHE DE BRIENNE WAS FOUND MURDERED.

FREDERICK GREULING.
× *Elene Popescu.*

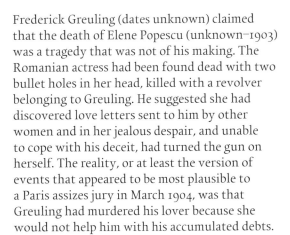

WEAPON.	TYPOLOGY.	POLICING.
REVOLVER.	RECKLESS ACT.	BERTILLONAGE.

HOTEL REGINA.

Frederick Greuling (dates unknown) claimed that the death of Elene Popescu (unknown–1903) was a tragedy that was not of his making. The Romanian actress had been found dead with two bullet holes in her head, killed with a revolver belonging to Greuling. He suggested she had discovered love letters sent to him by other women and in her jealous despair, and unable to cope with his deceit, had turned the gun on herself. The reality, or at least the version of events that appeared to be most plausible to a Paris assizes jury in March 1904, was that Greuling had murdered his lover because she would not help him with his accumulated debts.

Greuling, a Swiss national, had whisked Elene off her feet when they first met, charming her and treating her to days out and fancy eateries. In truth, he could not afford this lifestyle and had conned his way through life for years, building up debts that eventually caught up with him. As the creditors closed in, Greuling appealed to Elene for money, and when she refused him, he flew into a rage and shot her. The French court sentenced him to ten years in jail to be followed by expulsion from the country. ∎

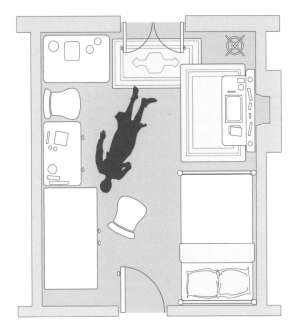

Above. ELENE POPESCU LYING DEAD IN A PARIS HOTEL ROOM. CRIME SCENE PHOTOGRAPH BY ALPHONSE BERTILLON.

Below. FLOOR PLAN SHOWING THE BEDROOM IN WHICH ELENE POPESCU WAS FOUND MURDERED.

CÉLESTIN-NICOLAS PIERSON, JULES MORROT, VICTOR PAGÈS, ANTHELME GAY.
× *Jeanne Bal.*

WEAPON. STRANGULATION.	TYPOLOGY. PROPERTY CRIME.	POLICING. BERTILLONAGE.

32 RUE DE TURENNE, 3E ARRONDISSEMENT.

CÉLESTIN-NICOLAS PIERSON.	JULES MORROT.	ANTHELME GAY.

On 25 March 1904, Madame Prainville (dates unknown), the wife of a local wine merchant, kissed her mother, Madame Bal (unknown–1904), as she always did, leaving her rooms at 4:30 p.m. and promising to visit the following day. At 5:00 p.m., the widow had another visitor, Marie Beer (*c.* 1854–unknown) who served as her 'companion', and so was someone she knew well and presumably trusted. As that guest was leaving, at around 5:30 p.m., she passed two young men on the stairs on their way towards her friend's apartment. The concierge also noticed the pair but thought nothing of it. They left half an hour later. Two days then passed without anyone – not even her daughter – seeing Madame Bal and concerns mounted. Monsieur Prainville (dates unknown) used his spare key to enter and, to his horror, found the apartment in a chaotic state, with the widow's possessions scattered everywhere. In the dining room, he found what he must have been dreading: the poor woman was stretched out on the floor, quite cold to the touch.

The police arrived and examined Madame Bal, concluding that she had suffocated about forty-eight hours earlier. A pair of diamond earrings was missing, as were a number of other valuables, but the thieves had been unable to break open her safe. It was local knowledge that the widow had a small fortune (even if she chose to live frugally and was considered something of a miser). The crime scene was photographed by Alphonse Bertillon (1853–1914) and a manhunt ensued. This proved fruitless for weeks until the police had a sudden tip-off, arresting four men and a woman, all of whom were part of an infamous gang of burglars and robbers.

The case came to trial in Paris in June 1905, some fifteen months after the widow was murdered. Jules Morrot (*c.* 1882–unknown) and Célestin-Nicolas Pierson (*c.* 1881–unknown) were regarded as the key protagonists, but neither was charged with murder for lack of proof. The jury convicted them of robbery and both received long prison sentences.

Anthelme Gay (*c.* 1859–unknown) and Victor Pagès (*c.* 1858–unknown) got five years for their involvement in disposing of the widow's property, but Marie Beer, the mysterious female companion and the person who had alerted the thieves to her wealth, walked away scot-free. ∎

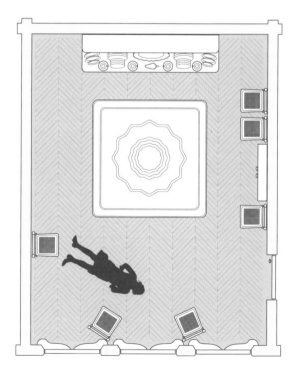

Above. FLOOR PLAN OF THE DINING ROOM WHERE WIDOW BAL'S BODY WAS DISCOVERED.

Right. ALPHONSE BERTILLON'S CRIME SCENE PHOTOGRAPHS RECORD THE RANSACKING OF JEANNE BAL'S APARTMENT BY THE ROBBERS WHO KILLED HER.

Above & Right. TWO VIEWS OF THE CRIME SCENE CAPTURED BY ALPHONSE BERTILLON, SHOWING JEANNE BAL LYING DEAD IN HER FLAT. DETECTIVES USED SUCH PHOTOS IN THEIR INVESTIGATIONS AFTER THE BODY HAD BEEN REMOVED FROM THE CRIME SCENE.

JEAN-JACQUES LIABEUF.
✕ *Célestin Deray.*

WEAPON. KNIFE.	TYPOLOGY. POLITICAL.	POLICING. BERTILLONAGE.

RUE AUBRY LE BOUCHER, 4E ARRONDISSEMENT.

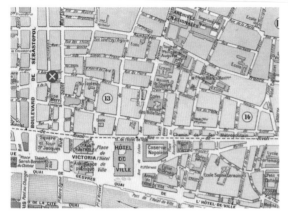

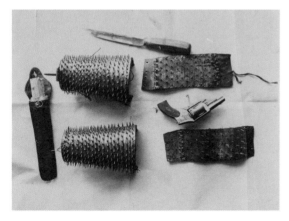

Above. MAP SHOWING RUE AUBRY LE BOUCHER WHERE JEAN-JACQUES LIABEUF MURDERED CÉLESTIN DERAY.

Below. JEAN-JACQUES LIABEUF USED THIS HOME-MADE ARMOUR AND CRUDE WEAPONS AS HE WAGED A GUERRILLA WAR ON THE POLICE HE BELIEVED HAD PERSECUTED HIM.

Jean-Jacques Liabeuf (1886–1910) was a man with a grudge against a society that had treated him unfairly. By July 1909, he had earned a string of convictions for petty crimes and had served time in the 'Bat d'Af', the French military units formed from convicted criminals. Then, while 'going straight' as a shoemaker, he was wrongly convicted of involvement in prostitution. Released on licence, he began a campaign of vengeance against the police who had persecuted him. Wearing protective body armour made from leather studded with nails, the shoemaker-turned-vigilante attacked officers in the Les Halles district of Paris. On 9 January 1910, cornered by a patrol, he killed Célestin Deray (1861–1910) and wounded several others before he was overpowered.

Liabeuf became a sort of working-class icon of the left, his case being described as the 'Dreyfus affair of the workers' (referencing the scandalous and anti-Semitic treatment of Alfred Dreyfus in the 1890s). The radical press took up his cause and when his trial resulted in a conviction for murder and a sentence of death there was a campaign to save his life. This failed and Liabeuf went to the guillotine on 1 July 1910. As he waited overnight in his cell, the Paris mob clashed with police, 10,000 rioters fought with 800 policemen and the cavalry had to be called in to disperse the crowds at the points of their swords. Among those swelling the ranks of the crowd that protested the execution of this would-be proletarian hero was the future leader of a more successful revolution, Vladimir Ilyich Ulyanov (1870–1924), better known as Lenin, and Jean Jaurès (1859–1914), the romantic figurehead of the French left who was assassinated just before the First World War engulfed Europe in bloody conflict.

Liabeuf was no revolutionary like Lenin or Jaurès, but he captured the imagination of those who saw oppression in the small acts of injustice he had suffered. Even as he lay on the plank awaiting the drop of the blade, Liabeuf continued to protest that he had never been a pimp in his life. ∎

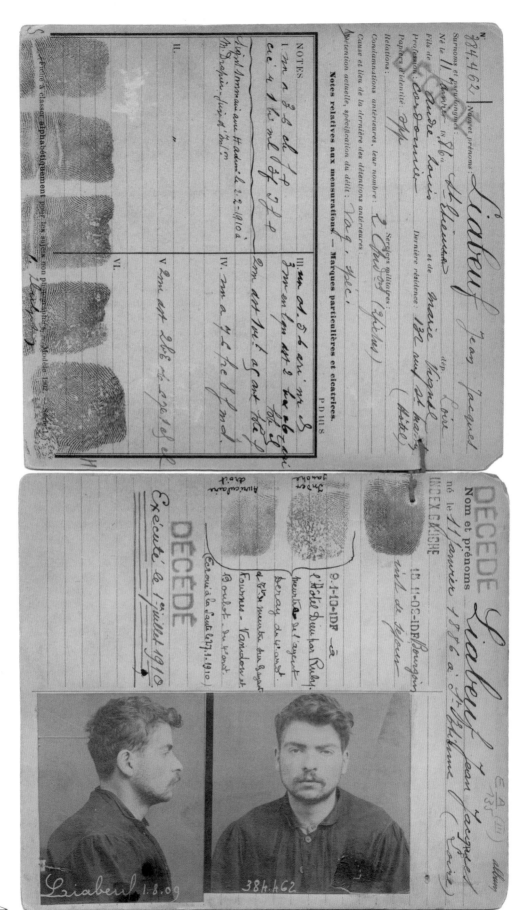

Right. JEAN-JACQUES LIABEUF'S *PORTRAIT PARLÉ* (SPEAKING PORTRAIT); INCLUDING HIS MUG SHOT, FINGERPRINTS, AND RECORD OF EXECUTION.

MARTIN DUMOLLARD & MARIE-ANNE MARTINET.
× *Marie Baday*.

WEAPON. BLOWS.	TYPOLOGY. PROPERTY CRIME.	POLICING. PHOTOGRAPHY.

DAGNEAUX, AIN.

MARTIN DUMOLLARD. | MARIE–ANNE MARTINET.

When, in 1814, Martin Dumollard (1810–62) witnessed the public execution by dismemberment of his father Pierre (unknown–1814), a known criminal who had fled arrest in Hungary for a series of crimes, little did anyone know that he was destined to share a similar fate. In 1842, Martin (under an assumed name) and his young wife Marie-Anne Martinet (1814–75) moved to Dagneux, near Lyon, France. There 'Raymond' might have enjoyed some sanctuary as accusations of thefts against him mounted elsewhere.

In the mid-1850s, Dumollard's criminal career took a new and twisted turn. In late February 1855, posing as a master looking for a maid, he met Marie Baday (unknown–1855) and offered her work before robbing and killing her. Baday's body was found in a nearby forest at Tramoyes, but it took months to identify her. Baday may not have been Dumollard's first victim. On 25 February 1855, Olympe Alubert (dates unknown) was offered a position by a 'good-natured' man who spoke good French and seemed plausible. When he assaulted her, she ran away. Josephte Charletty (dates unknown), Jeanne-Marie Bourgeois (c. 1833–unknown) and Victorine Perrin (c. 1833–unknown) all had a similar brush with Dumollard in late 1855, but avoided a worse fate. Then, in May 1861, Dumollard's attempt to kill Marie Pichon (dates unknown) led to his arrest. Pichon was assaulted in woods close to Dagneux and she was able to identify him. The authorities began an investigation and in July 1861, acting on information prised from his wife Marie-Anne by a judge, the police unearthed a dead body in Montmain woods.

In total, twelve charges of murder or attempted murder with robbery were levelled at Dumollard when he stood trial in early 1862. There were seventy-one witnesses to the various attacks and the police discovered property belonging to many of them in the couple's home. Marie-Anne was charged as his accomplice and the court convicted them both. Marie-Anne received twenty years' imprisonment, while her husband was sentenced to death. When it was announced that he would go to the guillotine, he simply said, 'I like it better than to be like my father, quartered on a wheel being pulled in all directions by horses.' So perhaps his father's death had made a profound impact on the 4-year-old witness to it. Dumollard was executed in front of a crowd of 5,000 and his body was buried in an unmarked grave on 7 March 1862.

He has the dubious honour of being regarded as the very first European serial killer to be so identified. The Lyon Medical School retained his head for examination, and in the 1980s researchers reconstructed his features from an analysis of it. Finally, Dumollard has a lasting place in French culture from being mentioned by Victor Hugo (1802–85) in *Les Misérables* as the 'orphan who became a bandit'. ∎

① ⟶

MARTIN DUMOLLARD STRUGGLES WITH ONE OF HIS VICTIMS.

② ⟶

THE BANKS OF THE RIVER RHÔNE, CLOSE TO WHERE DUMOLLARD STRUCK.

③ ⟶

THE POLICE UNEARTH A DEAD BODY IN THE WOODS, MOST LIKELY MARIE BADAY'S.

Above. THE HOUSE WHERE MARTIN DUMOLLARD WAS LIVING
WITH MARIE-ANNE MARTINET AT THE TIME OF HIS ARREST.

Above. PHOTOGRAPH OF THE BODY OF MARIE BADAY, TAKEN
IN FRONT OF THE CHURCH OF TRAMOYNES IN 1855.

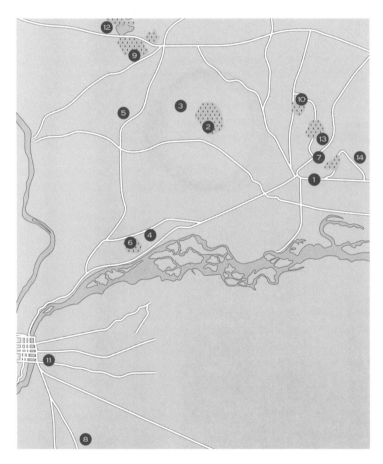

1
DUMOLLARD'S
HOUSE.
THE HOUSE WHERE
MARTIN DUMOLLARD
AND MARIE-ANNE
MARTINET LIVED.

2
MONTAVERNE
FOREST.
THE FOREST WHERE
MARIE BADAY'S
WAS FOUND.

3
MIONNAY.
THE AREA WHERE
MARTIN DUMOLLARD
ASSAULTED OLYMPE
ALUBERT.

4
MIRIBEL.
THE AREA WHERE
MARTIN DUMOLLARD
ASSAULTED JOSEPHTE
CHARLETTY.

5
POLLETINS.
THE AREA WHERE
MARTIN DUMOLLARD
ASSAULTED JEANNE-
MARIE BOURGEOIS.

6
SARRAZIN FARM.
THE FARM WHERE
MARTIN DUMOLLARD
ASSAULTED
VICTORINE PERRIN.

7
MONTMAIN WOODS.
THE WOODS WHERE
MARTIN DUMOLLARD
ASSAULTED AN
UNKNOWN WOMAN.

8
VÉNISSIEUX.
THE AREA WHERE
MARTIN DUMOLLARD
ASSAULTED AN
UNKNOWN WOMAN.

9
L'HÔPITAL WOODS.
THE WOODS WHERE
MARTIN DUMOLLARD
ASSAULTED JULIE
FARGEAT.

10
CASTLE WOODS.
THE WOODS WHERE
MARTIN DUMOLLARD
ASSAULTED AN
UNKNOWN WOMAN.

11
GUILLOTIÈRE, LYON.
THE AREA WHERE
MARTIN DUMOLLARD
ASSAULTED AN
UNKNOWN WOMAN.

12
BOIS DES ALLÉES.
THE WOODS WHERE
MARTIN DUMOLLARD
ASSAULTED LOUISE
MICHEL.

13
BOIS DES
COMMUNES.
THE WOODS WHERE
MARTIN DUMOLLARD
ASSAULTED MARIE-
EULALIE BUSSOD.

14
HERMITURE.
THE AREA WHERE
MARTIN DUMOLLARD
ASSAULTED MARIE
PICHON.

④ ⟶

MARTIN DUMOLLARD SKULKS AWAY, SHOVEL
IN HAND, TO DISPOSE OF ANOTHER VICTIM.

⑤ ⟶

MARTIN DUMOLLARD ATTEMPTS TO
DESTROY EVIDENCE IN THE WOODS.

JOSEPH VACHER.
× *11.* +

WEAPON. KNIFE & TEETH.	TYPOLOGY. SEXUAL.	POLICING. LACASSAGNE.

SOUTHEASTERN FRANCE.

In October 1897, the London weekly newspaper *The Pall Mall Gazette* carried a report from its French correspondent of the capture and confession of a serial murderer in Belley, near Lyon in France. The report noted that the killer wanted to tell his story through the newspapers, claiming he had been mistreated in the past and that his crimes (which were considerable) were motivated by a sense of injustice. Riding the political zeitgeist, the prisoner – Joseph Vacher (1869–98) – declared: 'I am an anarchist in my way and I have a grudge against society.'

Vacher, a former soldier, had injured himself severely in a failed suicide attempt that had left a bullet lodged in his head. It had been accompanied by an attempt on his sweetheart's life, and he ended up in a mental institution. Declared cured by doctors a year later, Vacher then wandered across central and southern France throughout the 1890s, posing as an ex-soldier to beg alms and win trust and brutally murdering and raping dozens of women, girls and teenage boys. It is hard to determine the extent of Vacher's crimes, but he confessed to several and others seem likely to have been committed by him, even if they were blamed on others at the time.

His first victim was Eugénie Delhomme (*c.* 1873–94), whose dead body appeared to have been ripped up by wild animals. She was discovered yards from the silk mill where she worked in Beaurepaire. Various local men were arrested and accused but the real culprit was already on the road, tramping his way across the rural landscape of late 19th-century France. In the autumn of 1894, he reached Var, close to the modern French Riviera. There, he killed Louise Marcel (*c.* 1881–94), a 13-year-old girl, who was found, raped and murdered, by searchers after she went missing. Again, no one pointed the finger at the strange vagabond who had been wandering in the vicinity, preferring to blame the local man who found her.

Months later, Adèle Mortureux (1878–95) was found by a friar walking his dog in the countryside near Étaules, just north of Dijon. She had been stabbed and her shoes were missing; the police tried to establish a cordon to prevent the killer escaping. When no suspect was found, they arrested a local businessman named Grenier (dates unknown) who had managed to make himself unpopular. While a 'modern' France was emerging at the end of the 1800s, it seems that in many rural areas the old superstitions and prejudices of the early modern period persisted and murders sparked unfounded witch-hunts for unpopular people against whom others held a grudge.

Meanwhile, Vacher continued to kill with impunity. He murdered the widow Morand (unknown–1895) in Savoi before killing teenage

❶ 19 MAY 1894. × *Eugénie Delhomme.* BEAUREPAIRE, ISÈRE.	❷ 20 NOVEMBER 1894. × *Louise Marcel.* VIDAUBAN, VAR.	❸ 12 MAY 1895. × *Adèle Mortureux.* DAROIS, CÔTE-D'OR.	❹ 24 AUGUST 1895. × *Widow Morand.* SAINT-OURS, SAVOIE.	❺ SEPTEMBER 1895. × *Victor Portalier.* BÉNONCES, AIN.	❻ 23 SEPTEMBER 1895 × *Aline Alaise* TRUINAS, DRÔME.

Above. VARIOUS ARTICLES BELONGING TO JOSEPH VACHER, INCLUDING HIS WALKING STICK, UMBRELLA AND ACCORDION.

shepherd Victor Portalier (*c.* 1879–95) in the mountains. He claimed at least six more victims before he was eventually caught by chance in 1897, after sexually assaulting a woman in the Ardèche. While Vacher was being held for attempted rape, it was noted that his description matched one being circulated by an investigating magistrate, Emile Forquet (1862–1936). Vacher was sent to Belley where he was questioned closely, if fruitlessly, for three weeks. Eventually, Forquet won the killer's trust and coaxed him into describing his travels. Vacher confessed and, egged on by the magistrate, agreed to give details of his murders to demonstrate that he was a madman who was not responsible for his crimes and so should not face the guillotine. When the press got wind of Vacher's confession, they descended on Belley in droves. Papers ran wild headlines such as 'The Shepherd Killer' or 'The French Jack the Ripper'. However, although they had a confession, the authorities were still not confident that they could secure Vacher's conviction and execution. For that, they needed the help of France's pre-eminent forensic scientist Dr Alexandre Lacassagne (1843–1924). Vacher was transferred to a prison in Lyon and interviewed by Lacassagne. The 'killer of little shepherds' tried his hardest to paint himself as criminally insane and unfit to stand trial, let

❼	❽	❾	❿	⓫	⓬ – ㉗
29 SEPTEMBER 1895.	10 SEPTEMBER 1896.	1 OCTOBER 1896.	MAY 1897.	18 JUNE 1897.	A FURTHER
✕ *Pierre Massot-Pellet.*	✕ *Marie Moussier.*	✕ *Rosine Rodier.*	✕ *Claudius Beaupied.*	✕ *Pierre Laurent.*	16 VICTIMS ALLEGED.
SAINT-ÉTIENNE-DE-BOULOGNE, ARDÈCHE.	BUSSET, ALLIER.	SAINT-HONORAT, HAUTE-LOIRE.	TASSIN-LA-DEMI-LUNE, RHÔNE.	COURZIEU, RHÔNE.	

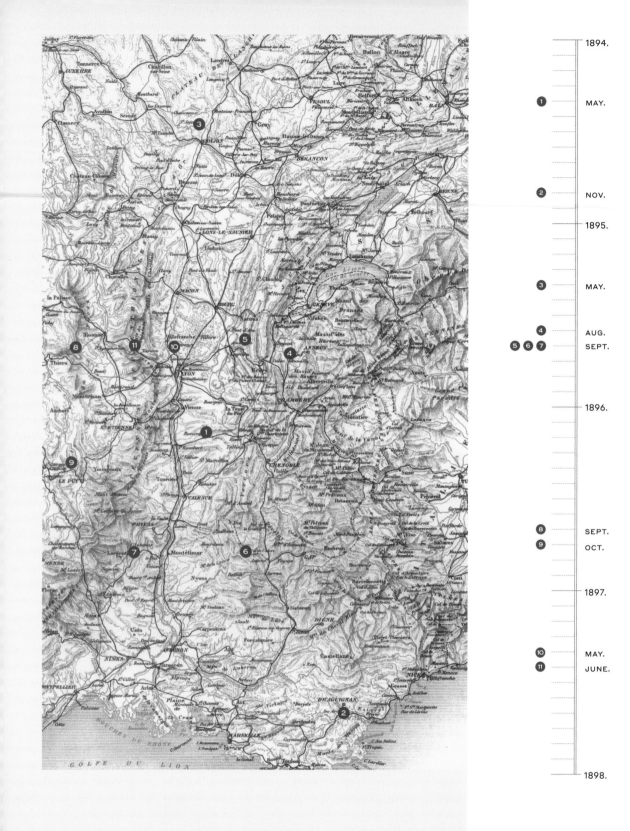

1894.

● 1   MAY.

● 2   NOV.

1895.

● 3   MAY.

● 4   AUG.

● 5 ● 6 ● 7   SEPT.

1896.

● 8   SEPT.
● 9   OCT.

1897.

● 10   MAY.
● 11   JUNE.

1898.

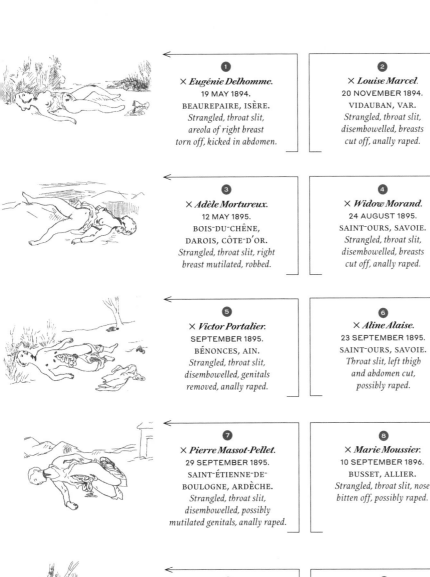

1

× *Eugénie Delhomme.*
19 MAY 1894.
BEAUREPAIRE, ISÈRE.
*Strangled, throat slit,
areola of right breast
torn off, kicked in abdomen.*

2

× *Louise Marcel.*
20 NOVEMBER 1894.
VIDAUBAN, VAR.
*Strangled, throat slit,
disembowelled, breasts
cut off, anally raped.*

3

× *Adèle Mortureux.*
12 MAY 1895.
BOIS-DU-CHÊNE,
DAROIS, CÔTE-D'OR.
*Strangled, throat slit, right
breast mutilated, robbed.*

4

× *Widow Morand.*
24 AUGUST 1895.
SAINT-OURS, SAVOIE.
*Strangled, throat slit,
disembowelled, breasts
cut off, anally raped.*

5

× *Victor Portalier.*
SEPTEMBER 1895.
BÉNONCES, AIN.
*Strangled, throat slit,
disembowelled, genitals
removed, anally raped.*

6

× *Aline Alaise.*
23 SEPTEMBER 1895.
SAINT-OURS, SAVOIE.
*Throat slit, left thigh
and abdomen cut,
possibly raped.*

7

× *Pierre Massot-Pellet.*
29 SEPTEMBER 1895.
SAINT-ÉTIENNE-DE-
BOULOGNE, ARDÈCHE.
*Strangled, throat slit,
disembowelled, possibly
mutilated genitals, anally raped.*

8

× *Marie Moussier.*
10 SEPTEMBER 1896.
BUSSET, ALLIER.
*Strangled, throat slit, nose
bitten off, possibly raped.*

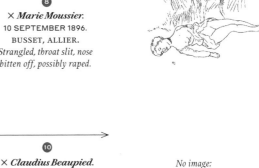

9

× *Rosine Rodier.*
1 OCTOBER 1896.
SAINT-HONORAT, HAUTE-LOIRE.
*Strangled, throat slit,
disembowelled, genitals removed.*

10

× *Claudius Beaupied.*
MAY 1897.
TASSIN-LA-DEMI-LUNE, RHÔNE.
*Strangled, throat slit, genitals
mutilated, anally raped.*

*No image:
skeleton found in a well.*

11

× *Pierre Laurent.*
18 JUNE 1897.
COURZIEU, RHÔNE.
*Strangled, throat slit, genitals
mutilated, possibly anally raped.*

alone execution, a stance he had maintained in his final months in Belley. The alienists (psychologists) who examined Vacher were split; one thought him mad, the other sane. They agreed he was 'a monster', but was he legally responsible for his actions? At Vacher's trial, Lacassagne established that the defendant was a 'sanguinary sadist', and since sadists were not deemed to be insane, this proved crucial in his conviction. On 31 December 1898, Vacher was guillotined. He had admitted to killing eleven people but had likely raped and murdered more than twenty-five. ∎

'It relieved me so much to bite, that in many of the cases
of the people I killed I bit them, even after having
killed them with a knife.'

JOSEPH VACHER'S CONFESSION TO THE BRUTAL MURDER OF MARIE MOUSSIER. 30 NOVEMBER 1898.

Above. VILLAGERS STANDING AROUND A COFFIN CONTAINING THE REMAINS OF CLAUDIUS BEAUPIED.

'You think to expiate the faults of France by having me die?
That will not be enough. You are committing another crime.
I am the great victim of the fin de siècle.'

JOSEPH VACHER TO HIS JAILERS BEFORE HIS EXECUTION BY GUILLOTINE, 31 DECEMBER 1898.

———

Above. JOSEPH VACHER POSES FOR THIS PORTRAIT WHILE IN BELLEY PRISON.

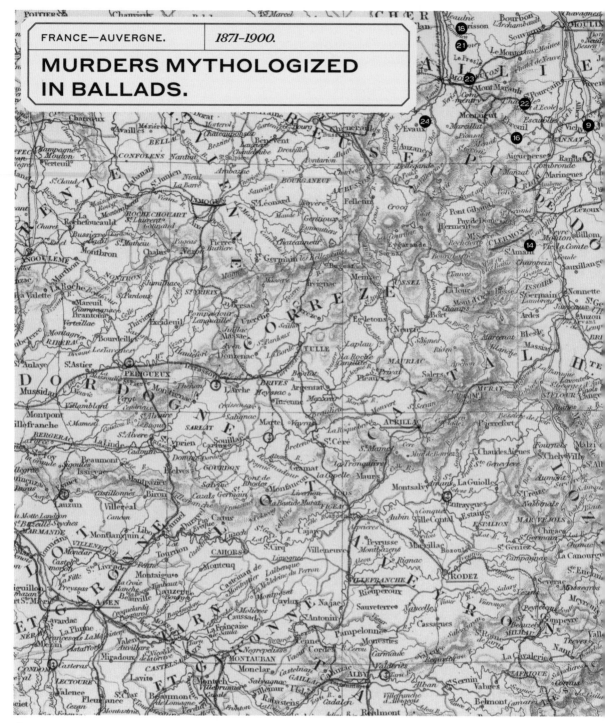

MURDERS MYTHOLOGIZED IN BALLADS.

1 1871. AMPUIS, RHÔNE. Barthélémy Bernard. ✕ BENOÎTE PARET. ✕ INFANT.

2 1871. MALTAVERNE, LOIRE. John Guillermet. ✕ PHILIPPE BERGER.

3 1872. LE CHAMBON-FEUGEROLLES, LOIRE. Jean-Marie Joubert. ✕ MME. JOUBERT.

4 1873. 20 RUE DES MAISONS-NEUVES, LYON. Jules-Joseph Seringer. ✕ HORTENSE POSTY. ✕ LOUIS GUERIN. ✕ MME. ESTHER.

5 1874. AMPUIS, RHÔNE. Pierre Montant. ✕ JEAN MONTANT. ✕ CLAUDINE DUCROS. ✕ MARIE MONTANT.

6 1878. GRENOBLE, ISÈRE. Pierre Chevalier & Jeanne Royer. ✕ PIERRE DELERT.

7 1879. SAINT-ETIENNE, LOIRE. Jean Chambes. ✕ ANTOINE CHAMBES.

8 1880. 14 RUE FRANÇOIS DAUPHIN, LYON. François Chalaye. ✕ MARIETTE CHALAYE.

9 1880. BAYET, ALLIER. J. B. Merlin. ✕ M. MERLIN. ✕ MME. MERLIN.

10 1882. SAINT-ARÇONS-SUR-ALLIER, HAUTE-LOIRE. Pierre Mallet. ✕ ABBOT RIVET.

11 1883. BOURG-EN-BRESSE, AIN. Louis-Frédéric Tanneur. ✕ HENRI MAISSIAT. ✕ MÉLANIE MAISSIAT.

12 1884. LAPALISSE, ALLIER. Unknown. ✕ FRÉDÉRIC LEBRUN.

13 1884. CHAPAREILLAN, ISÈRE. Joseph Jacquin. ✕ MOTHER. ✕ FATHER. ✕ BROTHER.

14 1884. PIBOULET, SAUVIAT, PUY-DE-DÔME. Pierre Biton

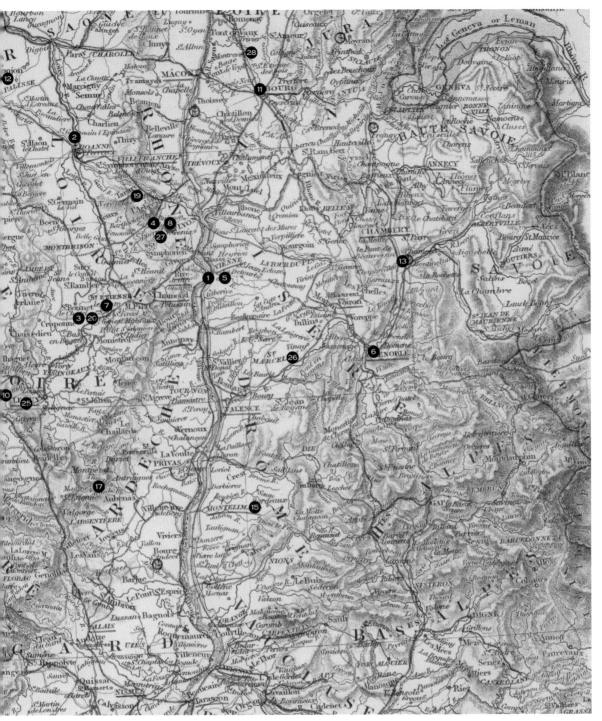

Guillaume, Bernard Claude & Molle Michel Jarles.
× JULIEN CHOSSIÈRE.

15 1884. POËT-LAVAL, DRÔME. Jean-Antoine Dauvier.
× IRMA DAUVIER.

16 1886. CHAMPS, PUY-DE-DÔME. Antoine Dayras. × PIERRE
FAURE.

17 1886. BARNAS, ARDÈCHE. Jean Faure. × CLAUDE FAURE.

18 1887. ÉPINEUIL-LE-FLEURIEL, CHER. Annette Chabance.
× INFANT.

19 1887. SAVIGNY, RHÔNE. Jean-Pierre Rivoire. × MME RIVOIRE.

20 1888. LE CHAMBON-FEUGEROLLES, LOIRE. Pierre Bertail.
× AUGUSTINE CELLE.

21 1890. AUDES, ALLIER. Abbot Martin. × HIS BROTHER.

22 1890. CHANTELLE, ALLIER. Mme. Achat. × M. LÉPINE.

23 1891. MONTLUÇON, ALLIER. M. Malherbe. × JEAN ANDRÉ.

24 1892. SAINT-PIERRE-LE-BOST, CREUSE.
Charles-Émile Legrand. × JULIA GIRAUD.

25 1893. PUY-EN-VELAY, HAUTE-LOIRE. M. Ouillon.
× M. DOMINIQUE.

26 1895. SAINT-MARCELLIN, ISÈRE. Benoit Faure &
Jean-Philippe Philidet. × CHRISTOPHE BASTIDE.

27 1898. RUE DE LA VILLETTE, LYON. Evariste Nouguier.
× THÉRÈSE FOUCHERAND.

28 1900. FOISSIAT, AIN. Frédéric Célard. × AMÉDÉE SOCHAY.

LE DRAME DE LA GUILLOTIERE

LE DRAME DE LA RUE PORT-DU-TEMPLE
Une Femme assassinée et jetée par la Fenêtre

FRANCE—AUVERGNE.	*23 April 1893.*

VICTOR GRENETIER.
✕ *Lucie Lamprand.*

WEAPON.	TYPOLOGY.	POLICING.
KNIFE.	DOMESTIC.	N/A.

16 RUE CHALOPIN, LYON.

Victor Grenetier (*c.* 1877–unknown) was in love, but the object of his affection had already been promised to another young man with better prospects than the 16-year-old Grenetier. Unable to have the girl he loved, Grenetier seems to have determined that no one else would. On 23 April 1893, he waited for Lucie Lamprand (*c.* 1874–93) and, as she descended the stairs at 16 Rue Chalopin, Lyon, he struck her violently with a knuckleduster. Lucie fled but Victor chased her into a grocery store and stabbed her repeatedly. She died in a pharmacy nearby, the victim of unrequited passion. ∎

Above. LE PROGRÈS ILLUSTRÉ, 23 APRIL 1893.
GRENETIER ATTACKS LUCIE LAMPRAND.

FRANCE—AUVERGNE.	*4 June 1894.*

LOUIS ALLAIN.
✕ *Marie Depalle.*

WEAPON.	TYPOLOGY.	POLICING.
PISTOL.	DOMESTIC.	N/A.

LA RUE PORT DU TEMPLE, LYON.

Marie Depalle (unknown–1894) and Louis Allain (dates unknown) appear to have had a tempestuous relationship. By early 1894 they had separated, but Allain appeared incapable of letting go. On the evening of 3 June he visited Marie at her lodgings in Rue Port Du Temple, four floors above a laundrette. The pair quarrelled into the early hours of the morning before Allain produced a revolver, took aim, and shot Marie five times. Depalle, almost certainly fatally wounded, stumbled to the balcony to shout for help but Allain rushed at her, toppled her over and sent her crashing to her death. ∎

Above. LE PROGRÈS ILLUSTRÉ, 17 JUNE 1894.
MARIE DEPALLE TUMBLES FROM A FIRST-FLOOR WINDOW.

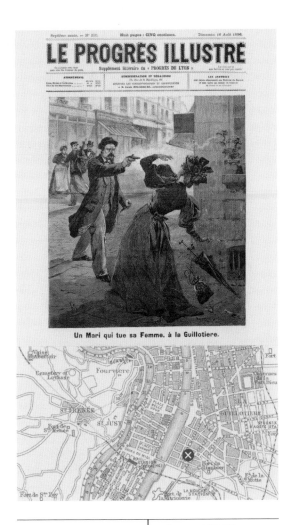

Un Mari qui tue sa Femme, à la Guillotiere.

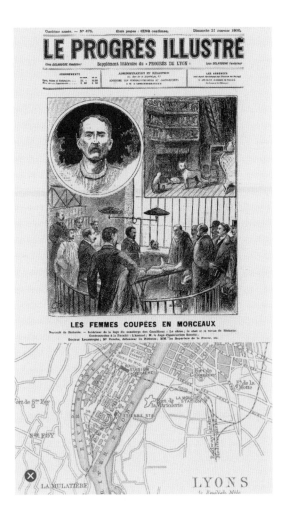

LES FEMMES COUPÉES EN MORCEAUX

FRANCE—AUVERGNE.	*August 1896.*

FRANÇOIS MARIOTTI.
✕ *Mme. Mariotti.*

WEAPON.	TYPOLOGY.	POLICING.
PISTOL.	DOMESTIC.	N/A.

CORNER OF RUE DE LA JANGOT AND RUE DE LA VITRIOLERIE, LYON.

A terrible marital tragedy occurred in mid-August 1896. At the corner of Rue de la Jangot and Rue de la Vitriolerie in Lyon, François Mariotti (dates unknown) finally tracked down his estranged wife. Madame Mariotti (dates unknown) had left the family home in Marseille to escape her husband and he had been searching for her ever since. He shot her twice in the street, before stabbing her unnecessarily in his rage. As poor Madame Mariotti succumbed to her wounds, François surrendered himself without resistance to the police, who had come rushing to the scene of the murder. ∎

Above. LE PROGRÈS ILLUSTRÉ, 18 AUGUST 1896.
FRANÇOIS MARIOTTI MURDERS HIS WIFE IN THE STREET.

FRANCE—AUVERGNE.	*1898–99.*

LUIGI GIOVANNI RICHETTO.
✕ *Mme Delorme.* ✕ *Mme Catinot.*

WEAPON.	TYPOLOGY.	POLICING.
KNIFE.	PROPERTY CRIME.	LACASSAGNE.

96 ROUTE DE FRANCHEVILLE, LYON.

Luigi Giovanni Richetto (1853–1901) was convicted at Lyon of the murder of two widows: Marguerite Delorme (c. 1835–98) and Augustine Catinot (unknown–1899). The investigation was launched when Catinot's butchered body was found in a local pond. The renowned pathologist Dr Alexandre Lacassagne (1843–1924) helped prove the case against Richetto, but while two further murders were alleged, insufficient evidence was produced to convict him of these. He stood trial and was sentenced on 29 June 1901 to imprisonment for life with hard labour. ∎

Above. LE PROGRÈS ILLUSTRÉ, 21 JANUARY 1900.
RICHETTO'S FEMALE VICTIMS' BODIES CUT INTO PIECES.

ANNET GAUMET & EVARISTE NOUGUIER.
✕ *Madame Foucherand.*

WEAPON. WINE BOTTLE.	TYPOLOGY. PROPERTY CRIME.	POLICING. LACASSAGNE.

RUE DE LA VILLETTE, LYON.

EVARISTE NOUGUIER.

The brutal murder of a widow in 1898 led to a manhunt and the eventual capture of six known members of a criminal gang. The victim, Madame Foucherand (dates unknown), was better known in her community as *'la petite vieille'*, the little old lady who ran a bistro on Rue de la Villette, in Lyon. Two were most suspected: Annet Gaumet (*c.* 1874–98) was only 24 years of age but had already accumulated fourteen convictions for a string of crimes. His close associate, Evariste Nouguier (*c.* 1878–98), nicknamed Emile, had managed just eight, but was a known pimp for local prostitutes.

The police believed Gaumet had first assaulted the bistro owner before Nouguier smashed her over the head with a bottle, splitting open her skull. The case turned on whether enough evidence could be found to convict the pair, and pathologist Dr Alexandre Lacassagne (1843–1924) was called in to help. He found bloodstains at the scene, which established she had been killed *in situ*, not elsewhere. In his laboratory his forensic skills revealed that at least two persons were involved: the bruising he found suggested she had been held down by one assailant and strangled by another, before being struck with a weapon, such as the wine bottle found next to her body. Lacassagne and Professor Lortet (dates unknown), an expert in parasitology, found traces of pinworms in faecal matter left at the scene, and when an examination of Gaumet's slop bucket in prison was made, pinworm eggs were identified.

At trial, four members of the gang, who admitted the robbery but not the murder, were sentenced to life in prison. Nouguier (the gang's leader) and Gaumet were sentenced to death. On the day he was set to face the guillotine, Gaumet requested that his skeleton be donated to Lacassagne, so impressed was he by the 'power of science'. Nouguier wrote his autobiography while he awaited execution. He gave his work, detailing his descent into a life of crime, to Lacassagne and also helped the forensic scientist compile a dictionary of criminal slang. ∎

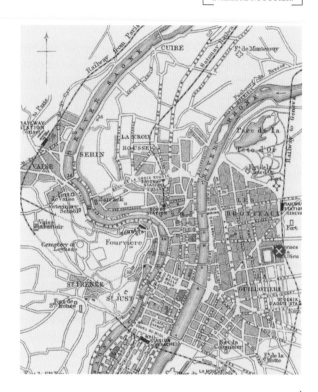

Above. MAP SHOWING THE ROAD ON WHICH MADAME FOUCHERAND WAS MURDERED BY ANNET GAUMET AND EVARISTE NOUGUIER.

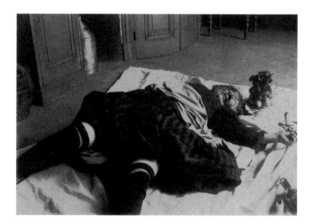

Above. THE BODY OF MADAME FOUCHERAND AS SHE WAS FOUND IN HER BISTRO IN LYON; THE MURDER WEAPON – A WINE BOTTLE – CAN BE SEEN BESIDE THE VICTIM.

VICTORINE GIRIAT
& HENRI BASSOT.

✕ *Eugénie Fougère.* ✕ *Lucie Maire.*

WEAPON. STRANGULATION.	TYPOLOGY. PROPERTY CRIME.	POLICING. BERTILLONAGE.

VILLA SOLMS, AVENUE DE TRESSERVE, AIX-LES-BAINS.

VICTORINE GIRIAT. | HENRI BASSOT.

On 20 September 1903, Eugénie Fougère (1861–1903) and one of her housemaids were found dead in the wealthy socialite's holiday villa at Aix-les-Bains in eastern France. Eugénie was a well-known member of the Paris demi-monde, who lived a hedonistic lifestyle, with frequent parties and love affairs as well as a conspicuous display of jewelry and high fashion. She was particularly notorious within her circle as a flirtatious and extravagant woman, never too far from the whiff of scandal. She was staying in the Villa Solms where she could enjoy the waters of the spa and the tables of chance in the casino. Sadly, her holiday was cut short when it appeared that burglars had broken in, bound her and two servants, Lucie Maire (dates unknown) and Victorine Giriat (dates unknown), hand and foot, and then strangled them. Only Giriat survived the ordeal, and the felons made off with money and jewelry estimated at 200,000 francs.

Detectives soon traced two men they believed were involved, naming them as Martin and Ceccaldi, but this soon proved to be little more than a cunning ruse. This arrest was a diversion so they could track the real culprits, the maid Giriat and her lover Henri Bassot (dates unknown). It took the police many months and several false trails before they were able to bring charges against those responsible for the murders. Along with Bassot and 'his instrument' Giriat, a man named Robardet (dates unknown) was accused of selling on some of the stolen goods, while another named César Ladermann (dates unknown) – purportedly the brains behind the operation – shot himself as the police descended on his lodgings in Lyon.

Bassot kept calm throughout his trial, writing letters in his prison cell denigrating the chief investigator, Monsieur Hamard (1861–unknown), and the French Criminal Investigation Department. On 3 June 1904, the court found all three defendants guilty. Bassot was sent to jail for ten years, while Robardet got just three months. Giriat was considered the worst offender because she had betrayed her mistress's trust; she was sentenced to fifteen years' penal servitude. ∎

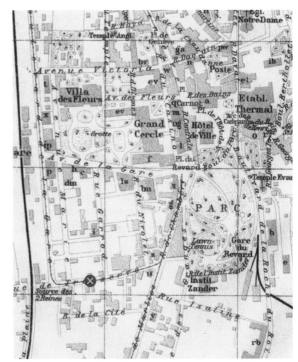

Above. MAP SHOWING THE LOCATION OF THE VILLA IN WHICH EUGÉNIE FOUGÈRE WAS MURDERED BY VICTORINE GIRIAT AND HENRI BASSOT.

Above. ALPHONSE BERTILLON'S CRIME SCENE PHOTOGRAPH OF EUGÉNIE FOUGÈRE'S BODY, FOUND IN HER BED FOLLOWING HER MURDER.

CHAUFFEURS OF DRÔME.
× *12.* +

WEAPON. FIRE.	TYPOLOGY. PROPERTY CRIME.	POLICING. N/A.

DRÔME.

OCTAVE-LOUIS DAVID.

PIERRE-AUGUSTIN-LOUIS BERRUYER.

URBAN-CÉLESTIN LIOTTARD.

In the early 1900s, the south of France was subjected to a wave of violent burglaries and murders. Four criminals terrorized Drôme in southeastern France. Octave-Louis David (1873–1909), Pierre-Augustin-Louis Berruyer (1873–1909), Urban-Célestin Liottard (1893–1909) and Jean Lamarque (unknown–1909) were responsible for perhaps as many as eighteen murders over the course of their criminal careers. They earned the unpleasant sobriquet of '*les chauffeurs* [heaters] *de la Drôme*' because they tortured householders by burning their feet until they revealed the whereabouts of their valuables. David, as the most infamous criminal among them, was the leader of the gang and met Lamarque when the pair served time together for a previous crime. Lamarque introduced him to Berruyer and Liottard, who shared rooms with him in Romans-sur-Isère, a small town in the Auvergne. The gang operated at night, targeting rural homes and farms, and maintained their cover by holding down regular jobs during the day.

The police eventually tracked down Berruyer and arrested him at his home; the arrests of David and Liottard soon followed but Lamarque evaded capture. The trio were tried and convicted at Valence, with the large haul of stolen goods found in Berruyer's room a significant indicator of their guilt. The French president, an opponent of the death penalty, might have spared their lives, but public opinion was outraged by their use of violence and all three were sent to the guillotine. Lamarque was sentenced *in absentia* but avoided execution. He was captured a year later and sent to Devil's Island, the notorious penal colony in French Guiana immortalized by Henri Charrière (1906–73) in his novel *Papillon* (1969). The other three faced the guillotine in their own ways.

Berruyer was angry with the decision to kill him, remonstrating with his jailers and protesting to the last minute. Liottard went calmly to his death whereas David drank and smoke the night before, seemingly unconcerned. When the blade fell, his head stayed in place and had to be pushed into the basket by the executioner. Despite a prohibition on photography at the execution, numerous images were taken and reproduced as postcards for eager buyers. ∎

❶ 26 RUE PÊCHERIE, ROMANS-SUR-ISÈRE, DRÔME.
THE LOCATION OF THE CHAUFFEURS' HEADQUARTERS.

❷ MONDY, BOURG-DE-PÉAGE, DRÔME.
THE TOWN WHERE MLLE. JUDGE WAS MURDERED IN 1906.

❸ ALIXAN, DRÔME.
THE TOWN WHERE PÈRE DELAYE WAS MURDERED IN 1907.

❹ SAUT DU CHAT, SAINT-LATTIER, ISÈRE.
THE TOWN WHERE M. AND MME. REY WERE MURDERED IN 1907.

❺ PEYRINS, DRÔME.
THE TOWN WHERE FRÉDÉRIC LARDY WAS MURDERED IN 1907.

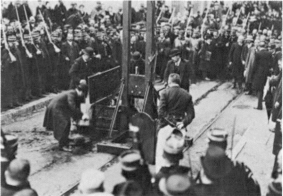

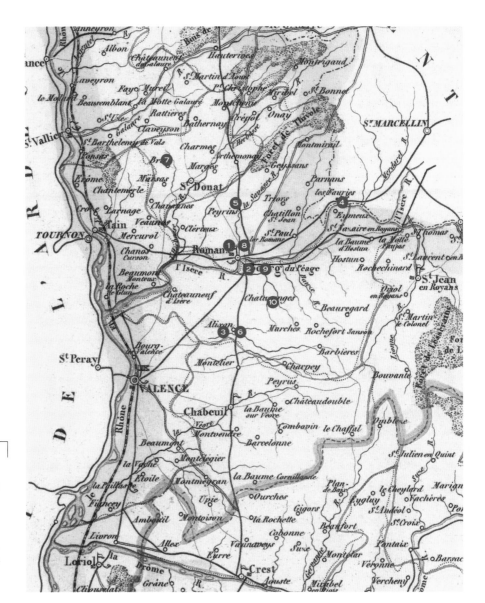

6

ALIXAN, DRÔME.
THE TOWN WHERE
PÈRE DORIER AND
NOEMIE DORIER WERE
MURDERED IN 1907.

7

CORINS, BREN,
DRÔME.
THE TOWN WHERE
PÈRE JEAN MALBOURRET
WAS MURDERED IN 1907.

8

ROMANS-SUR-ISÈRE,
DRÔME.
THE TOWN WHERE
EUGÈNE GIRARD WAS
MURDERED IN 1907.

9

CHAMBOIS, BOURG-DE-
PÉAGE, DRÔME.
THE TOWN WHERE
FRANÇOIS AND JULIE
TORTEL WERE MURDERED
IN 1908.

10

TRIMOLLET,
CHATUZANGE-LE-
GOUBET, DRÔME.
THE TOWN WHERE
ROMARIN WAS
MURDERED IN 1908.

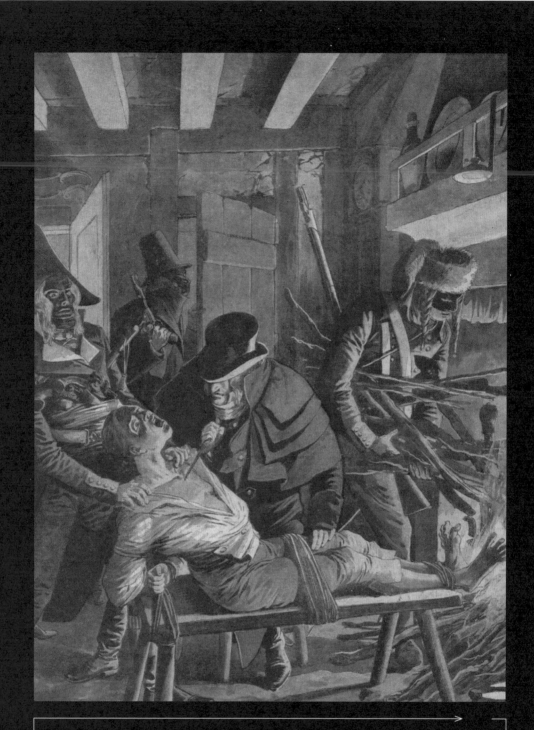

'Listen to the horrible tales of the awful blood that this
filthy band have spread across the country.'

CONTEMPORARY BALLAD ABOUT THE CRIMES OF THE CHAUFFEURS OF DRÔME.

Above. LE PETIT JOURNAL, 15 NOVEMBER 1908, BACK PAGE.
THE CHAUFFEURS TORTURING A VICTIM.

'For three years they have traced a furrow full of blood
through our countryside.'

CONTEMPORARY BALLAD ABOUT THE CRIMES OF THE CHAUFFEURS OF DRÔME.

———

Above. LE PETIT JOURNAL, 15 NOVEMBER 1908, FRONT PAGE.
THE CHAUFFEURS TORTURING A VICTIM.

FERDINAND GUMP.
× *Eduard Gänswürger.* × *3.*

WEAPON.	TYPOLOGY.	POLICING.
GUN.	GANG.	PHOTOGRAPHY.

NIEDERFELD, INGOLSTADT.

On 12 December 1872, three farmers were making their way home from the annual cattle market at Mainburg, Germany. As they reached the outskirts of Meilenhofen, they encountered three strangers whom they thought might have been former French prisoners (from the recent Franco-Prussian conflict). The men were armed, and when one of them asked Franz-Xaver Gruber (unknown–1872) to put down his weapon the farmer laughed it off. It was a mistake, and Gruber was instantly shot dead. Another was murdered before the third farmer surrendered all his money and the gang ran off. The dead body of one of the robbers was soon found nearby, his companions having dispatched him as well, and a police manhunt was launched.

The two remaining robbers were Eduard Gänswürger (1843–73) and Ferdinand Gump (1844–73), two misfit school friends who had teamed up to pursue a life of crime. Wanted for at least twenty-eight robberies, the pair evaded the police and large numbers of vigilantes for several months. At Karlskron, Gänswürger shot a shopkeeper, Margarethe Kufer (unknown–1873), who had been unwittingly helping them. The pair fell out over this murder and Gump killed his associate by the Sanbach River, shooting him at close range.

The photograph the police made of the scene of the crime was one of the first used by the Bavarian justice system, as authorities across the world began to recognize the value that the new science of photography could bring to criminal investigations. There was now a price on Gump's head and he had to disguise himself to avoid his pursuers. In April, he shot at two officers who had found his hideout, killing one of them. At Ingolstadt, he managed to avoid capture by disguising himself as a solider in the crowds mourning the dead lawman. He was finally arrested at Wolznach when a shopkeeper grew suspicious of him and called the gendarmerie. He admitted many of his crimes but denied murder, probably because he knew that such an admission was likely to result in the death penalty. However, Gump (nicknamed 'Seitzfendi' by classmates who were scared of him at school) never came to trial because he succumbed to tuberculosis in prison and died. ∎

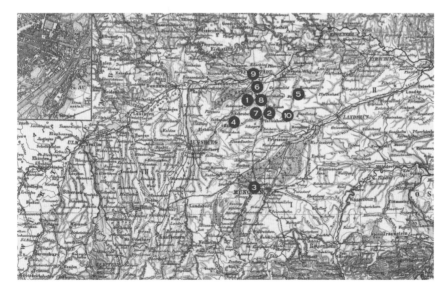

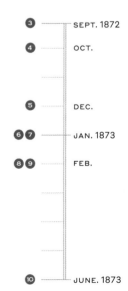

③	SEPT. 1872
④	OCT.
⑤	DEC.
⑥⑦	JAN. 1873
⑧⑨	FEB.
⑩	JUNE. 1873

1. KARLSKRON, NEUBURG-
SCHROBENHAUSEN.
THE TOWN WHERE FERDINAND
GUMP AND EDUARD GÄNSWÜRGER
ATTENDED SCHOOL.

2. REICHERTSHOFEN,
PFAFFENHOFEN.
THE TOWN WHERE FERDINAND
GUMP AND EDUARD GÄNSWÜRGER
WERE CARPENTRY APPRENTICES
IN 1860.

3. BAADERSTRASSE, MUNICH.
THE LOCATION OF THE MUNICH
DISTRICT COURT PRISON FROM
WHICH EDUARD GÄNSWÜRGER
ESCAPED IN 1872.

4. OBERLAUTERBACH, ARESING.
THE TOWN WHERE FERDINAND
GUMP AND EDUARD GÄNSWÜRGER
RAIDED A VICARAGE IN 1872.

5. MEILENHOFEN, MAINBURG.
THE TOWN WHERE FERDINAND
GUMP AND EDUARD GÄNSWÜRGER
ROBBED THREE FARMERS IN 1872.

6. MÄNDLFELD, KARLSKRON.
A TOWN WHERE FERDINAND GUMP
AND EDUARD GÄNSWÜRGER HID
FROM THE POLICE.

7. WALDING, KARLSKRON.
A TOWN WHERE FERDINAND GUMP
AND EDUARD GÄNSWÜRGER HID
FROM THE POLICE.

8. KARLSKRON, NEUBURG-
SCHROBENHAUSEN.
THE TOWN WHERE MARGARETHE
KUFER WAS MURDERED IN 1873.

9. NIEDERFELD, INGOLSTADT.
THE TOWN WHERE THE BODY
OF EDUARD GÄNSWÜRGER
WAS FOUND IN 1873.

10. WOLZNACH, PFAFFENHOFEN.
THE TOWN WHERE FERDINAND
GUMP WAS ARRESTED IN 1873.

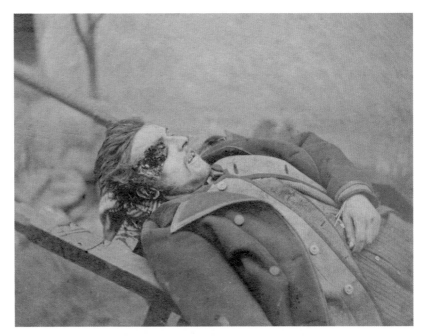

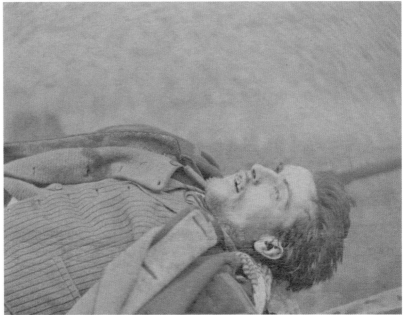

Top. THE BODY OF EDUARD
GÄNSWÜRGER ON A POLICE
STRETCHER SHORTLY AFTER
IT WAS DISCOVERED BY THE
BANKS OF THE SANBACH
RIVER. THIS VIEW SHOWS
WHERE HIS FORMER
ACCOMPLICE FERDINAND
GUMP SHOT HIM IN THE FACE.

Above. A SECOND VIEW OF
GÄNSWÜRGER'S MURDERED
BODY, REVEALING HIS
RELATIVE YOUTH. THE
MILITARY-STYLE UNIFORM
CONVINCED THE FARMERS
THAT THE THREE ROBBERS
WERE PRISONERS FROM THE
FRANCO-PRUSSIAN WAR.

UNKNOWN.
✕ *Ludwig II of Bavaria.*

WEAPON. DROWNING.	TYPOLOGY. ASSASSINATION.	POLICING. N/A.

LAKE STARNBERG, UPPER BAVARIA.

The death of Ludwig II (1845–86), king of Bavaria, has all the elements of a 19th-century murder mystery. On 13 June 1886, Ludwig disappeared, along with his physician, Dr Bernhard von Gudden (1824–86), after the pair had been seen walking in the grounds of Berg Castle. At 10:30 p.m. that night, a fisherman, Jakob Lidl (dates unknown), found the bodies of the king and his doctor. Both were drowned, and Gudden appeared to have also been strangled. Ludwig had been treated for a form of insanity (although it is far from clear that modern medicine would have so diagnosed him) and had been deposed. Rumours persist that Ludwig and his doctor were shot and killed while trying to escape from the castle, the 'drowning' incident being used as a cover. According to official sources, Ludwig had walked into the lake to take his own life and Dr Gudden had died while trying to save him. The story has enjoyed several twists and turns as new evidence emerges and rumours are revived, but we are unlikely to ever know the truth. ∎

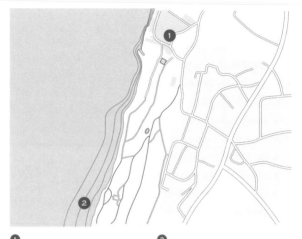

❶ BERG CASTLE.
THE CASTLE WHERE LUDWIG II WAS STAYING, AND BEGAN THE WALK THAT WOULD END IN HIS DEATH.

❷ LAKE STARNBERG.
THE LAKE IN WHICH LUDWIG II'S BODY WAS FOUND.

Above. BERG CASTLE IN BAVARIA WHERE KING LUDWIG II WAS STAYING WHEN HE DIED IN MYSTERIOUS CIRCUMSTANCES. HIS BODY WAS FOUND FLOATING IN THE LAKE BY ONE OF THE ESTATE'S FISHERMEN.

Below. KING LUDWIG II'S BODY LIES IN STATE SURROUNDED BY CANDLES. RUMOURS PERSIST THAT LUDWIG, WHO HAD BEEN TREATED FOR WHAT CONTEMPORARIES THOUGHT WAS 'MADNESS', MAY HAVE TAKEN HIS OWN LIFE.

JOHANN BERCHTOLD.
✕ *Julie von Roos.* ✕ *Karoline von Roos.* ✕ *Maria Gradl.*

WEAPON.	TYPOLOGY.	POLICING.
STRANGULATION.	PROPERTY CRIME.	FORENSIC PSYCHOLOGY.

33 KARLSTRASSE, MUNICH.

The discovery of three dead bodies at the Roos family's apartment on Karlstrasse, Munich, initially presented the police with a mystery. Mrs von Roos (unknown–1896) and Marie Gradl (unknown–1896) – her cook – were found one on top of the other in the water closet, while Julie von Roos's (unknown–1896) body was laid out on her bed. Investigators first suspected a gas leak had killed the trio, but post-mortems revealed that they had been strangled. The motive was initially and mistakenly assumed to be sexual. In fact the household had been killed for their money, as 800 reichsmark was missing. Suspicion eventually fell on a builder who had worked there the previous year. Johann Berchtold (1862–1925) was arrested and, after five months of evidence gathering, he was put on trial in Munich accused of triple murder. This was the first recorded case where a forensic psychologist's testimony was deployed. Berchtold was sentenced to death but this was commuted to life imprisonment. ∎

① 33 KARLSTRASSE, MAXVORSTADT. THE HOUSE WHERE JOHANN BERCHTOLD MURDERED JULIE AND KAROLINE VON ROOS AND MARIE GRADL.

② QUELLENSTRASSE, AU-HAIDHAUSEN. THE HOUSE WHERE JOHANN BERCHTOLD WAS RUMOURED TO HAVE MURDERED FRAU EMETSKOFERIN.

③ PAULANERPLATZ, AU-HAIDHAUSEN. THE HOUSE WHERE JOHANN BERCHTOLD WAS RUMOURED TO HAVE MURDERED JOHANN SCHNEIDER.

Above. THE ROOS FAMILY'S APARTMENT BLOCK ON KARLSTRASSE, MUNICH, WHERE THE THREE VICTIMS WERE DISCOVERED.

Below. THE HOUSE IN QUELLENSTRASSE WHERE FRAU EMETSKOFERIN WAS MURDERED.

MATHIAS KNEISSL.
✕ *Gendarmerie Commander Brandmeier.*
✕ *His Sergeant.*

WEAPON. GUN.	TYPOLOGY. GANG.	POLICING. N/A.

IRCHENBRUNN.

Mathias Kneissl, or Kneißl, (1875–1902) was something of a legendary figure in Bavarian popular folklore, akin to Robin Hood in England or Ned Kelly (1854–80) in Australia. He went to his death on 21 February 1902, having been convicted of a string of robberies with murder. He took his Monday sentencing casually, reportedly telling the judge, 'well that's a good start to the week', and this appears to have been a part of Kneissl's popular 'bandit' image.

Born into a large but poor family, he followed his father and brother into a life of crime, serving his first term of imprisonment at the age of 16. By 1893, his father and one of his brothers had died in jail. Mathias went down for five years in 1893 for his part in the family's cattle-rustling escapades. He went straight for all of six months before losing his job as a carpenter and reverting to robbery and violence. As his armed raiding drew down the ire of the German authorities, he went on the run and, like his Australian equivalent, fought armed police in a huge gun battle on 30 November 1900. Kneissl survived, but two officers died and the manhunt continued. In March, his luck ran out, as surrounded by up to sixty policemen Kneissl was wounded in the stomach and finally captured.

He stood trial at Augsburg in November 1901, where he admitted several charges of robbery but denied murder. The court convicted him, nonetheless, finding him guilty of armed robbery, murder and extortion. The press reported the five days of the trial in great detail and Kneissl, probably relishing his notoriety, obliged them with quotes such as: 'I cannot bend, I would rather kill myself.' The small farmers of Bavaria might have viewed Kneissl as some sort of revolutionary hero but, like many outlaws in history, he was mostly a violent thief who refused to bow to authority. He had no political creed, just a base desire to serve his own self-interest. ∎

Above. MATHIAS KNEISSL BEING RESTRAINED BY A POLICEMAN FOLLOWING HIS ARREST.

Above. GERMAN DETECTIVES DISPLAY THEIR WOUNDED CAPTIVE MATHIAS KNEISSL FOR THE PRESS.

Above. MATHIAS KNEISSL, WHO RESISTED ARREST, WAS AFTERWARDS CONFINED TO A WHEELCHAIR.

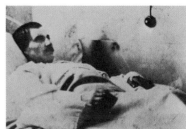

❶

UNTERWEIKERTSHOFEN, ERDWEG.
THE TOWN WHERE MATHIAS KNEISSL WAS BORN IN 1875.

❷

MUNICH DISTRICT COURT PRISON, MUNICH.
THE PRISON WHERE MATHIAS KNEISSL WAS IMPRISONED IN 1893.

❸

NUSSDORF AM INN, ROSENHEIM.
THE TOWN WHERE MATHIAS KNEISSL BECAME A CARPENTER IN 1899.

❹

IRCHENBRUNN, ALTOMÜNSTER.
THE TOWN WHERE MATHIAS KNEISSL MURDERED GENDARMERIE COMMANDER BRANDMEIER AND HIS SERGEANT.

❺

GEISENHOFEN, EGENHOFEN.
THE TOWN WHERE MATHIAS KNEISSL WAS ARRESTED.

❻

AUGSBURG.
THE TOWN WHERE MATHIAS KNEISSL WAS TRIED BEFORE A JURY.

JAN JIŘÍ GRÁZL, JAKOB FÄHDING & IGNAZ STANGEL.
✕ *Multiple – Unknown.*

WEAPON. SWORD.	TYPOLOGY. GANG.	POLICING. N/A.

LOWER AUSTRIA & SOUTH MORAVIA.

JAN JIŘÍ GRÁZL.	JAKOB FÄHDING.	IGNAZ STANGEL.

In November 1815, the Hapsburg authorities issued a reward for the capture of a notorious bandit 'captain' and his 'gang' of robbers. Jan Jiří Grázl (1790–1818) was born in Nové Syrovice (in what is now the Czech Republic), just as Europe entered the turmoil of the French revolutionary wars. The son of skinners, Grázl soon recognized that crime offered a better life than animal hides. Starting with petty theft, he progressed to burglary before allying himself with outlaws and taking up robbery. Whether Grázl deserved his reputation as a bandit captain is extremely doubtful; in reality, he seems to have been someone trying to survive in what were very difficult times for the populace of the Hapsburg Empire. While the emperor and his court enjoyed all the luxuries that aristocratic wealth could buy, the poorer classes eked out a desperate existence in a country ravaged by war. The reward did its job, though, and Grázl was arrested in an inn near the city of Horn.

The authorities took him to Vienna, but it was a couple of years before he was finally brought to trial. Grázl confessed to more than 200 offences and he was sentenced to death along with two others. On 31 January 1818, he was executed in front of the Schottentor on the Glacis, the traditional site of public hangings in Vienna since the middle of the 1700s. A crowd of 60,000 came to watch, prompting him to remark: 'Jesus, so many people!' Grázl has passed into legend in Austria, accorded the status of a Robin Hood-style character by some, with the phrase 'you grázl' being used to mean 'you crook'. Whatever the truth of his criminal life, it seems likely that the former skinner did lead an adventurous, if fairly short, life as one of Austria's most notorious and violent robbers. Ultimately, he paid for his actions with his life, but in an age where thousands of young Austrians were dying on the battlefield he may have felt he had at least enjoyed the time he had. ∎

Below. A CONTEMPORARY PAMPHLET REVIEWING THE LIFE OF JAN JIŘÍ GRÁZL.

Below. A 19TH-CENTURY 'TRUE CRIME' PUBLICATION REVEALS THE LIFE 'AND HUSTLE AND BUSTLE' OF THE 'ROBBER CAPTAIN' JAN JIŘÍ GRÁZL.

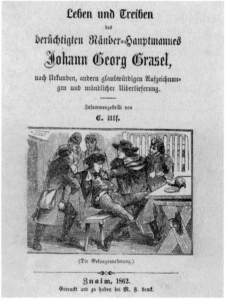

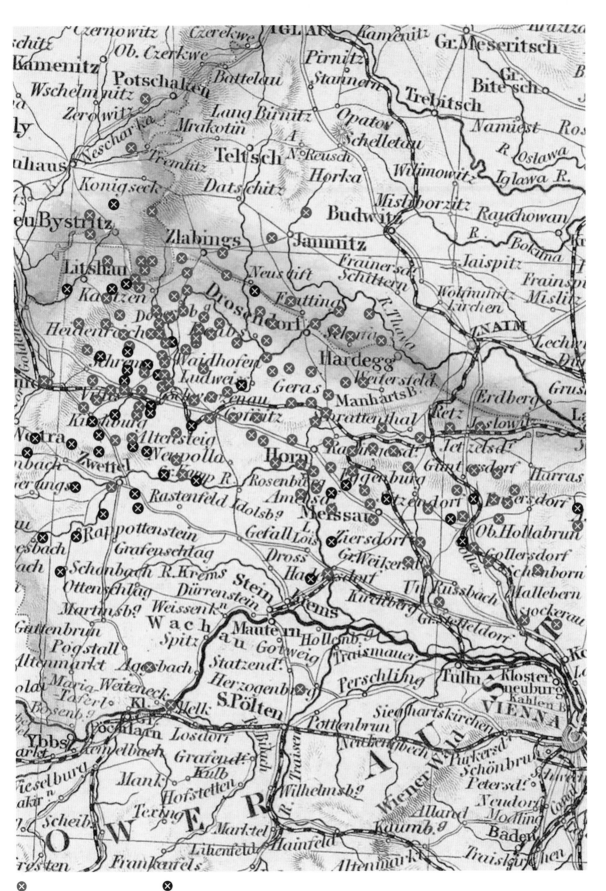

HUGO SCHENK.
× 4.

WEAPON.	TYPOLOGY.	POLICING.
VARIOUS.	PROPERTY CRIME.	N/A.

STATE OF VIENNA, AUSTRIA.

Vienna was no stranger to murder in the late 19th century. The capital of the Hapsburg Empire was a busy metropolis of more than a million souls, with all the associated social problems that brought. In the 1880s, the Viennese public were rudely shocked by newspaper reports of a serial killer at large. Hugo Schenk (1849–84) had started his criminal career in the late 1860s as a fraudster who attempted to trick young women out of their marriage dowries. He went to prison; however, on his release he teamed up with a former cell mate – Karl Schlossarek (1858–1884) – and escalated fraud to murder. In January 1883, Schenk raped and murdered Josefine Timal (1849–83), a 34-year-old Viennese servant, dumping her body in the Hranice Abyss (the deepest underwater cave in the world). He had tricked her into believing they would marry. Josefine had left her position as a maid and had run off with him to Warsaw, little suspecting that the man she hoped to call her husband would turn out to be her murderer. Schlossarek and Schenk then murdered Josefine's aunt, drowning her in the Danube because they feared she would report them.

Six weeks later, emboldened by his success in getting away with murder and what little wealth Josefine possessed, Schenk targeted another maid, Theresia Ketterl (unknown–1883). While Schenk drowned most of his victims, he tricked Theresia into taking her own life. Instigating a game of Russian roulette, Schenk secretly loaded the pistol and allowed her to shoot herself, then toppled her body into a gorge. Finally, in December 1883, the pair killed Rosa Ferenszi (unknown–1883).

Although none of the girls that Schenk murdered were rich, they were persuaded by him to hand over all the savings and valuables they possessed. In all the contemporary press reports, Schenk was described as 'handsome and gentlemanly', the archetypal melodrama villain. These characteristics help explain how Schenk was able to get so close to his victims. That most dangerous of killers, Schenk was a plausible and attractive man who had the ability to manipulate vulnerable young women. Once he had seduced them away from family and friends, he sexually assaulted his victims before tying a large stone to their legs and tossing them into a river to drown. Schenk probably made very little money from his crimes and so robbery was unlikely to have been his prime motive. As is the case with many serial murderers, Schenk likely enjoyed the feeling of power that he gained from tricking and then terrorizing his victims.

He was eventually captured by police, put on trial and hanged in 1884 along with his accomplices, his brother Karl and Karl Schlossarek. After his execution, Schenk's skull was examined by the neurologist Moritz Benedikt (1835–1920) as part of his ongoing work on identifying so-called 'criminal' brains. The skull is still on display in Vienna's crime museum today. ∎

HUGO SCHENK.
1849–84.
MURDERER.
HANGED.

KARL SCHLOSSAREK.
1858–84.
ACCOMPLICE.
HANGED.

KARL SCHENK.
DATES UNKNOWN.
ACCOMPLICE.
HANGED.

EMILIE HOCHSMANN.
1859–UNKNOWN.
FIANCÉE.
SURVIVED.

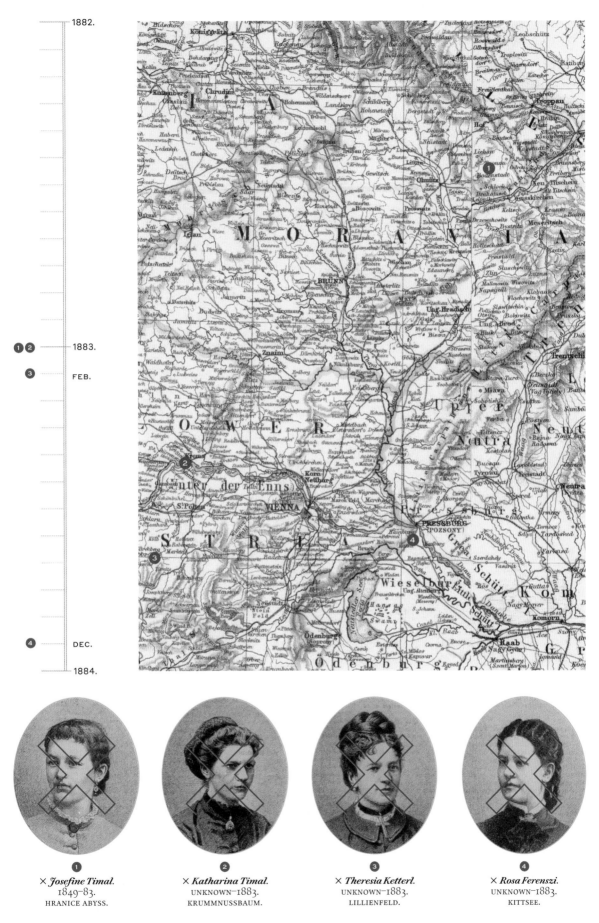

1883.

FEB.

DEC.

1884.

✕ *Josefine Timal.*
1849–83.
HRANICE ABYSS.

✕ *Katharina Timal.*
UNKNOWN–1883.
KRUMMNUSSBAUM.

✕ *Theresia Ketterl.*
UNKNOWN–1883.
LILLIENFELD.

✕ *Rosa Ferenszi.*
UNKNOWN–1883.
KITTSEE.

Left above. HUGO SCHENK PERSUADES THERESIA KETTERL TO PLAY A DANGEROUS GAME OF RUSSIAN ROULETTE.

Left centre. JOSEFINE TIMAL IS THROWN INTO THE DEPTHS OF THE HRANICE ABYSS.

Left below. KARL SCHLOSSAREK ROBS FRANZ PODPERA IN THE KRAKOW FOREST WHILE HUGO SCHENK LURKS IN WAIT.

Right above. HUGO SCHENK AND KARL SCHLOSSAREK MURDER ROSA FERENSZI AND DISPOSE OF HER BODY.

Right centre. JOSEFINE'S AUNT, KATHARINA TIMAL, BECOMES THE NEXT VICTIM OF HUGO SCHENK.

Right below. HUGO SCHENK AND KARL SCHLOSSAREK MURDER FRANZ BAUER, A COACHMAN, IN THE WOODS.

Below. MORGEN-POST, 27 JANUARY 1884. HUGO SCHENK PICTURED
IN PRISON BEFORE HIS EXECUTION. DESCRIBED AS A 'WOMAN
MURDERER', SCHENK IS CHARACTERIZED AS HANDSOME AND
GENTLEMANLY, WHICH EXPLAINS HOW HE WAS ABLE TO GET
CLOSE TO HIS FEMALE VICTIMS. IN REALITY HE WAS A SADISTIC
MURDERER WHO ENJOYED THE POWER THAT KILLING GAVE HIM.

Der Frauenmörder Hugo Schenk.
Nach der letzten photographischen Aufnahme im Polizei-gefangenhause.

SIMON SCHOSTERITZ.
✕ *Franciska Hofer.* ✕ *Anna Spilka.*

WEAPON.	TYPOLOGY.	POLICING.
KNIFE.	SEXUAL.	SUSPECT IMAGE CIRCULATED.

27 HAYMERLEGASSE, OTTAKRING.

In 1886, Richard von Krafft-Ebing (1840–1902) first published his seminal work on sexuality and psychology, *Psychopathia Sexualis*. In later editions, he referenced the Whitechapel murderer Jack the Ripper and what seemed like a copycat case in Vienna. Krafft-Ebing described the murder of Franciska Hofer (unknown–1898) as 'a lust murder of the most terrible kind'. The victim was a prostitute, known to the police, who on the night she died was seen returning to her lodgings at 27 Haymerlegasse, Vienna, with a man apparently carrying a rolled-up apron. The next day, Franciscka's body was found by her stepsister, who had brought round some new clothes for her. What she found must have shocked her to the core because, as it was later reported: 'There laid Franciska Hofer, completely undressed, her feet hanging over the sofa, arms on her hips. The whole body was slashed up to the breasts with a sharp, rectangular-shaped cut. The intestines came out of the opened abdominal cavity. The liver was cut out and discarded, found under the divan. The floor was soaked in blood. Blood was also found in the washbasin, as well as a print of a bloody hand and bloody footprints on the corridor.'

Only a decade after 'Jack' had terrorized the East End, Vienna had its own 'Ripper' to rival London's. Descriptions of the killer were circulated and more than one of the city's 'unfortunates' reported seeing men that matched it. Nevertheless, the Austrian police, like their London equivalents, struggled to catch a serial killer who chose such vulnerable targets. Then, just a few days later, another Viennese prostitute – Anna Spilka (unknown–1898) – was killed by someone the police also identified as a 'perverted lust killer'. Although she was not mutilated as Hofer had been, this was put down to the killer being disturbed. As one of Anna's flatmates went to her room, a strange man rushed out, blood spattered on his face and hands. A lynch mob pursued the killer before the police rescued him. The man was identified as Hungarian butcher Simon Schosteritz (dates unknown) and he was convicted for Spilka's murder. ∎

Below. FLOOR PLAN OF THE MURDER SCENE AT 27 HAYMERLEGASSE, SHOWING FRANZISKA HOFER'S BODY ON HER SOFA.

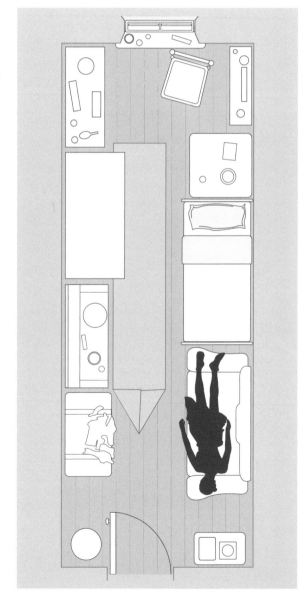

Below left. A POLICE PHOTOGRAPH
OF THE MURDER SCENE. FRANZISKA
HOFER'S MURDER WAS LIKENED
TO THAT OF MARY JANE KELLY IN
LONDON, ENGLAND, IN 1888.

Bottom left. FRANCISKA HOFER'S FEET.
THEY WERE HANGING OVER THE EDGE
OF THE SOFA WHEN SHE WAS DISCOVERED.

Below right. THE *WIENER BILDER*
NEWSPAPER'S ILLUSTRATION OF THE
CAPTURE OF SIMON SCHOSTERITZ
BY THE LYNCH MOB.

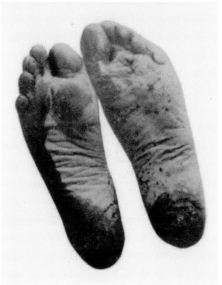

PÁL SPANGA, MIHÁLY OLÁH PITÉLI & JÁNOS BERECZ. × *György Majláth.*

WEAPON. STRANGULATION.	TYPOLOGY. PROPERTY CRIME.	POLICING. EARLY FORENSICS.

BUDA CASTLE DISTRICT.

PÁL SPANGA.

MIHÁLY OLÁH PITÉLI.

JÁNOS BERECZ.

Count Georg (or György) von Majláth (1818–83) had served Austria-Hungary as a politician and judge for many years. Then, on 29 March 1883, at the age of 64, Majláth's career was cut short. The count was a member of the Knights of the Golden Fleece (an ancient order of chivalry created in the 15th century). Even today, the gilded collar that the knights wear makes it the most expensive chivalrous order in existence and this may have attracted thieves to Majláth's home that evening.

The count retired to bed at around 11:00 p.m., and that was the last time he was seen alive. One of his manservants found him dead the next morning, lying on the floor of his chamber, his nightshirt spattered with blood and his face blackened. The count had been strangled to death, but he had clearly put up a fight, scratching at his assailant and drawing blood. The room had been trashed and a strongbox had been forced open and jewelry stolen.

The police quickly decided that robbery, and not political assassination, was the reason for the crime and the telltale footprints of heavy boots outside seemed to confirm that this incident was the work of ordinary criminals. A Czech labourer named Mihály Oláh Pitéli (1857–84) had been seen talking to Majláth's valet, János Berecz (1856–84), a day or so before the murder and he and another man, Pál Spanga (1854–84), became the main culprits sought by the authorities. Aided by a glove that one of the murderers had dropped as he fled, the police were able to successfully prosecute the three criminals and they were all hanged on 23 February 1884. ∎

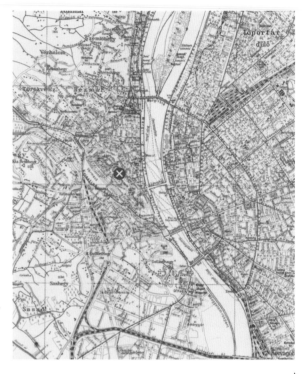

Above. MAP SHOWING THE LOCATION OF THE DISTRICT IN WHICH COUNT GEORG MAJLÁTH LIVED WHEN HE WAS MURDERED.

Above. THE BUDA CASTLE DISTRICT IN BUDAPEST WHERE COUNT GEORG MAJLÁTH LIVED.

Above. THE BUDA CASTLE GARDENS IN 1883, IN THE DISTRICT WHERE THE MURDER TOOK PLACE.

Above. ILLUSTRATED *POLICE NEWS* SHOWS COUNT GEORG MAJLÁTH'S MURDER.

Above. MURDERER PÁL SPANGA'S CRIMINAL RECORD.

COUNT GEORG MAJLÁTH. 1818–83.

BÉLA KISS.
✕ *24.*

WEAPON. STRANGULATION.	TYPOLOGY. PROPERTY CRIME.	POLICING. N/A.

CINKOTA.

As the First World War ravaged Europe, Mrs Jakubec (dates unknown) thought she ought to 'do her bit' for the war effort by alerting the Austro-Hungarian authorities to what she believed to be a stash of petrol kept by her employer in his home near Budapest. When police opened the first of seven large metal drums at Béla Kiss's (1877–unknown) property, the smell was overpowering. Instead of much-needed fuel, the drum contained the body of a woman. The other six held similarly gruesome contents, and a thorough search of the Kiss estate uncovered twenty-four dead women, each of whom had been strangled and drained of blood.

Kiss was nowhere to be seen; he had gone off to fight and despite the best efforts of the police and military he evaded capture. Mrs Jakubec, the housekeeper, showed the police to a sealed room that she had never been allowed to enter. There, they found letters from over seventy women whom Kiss had been corresponding with, a number of photographs, and books on poisons and methods of killing. It appeared that the sometime occultist and astrologer had been placing advertisements in the 'lonely hearts' columns of the newspapers to lure moneyed middle-aged women to his home by promising marriage and future happiness. Once at the house, he murdered them, seizing any wealth they possessed. At least two had escaped his clutches and initiated court proceedings, but the war gave him the opportunity to disappear, and he was never brought to justice for his crimes. ∎

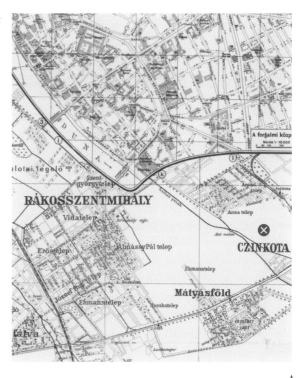

Above. MAP SHOWING THE LOCATION OF BÉLA KISS'S HOME IN CINKOTA, OUTSIDE BUDAPEST.

Above. THE WOODSHED AT BÉLA KISS'S PROPERTY WHERE HE PLOTTED HIS CRIMES.

Above. THE METAL DRUMS THAT WERE FOUND TO CONTAIN SEVEN DECOMPOSING BODIES.

Above. INSIDE THE WOODSHED AT BÉLA KISS'S PROPERTY.

MARGARET TOTH. UNKNOWN– 1906.

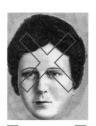

KATHERINE VARGA. DATES UNKNOWN.

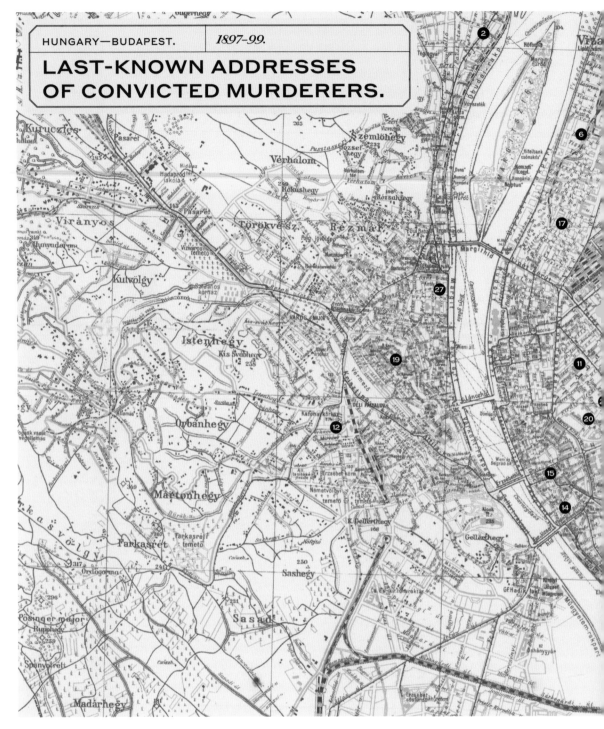

LAST-KNOWN ADDRESSES
OF CONVICTED MURDERERS.

1 1897. BUDAPEST VIII, FECSKE ÚTCA 5. Lente Antal. × UNKNOWN.

2 1897. BUDAPEST III, ÓBUDA LAJOS ÚTCA 203. Singer Zsigmond.
× UNKNOWN.

3 1897. BUDAPEST VIII, NÉPSZÍNHÁZ ÚTCA 26. Gitzl Hermin.
× UNKNOWN.

4 1897. BUDAPEST IX, FERENC ÚTCA 13. Bujna János. × UNKNOWN.

5 1897. BUDAPEST IX, GYÁLI ÚTCA 18. Hetzendorfer István.
× UNKNOWN.

6 1897. BUDAPEST V, DRÁVA ÚTCA. Hradil Adolf. × UNKNOWN.

7 1897. BUDAPEST VIII, KEREPESI ÚTCA 11.
Tóth Gyuláné Kovács Mari. × UNKNOWN.

8 1897. BUDAPEST VI, EÖTVÖS ÚTCA 33. Hegyi Károly. × UNKNOWN.

9 1897. BUDAPEST IX, ÜLLŐI ÚTCA 101. Lőrincz Rozália.
× UNKNOWN.

10 1897. BUDAPEST IX, SOROKSÁRI ÚTCA 26. Tánczos Sándor.
× UNKNOWN.

11 1897. BUDAPEST VI, HAJÓS ÚTCA 7. Fuchs Mátyás. × UNKNOWN.

12 1897. BUDAPEST I, ALKOTÁS ÚTCA 15. Monaszni György József.
× UNKNOWN.

13 1897. BUDAPEST VI, SZABOLCS ÚTCA 11.
Jancsik Ágoston Gusztáv. × UNKNOWN.

14 1897. BUDAPEST IV, SZARKA ÚTCA 5. Gárdos Lajos ifj.
× UNKNOWN.

15 1897. BUDAPEST V, VÁCI ÚTCA 182. Kainer János. × UNKNOWN.

16 1898. BUDAPEST VII, KEREPESI ÚTCA 14. Striegel Rudolf.
× UNKNOWN.

17 1898. BUDAPEST V, CSÁKY ÚTCA 17. Hladnyi István. × UNKNOWN.

18 1898. BUDAPEST VIII, ŐR ÚTCA 7. Pátkai Elek. × UNKNOWN.

19 1898. BUDAPEST I, FORTUNA ÚTCA 2. Mader Ferenc ifj.
× UNKNOWN.

20 1898. BUDAPEST VII, DOB ÚTCA 8. Návay Árpád. × UNKNOWN.

21 1898. BUDAPEST IX, MESTER ÚTCA 19. Benkő Lajos. × UNKNOWN.

22 1898. BUDAPEST VIII, PRÁTER ÚTCA 41. Angyal József.
× UNKNOWN.

23 1898. BUDAPEST VIII, TÖMŐ ÚTCA. 62 I/24. Gyagyó András.
× UNKNOWN.

24 1898. BUDAPEST VI, LEHEL ÚTCA 12. Dancsó Mátyás.
× UNKNOWN.

25 1899. BUDAPEST VI, RÓZSA ÚTCA. Moór János. × UNKNOWN.

26 1899. BUDAPEST VII, KERTÉSZ ÚTCA 46. Prda Antal.
× UNKNOWN.

27 1899. BUDAPEST II, FŐ ÚTCA 73. Bizovszki Mária. × UNKNOWN.

28 1899. BUDAPEST X, MAGLÓDI ÚTCA TÉGLAGYÁR.
Szlodiczka Ágnes. × UNKNOWN.

29 1899. BUDAPEST VII, DOB ÚTCA 34. Bayer János. × UNKNOWN.

30 1899. BUDAPEST VI, FELSŐ ERDŐSOR ÚTCA 5. Szalai Julianna.
× UNKNOWN.

31 1899. BUDAPEST IX, MESTER ÚTCA 6. Lojdl Mária. × UNKNOWN.

OTAKAR DOLEŽAL, FRANTIŠEK DRAGOUN & JOSEF KŘÍŽ.
× *Rudolf Mrva.*

WEAPON.	TYPOLOGY.	POLICING.
KNIFE.	POLITICAL.	N/A.

MOSTECKÁ STREET, MALÁ STRANA.

OTAKAR DOLEŽAL. | FRANTIŠEK DRAGOUN. | JOSEF KŘÍŽ.

On Christmas Eve 1893, the hunchback Rudolf Mrva (1873–93) was murdered in his home by two erstwhile friends. They had been playing cards and decorating Mrva's Christmas tree, and so it is unlikely he saw the attack coming. However, Mrva was a suspected police informant, and tensions had been running high in Prague.

The year 1848 had been the 'year of revolutions' in Europe, as nationalist and radical groups rattled the yoke of the continent's *anciens régimes*. Then, in 1871, in the aftermath of the Franco-Prussian War and the failed Paris Commune, several radical independence movements resurfaced. In Bohemia (the modern-day Czech Republic), radicalism was spearheaded by the National Liberal (or Young Czech) Party, which was formed in 1874. Its rise was dramatic, winning seats in the Austro-Hungarian Parliament and even taking control of the Bohemian Diet. The Young Czechs espoused universal suffrage and a reform of employment law, demanding a greater say for the working classes. Radical newspapers such as *Omladina* helped spread their message. In March 1893, they put down a motion for universal suffrage in Parliament and as the bill was debated and resisted, popular demonstrations followed. Huge crowds, predominantly made up of politically aware students, filled the streets and on 15 May a noose was strung around the neck of Emperor Franz I's statue in a symbolic gesture of revolution. It was too much for the authorities, who ordered a clampdown and the imposition of martial law.

Mrva's murder gave the government the excuse it needed to round up radicals and put them on trial. Seventy-six *Omladina* 'conspirators' were arrested, and two were charged with the killing. Six people received prison sentences and the radical movement was crushed, but only temporarily. It resurfaced after the First World War. ∎

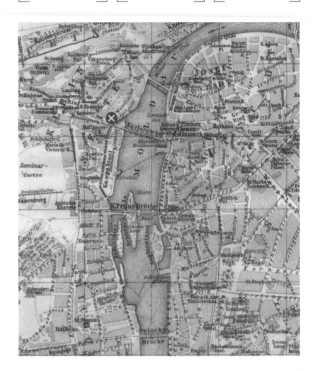

Above. MAP SHOWING THE LOCATION OF MOSTECKÁ STREET WHERE RUDOLF MRVA LIVED, AND WAS MURDERED.

Below. THE IMPERIAL ROYAL REGIONAL CRIMINAL COURT IN CHARLES SQUARE, PRAGUE, WHERE THE TRIAL TOOK PLACE.

LEOPOLD HILSNER.
✕ *Anežka Hrůzová.*

WEAPON.	TYPOLOGY.	POLICING.
KNIFE.	RECKLESS ACT.	N/A.

BREZINA FOREST, POLNÁ.

In March 1899, Anežka Hruzová (1879–99) disappeared. The seamstress was on her way home from Polná in Bohemia (now in the Czech Republic), a journey of about 3 kilometres (2 mi). Three days later, her dead body was discovered in woods nearby; she had been strangled, her throat was cut and her clothes strewn over the crime scene. Suspicion fell on four vagrants seen in the area, one of whom – Leopold Hilsner (1876–1928) – was quickly apprehended. Hilsner and the other wanted men were poor Jews, and as anti-Semitism was rife in the Hapsburg Empire it was quickly decided that not only was Hilsner guilty of murder but he had probably also been involved in ritual killing.

In 19th-century Europe, the unfounded allegation that Jews practised a form of blood sacrifice, killing Christian children and using their blood in religious ceremonies, was widely believed. Thus, without any clear evidence and with no attempt to track down anyone else for the murder, Hilsner was put on trial, convicted and sentenced to death. Czech nationalist activist Tomáš Masaryk (1850–1937) took up Hilsner's cause and forced a retrial, but while he was held in prison Hilsner was intimidated by fellow inmates and confessed to the murder. Although he later retracted his confession, he was tried for Anežka's murder and that of another girl, Marie Klimová (unknown–1898), whose dead body had been found in the same forest. His death sentence was commuted but he served nineteen years before being exonerated of a crime he did not commit. ∎

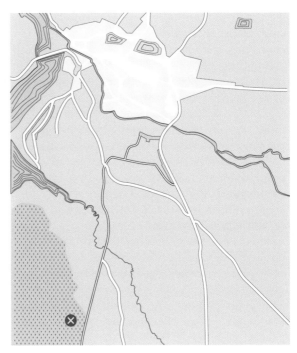

Above. MAP SHOWING THE LOCATION OF THE BREZINA FOREST, JUST OUTSIDE POLNÁ, WHERE THE BODY OF ANEŽKA HRUZOVÁ WAS DISCOVERED.

Below. AN ILLUSTRATION SHOWING THE DISCOVERY OF ANEŽKA HRUZOVÁ'S BODY IN THE FOREST NEAR POLNÁ. THE BLAME WAS PUT ON LEOPOLD HILSNER, A VAGRANT, BUT THERE WAS LITTLE EVIDENCE THAT HE HAD KILLED HER.

STEFANO 'IL PASSATORE' PELLONI.
× *Multiple – Unknown.*

WEAPON.	TYPOLOGY.	POLICING.
GUN.	GANG.	N/A.

EMILIA ROMAGNA.

The history of crime has thrown up a number of popular bandits, such as Robin Hood, who robbed the rich to help the poor. In reality, most of these stories are embroidered to emphasize their anti-hero status and downplay their criminality. Stefano Pelloni (1824–51) was just such a character: a ferryman turned street robber, who forged connections with Romagna's criminal networks and set himself up as a bandit chief, adopting the sobriquet 'Il Passatore' to reflect his former trade. He assembled a gang of 130 brigands, who robbed their way across Romagna during a period of civil chaos when the rule of law was fragile.

On 25 January 1851, Pelloni pulled off his most audacious heist, taking control of the theatre at Forlimpopoli, northeastern Italy, and forcing the audience to hand over their money and jewelry at gunpoint. In March 1851, Pelloni's luck ran out. Surrounded, he was shot and killed in a gun battle with the gendarmerie. His body was paraded through the streets and then unceremoniously dumped in desconsecrated hole at Certosa. ∎

Below. STEFANO PELLONI AND HIS GANG TAKE THE STAGE AT FORLIMPOPOLI, FORCING THE THEATRE-GOERS TO HAND OVER THEIR VALUABLES AT GUNPOINT.

1
BONCELLINO, RAVENNA.
THE TOWN WHERE
STEFANO PELLONI
WAS BORN.

2
BAGNARA DI ROMAGNA,
RAVENNA.
A TOWN 'IL PASSATORE'
RAIDED IN 1849.

3
COTIGNOLA, RAVENNA.
A TOWN 'IL PASSATORE'
RAIDED IN 1850.

4
CASTEL GUELFO, BOLOGNA.
A TOWN 'IL PASSATORE'
RAIDED IN 1850.

5
BRISIGHELLA, RAVENNA.
A TOWN 'IL PASSATORE'
RAIDED IN 1850.

6
LONGIANO, FORLÌ-CESENA.
A TOWN 'IL PASSATORE'
RAIDED IN 1850.

7
CONSANDOLO, FERRARA.
A TOWN 'IL PASSATORE'
RAIDED IN 1851.

8
FORLIMPOPOLI, FORLÌ-CESENA.
THE TOWN WHERE 'IL PASSATORE'
ROBBED AN ENTIRE THEATRE
IN 1851.

9
FARMHOUSE, MANDRIOLE,
RAVENNA.
THE FARM WHERE 'IL PASSATORE'
ROBBED THE RAVAGLIA FAMILY
AND KILLED GIUSEPPE RAVAGLIA.

10
MOLESA ESTATE, RUSSI,
RAVENNA.
THE ESTATE WHERE
'IL PASSATORE' WAS KILLED
IN A GUNFIGHT WITH THE POLICE.

GAETANO 'LO SPIRITO' PROSPERI.
✕ *Giacomo Sondaz.*

WEAPON.	TYPOLOGY.	POLICING.
GUN.	GANG.	N/A.

CA DE ROSSI, MODENA.

In August 1860 the National Guard in Monghidoro, just south of Bologna, found themselves surrounded by an angry crowd. Those gathered were protesting against the attempt by their new rulers to enforce compulsory military service and they were led by a local miller, Gaetano Prosperi (unknown–1863). The protest soon subsided, with many arrests made, but Prosperi escaped. Dubbed 'Lo Spirito' ('the spirit') for his ability to evade capture, he was viewed as a brigand by the authorities and hunted down. As the *Carabinieri* closed in, Prosperi shot and killed one of them, Giacomo Sondaz (1833–1861) and so became notorious as a murderer and fugitive from justice. Having wounded himself whilse cleaning his gun, Prosperi was finally captured and confined in prison in Bologna. Tried and convicted for the shooting of Sondaz, he was executed by guillotine outside the medieval gate at the end of the Via Lame. 'Lo Spirito' may have been characterized as a violent criminal by the police and government but recent research suggests he is best viewed as a social bandit and political rebel. ∎

Below. GAETANO 'LO SPIRITO' PROSPERI PICTURED DURING THE RIOTS AGAINST FORCED CONSCRIPTION IN MONGHIDORO, SOUTH OF BOLOGNA.

1 BETWEEN LOIANO AND MONGHIDORO, BOLOGNA. THE LOCATION OF 'LO SPIRITO'S' MILL.

2 MONGHIDORO, BOLOGNA. WHERE 'LO SPIRITO' JOINED A RIOT AGAINST MILITARY CONSCRIPTION IN 1860.

3 CA DE ROSSI, MODENA. THE TOWN WHERE 'LO SPIRITO' SHOT THE POLICEMAN GIACOMO SONDAZ IN 1861.

4 SAN BENEDETTO VAL DI SAMBRO, BOLOGNA. WHERE 'LO SPIRITO' WAS ARRESTED.

5 PORTA LAME, BOLOGNA. THE PLACE WHERE 'LO SPIRITO' WAS GUILLOTINED IN 1863.

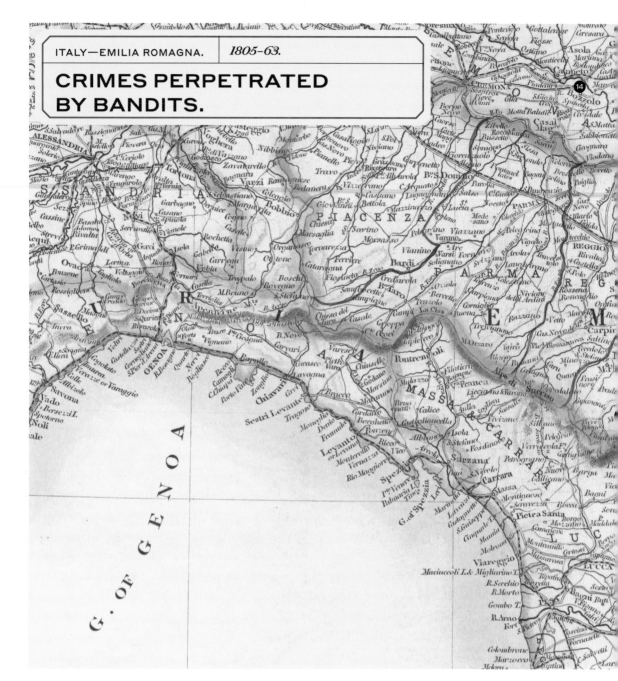

CRIMES PERPETRATED BY BANDITS.

ITALY—EMILIA ROMAGNA. | 1805–63.

1 1805–10. BAGNACAVALLO, RAVENNA. Michele 'Falcone' Botti. ACTIVE IN THIS AREA.

2 1810. FONDO RONCOROSSO, BAGNARA. Michele 'Falcone' Botti. GUNFIGHT WITH THE POLICE ENDED FALCONE'S CAREER.

3 1834. CASA ROTONDA, MONTEGUIDUCCIO, PESARO & URBINO. Antonio 'Fabrizj' Cola. ROBBERY OF A FARM.

4 1849. BAGNARA DI ROMAGNA, RAVENNA. Stefano 'Il Passatore' Pelloni. ROBBERY IN THE TOWN.

5 1849. GUICCIOLI FARM, MANDRIOLE, RAVENNA. Stefano 'Il Passatore' Pelloni. × GIUSEPPE RAVAGLIA.

6 1850. COTIGNOLA, RAVENNA. Stefano 'Il Passatore' Pelloni. ROBBERY IN THE TOWN.

7 1850. CASTEL GUELFO, BOLOGNA. Stefano 'Il Passatore' Pelloni. ROBBERY IN THE TOWN.

8 1850. BRISIGHELLA, RAVENNA. Stefano 'Il Passatore' Pelloni. ROBBERY IN THE TOWN.

9 1850. LONGIANO, FORLÌ-CESENA. Stefano 'Il Passatore' Pelloni. ROBBERY IN THE TOWN.

10 1850. VEDRANA DI BUDRIO, BOLOGNA. Bandit gang. × SIG.RA BELLETTI.

11 1850. MEDICINA, BOLOGNA. Bandit gang. × SIG.RA LAZZARETTI.

12 1850. BUDRIO, BOLOGNA. Bandit gang. ROBBERY OF GIUSEPPE PALMIERI.

13 1850. SELVA DI BUDRIO, BOLOGNA. Bandit gang. ROBBERY OF CARLO FERRI, ALESSANDRO ALTOBELLI & GAETANO PASQUALI.

14 1850. SAN MARTINO DALL'ARGINE, MANTUA. Bandit gang. ROBBERY OF CARLO PRESTI, ISAIAH ORSONI & GIUSEPPE MARTELLI.

15 1850. CASTEL SAN PIETRO, BOLOGNA. Bandit gang. ROBBERY OF ANTONIO BALDAZZI, DON ANTONIO CAZZANI, DOMENICO SGARZI & GIUSEPPE ZERBINI.

16 1850. GANZANIGO, BOLOGNA. Bandit gang. ROBBERY OF PAOLO DARDANI.

17 1850. VILLA FONTANA, BOLOGNA. **Bandit gang.** ROBBERY OF DOMENICO RODA.

18 1850. BAGNAROLA DI BUDRIO, BOLOGNA. **Bandit gang.** ROBBERY OF SANTE FIORINI, GIOVANNI FIORINI & STEFANO FIORINI.

19 1850. BUDRIO, BOLOGNA. **Bandit gang.** ROBBERY OF GAETANO ACCORSI.

20 1851. CONSANDOLO, FERRARA. **Stefano 'Il Passatore' Pelloni.** ROBBERY IN THE TOWN.

21 1851. TEATRO COMUNALE, FORLIMPOPOLI. **Stefano 'Il Passatore' Pelloni.** ROBBERY OF THE ENTIRE THEATRE AUDIENCE.

22 1851. RUSSI, RAVENNA. **Stefano 'Il Passatore' Pelloni.** GUNFIGHT WTTH THE POLICE AND DEATH OF 'IL PASSATORE'.

23 1851. CASETTO FARM, BETWEEN TREDOZIO & MODIGLIANA, FORLÌ-CESENA. **Angiolo 'Lisagna' Lama.** × GIUSEPPE LOMBARDI. × MARIA LOMBARDI. × DOMINICA LOMBARDI. × LUIGI LOMBARDI.

24 1853. SAN VALENTINO NEAR TREDOZIO, FORLÌ-CESENA. **Pietro 'Don Stiffelone' Valgimigli.** × ANGIOLO 'LISAGNA' LAMA. × ANTONIO 'CALABRESE' RAVAIOLI.

25 1854. CASTEL BOLOGNESE, BOLOGNA. **Giuseppe 'Lazzarino' Afflitti.** × FRANCESCO GOTTARELLI.

26 1857. ALPICELLA, SAVONNA. **Giuseppe 'Lazzarino' Afflitti.** THE CAPTURE OF LAZZARINO.

27 1857. BOLOGNA. **Giuseppe 'Lazzarino' Afflitti.** THE EXECUTION OF LAZZARINO.

28 1861. CA DE ROSSI, MODENA. **Gaetano 'Lo Spirito' Prosperi.** × GIACOMO SONDAZ.

29 1863. SAN BENEDETTO VAL DI SAMBRO, BOLOGNA. **Gaetano 'Lo Spirito' Prosperi.** ARREST OF 'LO SPIRITO'.

30 1863. PORTA LAME, BOLOGNA. **Gaetano 'Lo Spirito' Prosperi.** THE EXECUTION OF 'LO SPIRITO'.

PIETRO CENERI.
✕ *Deputy Quaestor Grasselli.*
✕ *Police Inspector Fumagalli.*

WEAPON.	TYPOLOGY.	POLICING.
GUN.	GANG.	MAJOR COURT CASE.

STRADA MAGGIORE, BOLOGNA.

In April 1864, the assize courthouse in Bologna, Italy, was packed as dozens of curious onlookers, many of them women from the upper echelons of Italian society, struggled to get a look at the 110 criminals imprisoned in an iron cage. The prisoners were collectively and individually accused of robbery, extortion, threatening behaviour and murder. At the heart of the group sat the man everyone wanted to see: Pietro Ceneri (1836–unknown), a man possessed of what we might today call 'matinée idol' good looks. Ceneri had been born in the town in 1836 and trained as a butcher before he fell into a life of crime. When things got too hot for him and his brother Giacomo (dates unknown), they left Bologna and started raiding caravans and travellers in the region before they were captured.

Above. THE *BALLA GROSSA* GANG MEMBERS CONFINED IN A CAGE AT THE COURTHOUSE IN BOLOGNA.

Below. A SCENE OF THE TRIAL INSIDE THE COURTHOUSE. THE TRIAL DREW HUGE CROWDS.

The trial of Ceneri and the others opened on 26 April and evidence was heard from hundreds of witnesses who had fallen victim to their depredations. Ceneri's gang, known as the *Balla Grossa* (Big Gang), was one of many proto-Mafia criminal organizations that proliferated in the chaos of 19th-century Italy – and just one of the many *Ballas* operating in Bologna. They had terrorized Bologna and its environs before and after the wars for Italian unification in the late 1850s and 1860s. However, it was the killing of a police inspector and a local official in 1861 that prompted the authorities to actively hunt down the gang, something not achieved until Cavour (1810–61) and Garibaldi's (1807–82) forces gained control of the country and its governance.

Appropriately enough, it was a 'hero' of the Risorgimento (the popular name of the independence movement), Raffaele Feoli (dates unknown), who now presided over the trial of Ceneri's 'Association of Evildoers'. The newspapers gave a blow-by-blow account of the hearings, reporting back to those who had been unable to gain access to what was the criminal justice event of the year. Seats were at a premium, and the authorities were forced to issue day tickets for the trial. The case against the defendants lasted for six months, and in the process the whole court was moved to a larger venue, at Bologna's town hall. Not all of those accused were present at the beginning of the proceedings, but the police picked up a handful of fugitives as they went along. A couple of prisoners even died in prison before they could be brought to stand trial for their crimes.

The trial ended with all but six of the prisoners being convicted. In total, the judges handed down sentences of around 700 years in prison, with Ceneri, as the chief protagonist and ringleader, getting life. The group's accountant, Maria Mazzini (dates unknown), was acquitted and she later helped fund Ceneri after he escaped as he was being taken away to start his sentence. The bandit leader fled to Peru where he was recaptured several years later; he was brought back to Italy and locked up in a prison in Genoa to complete his sentence. ∎

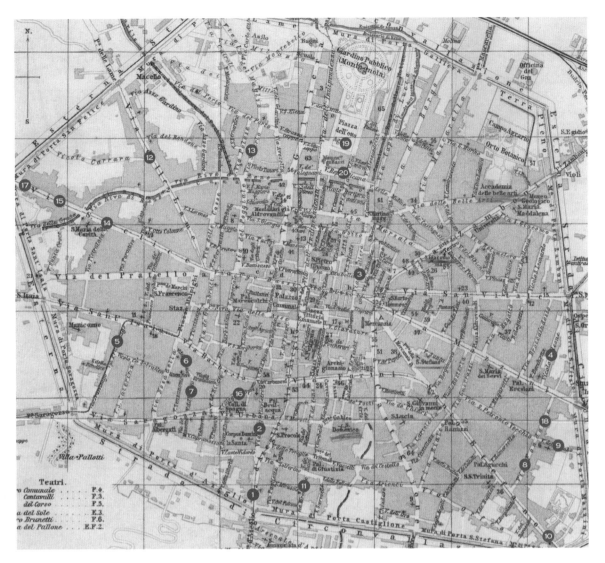

①

OSTERIA DELLA PALAZZINA,
PORTA SAN MAMOLO.
A HAUNT OF THE *BALLA
GROSSA.*

②

LOCANDA DI ALESSIO.
A HAUNT OF THE *BALLA
GROSSA.*

③

LOCANDA DELLA PIGNA,
VIA CAVALIERA 1618/2.
A HAUNT OF THE *BALLA
GROSSA.*

④

BETTOLA ZUCCHI,
VIA TORLEONE 151.
A HAUNT OF THE *BALLA
DI TORLEONE.*

⑤

OSTERIA DELLA CAMPANA,
VIA FRASSINAGO.
A HAUNT OF THE *BALLA
DI SARAGOZZA.*

⑥

OSTERIA DELLA TROMBA,
VIA DEL FOSSATO.
A HAUNT OF THE *BALLA
DI SARAGOZZA.*

⑦

OSTERIA AL CARRO,
VIA DEL FOSSATO.
A HAUNT OF THE *BALLA
DI SARAGOZZA.*

⑧

OSTERIA DELLA FONTANA,
VIA DELLA FONDAZZA 381.
A HAUNT OF THE *BALLA
DI STRADA STEFANO.*

⑨

OSTERIA ALLE STREGHE,
VIA DEL PIOMBO.
A HAUNT OF THE *BALLA
DI STRADA STEFANO.*

⑩

LOCANDA DEL PELLEGRINO,
PORTA SANTO STEFANO.
A HAUNT OF THE *BALLA
DI STRADA STEFANO.*

⑪

OSTERIA DEL FALCONE,
VIA MIRAMONTE 555.
A HAUNT OF THE *BALLA
DI MIRASOLE.*

⑫

OSTERIA DELL'ANCORA,
STRADA DELLE LAME 239.
A HAUNT OF THE *BALLA
DELLE LAME.*

⑬

OSTERIA DEL CARRO,
VIA SAN CARLO.
A HAUNT OF THE *BALLA
DELLE LAME.*

⑭

OSTERIA BAZZANESE,
STRADA SAN FELICE.
A HAUNT OF THE *BALLA
DI SAN FELICE.*

⑮

OSTERIA DELLA CORONA,
STRADA SAN FELICE 3.
A HAUNT OF THE *BALLA
DI SAN FELICE.*

⑯

CAFFÉ DEGLI SPAGNOLI, VIA
DEL COLLEGIO DI SPAGNA 368.
A HAUNT OF THE *BALLA
DI SAN FELICE.*

⑰

OSTERIA DEL CHIU, IN FRONT
OF THE PORTA SAN FELICE.
A HAUNT OF THE *BALLA
DI SAN FELICE.*

⑱

OSTERIA DELLA PRETINA,
VIA FONDAZZA.
A HAUNT OF THE *BALLA
DELLA FONDAZZA.*

⑲

OSTERIA ALLA COLONNA,
PIAZZA DELL OTTO AGOSTO.
A HAUNT OF THE *BALLA DELLA
MONTAGNOLA.*

⑳

OSTERIA ALLA PORTANTINA,
VIA REPUBBLICANA 2055.
A HAUNT OF THE *BALLA
DELLA MONTAGNOLA.*

TULLIO MURRI.
✕ *Count Francesco Bonmartini.*

WEAPON.	TYPOLOGY.	POLICING.
KNIFE.	DOMESTIC.	LOMBROSO.

39 VIA MAZZINI, BOLOGNA.

TULLIO MURRI.   FRANCESCO BONMARTINI.

Count Francesco Bonmartini (unknown–1902) had been dead for a couple of days by the time police broke into his Bologna apartment at the end of August 1902. The playboy aristocrat was lying in a dried pool of blood, with violent wounds to his chest, hands and face. Initial thoughts that he had taken his own life were soon dismissed and the police settled on the obvious theory that this was a robbery. Bonmartini, married with children, had a reputation for philandering. When his family home near Padua was searched, detectives found numerous letters from '*donne allegre*' (Italian slang for women with loose morals). The murder was a huge scandal, exposing Bonmartini's disreputable lifestyle, and dragging his wife, Linda Murri (1871–1957), and her respectable family through the pages of the national press.

Linda had been legally separated from her husband for some time by 1902 on account of adultery and had begun an affair with her childhood sweetheart, Carlo Secchi (dates unknown). Her brother, Tullio (dates unknown), a local politician, had clashed with the count, even challenging him to a fight. As the investigation progressed, it emerged that more than simple robbery was behind Bonmartini's murder. It had seemed odd that while Linda's jewelry had been stolen the thieves had not bothered to remove the valuable rings from the dead count's fingers. Police discovered that Linda had rented the apartment next to her estranged husband's under a false name to use as a place to meet with Secchi. Tullio had organized the murder, recruiting Pio Naldi (dates unknown) and his lover Rosina Bonetti (dates unknown). The plan was for Rosina to distract the count so that Tullio could gain entry to his rooms and kill him.

A six-month trial began on 21 February 1903, with each twist being reported to a fascinated public audience by the media, before all those involved were convicted. The trial involved the famous criminal anthropologist, Cesare Lombroso (1835–1909), who was a professor at the University of Turin, and had developed the idea that criminals were identifiable by their physical characteristics.

Before her trial, Linda had her cranium examined by Lombroso, and his theories were also used in Tullio Murri's defence case, as his lawyers drew on the idea that criminals do not wilfully choose to commit crimes but are instead driven by innate tendencies. This defence did not work, however, and Tullio was given thirty years, and Naldi got thirty for conspiracy. Linda Murri, Carlo Secchi and Rosina Bonetti also received long sentences for their involvement in the murder.

In a final twist, Victor Emmanuel III (1869–1947) pardoned Linda in 1906, as a gesture of thanks to her father, a prominent physician, who had saved his daughter's life. ∎

Above. MAP SHOWING THE LOCATION OF 39 VIA MAZZINI, WHERE COUNT FRANCESCO BONMARTINI WAS FOUND DEAD.

Below left. LA TRIBUNA ILLUSTRATA,
19 MARCH 1903. LINDA MURRI
APPEARS IN COURT.

Below right. LA TRIBUNA ILLUSTRATA,
27 AUGUST 1903. LINDA MURRI BIDS
FAREWELL TO HER FATHER IN PRISON.

Bottom. TULLIO MURRI QUESTIONED
BY A LAWYER AT HIS TRIAL FOR
COUNT BONMARTINI'S MURDER.

Il dramma psicologico di Linda Murri

Lo straziante incontro di Linda Murri con suo padre dopo la sentenza

CLARA MARINA & ANTONIO MARINA.
✕ *José Lafuente.* ✕ *Unknown.*

WEAPON. STRANGULATION.	TYPOLOGY. PROPERTY CRIME.	POLICING. N/A.

56–58 CALLE DE LA MONTERA, CENTRO.

CLARA MARINA. | ANTONIO MARINA.

Passers-by watched in horror as a body tumbled out of a second-floor window and fell to the Madrid street below. Locals rushed into 56–58 Calle de la Montera and raced upstairs. They banged on the door for fifteen minutes before it was opened by a young woman and her brother. Inside, they found Don José Lafuente (unknown–1849), a local tailor and the property landlord, who had been strangled to death. The occupants were Clara (unknown–1849) and Antonio Marina (unknown–1849) and they were immediately suspected of murdering both Lafuente and the unknown man in the street.

In 1849, forensic science was in its infancy and without fingerprint technology or even the ability to determine whether the blood found on the siblings' clothing was that of their landlord, the authorities had little to go on. Not that they allowed this to hamper their prosecution of the Marinas, who were questioned rigorously. The motive for Lafuente's murder was deemed to be robbery: according to the investigating judge, Clara had conspired with her lover and brother to rob and murder their landlord. When her paramour demanded a higher cut of the man's treasure, the Marinas objected and killed him, throwing him out of the window. At their trial they claimed he had tied them up and then fled, falling accidentally to his death. It seemed far-fetched and the jury agreed. Clara and Antonio were convicted and executed by garrotting on 31 October 1849. ∎

Below. MAP SHOWING THE LOCATION OF CALLE DE LA MONTERA, WHERE JOSÉ LAFUENTE AND AN UNKNOWN MAN WERE MURDERED BY CLARA AND ANTONIO MARINA.

Below, clockwise from left. AN UNKNOWN MAN FALLS TO HIS DEATH FROM THE SECOND FLOOR; JOSÉ LAFUENTE'S BODY IS DISCOVERED; CLARA MARINA AND HER BROTHER ANTONIO ARE TAKEN INTO CUSTODY; THE PAIR ARE PUBLICLY GARROTTED ON 31 OCTOBER 1849.

HIGINIA DE BALAGUER OSTALÉ & DOLORES ÁVILA.
× *Luciana Borcino.*

WEAPON.	TYPOLOGY.	POLICING.
KNIFE.	PROPERTY CRIME.	TOXICOLOGY.

CALLE DE LA FUENCARRAL, MALASAÑA.

HIGINIA DE BALAGUER OSTALÉ.

DOLORES ÁVILA.

The murder of Luciana Borcino (1838–88) became one of *the* crime sensation stories in the Spanish press. The middle-aged widow lived alone, with only a fierce bulldog for company and protection. Her son, José Vázquez Varela (dates unknown), was a petty thief serving time for stealing a cape. At the time of his mother's murder, he was locked up in prison. Luciana had recently acquired a maid, Higinia de Balaguer Ostalé (unknown–1890), although doubts circulated as to her motives for taking the position.

Neighbours were alerted to the house when smoke was seen billowing from the property in July 1888. When they gained access, they found the widow stabbed to death in her bedroom and half burnt by the fire. Her dog was out cold, apparently having been drugged, and the maid Higinia was found unconscious. On questioning, Higinia denied any involvement in her mistress's death, but the discovery that she had given a false name when taking up the role helped convince the authorities that she had planned to rob Señora Borcino all along. It was suggested that José might have been involved but, despite some inconsistencies, his alibi (that he was in jail) stuck. The press carried the story's developments daily and helped make up the mind of the court against Higinia. She was found guilty, along with an accomplice, Dolores Ávila, and was garrotted on 19 July 1890, the last person to be publicly executed in Madrid. ∎

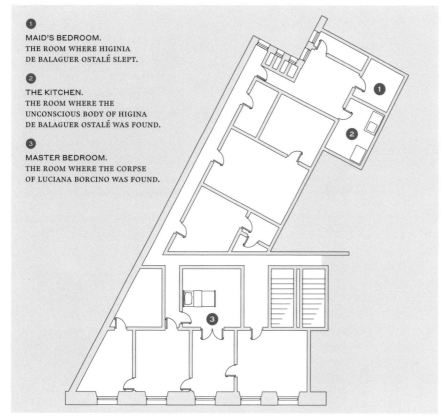

1
MAID'S BEDROOM.
THE ROOM WHERE HIGINIA DE BALAGUER OSTALÉ SLEPT.

2
THE KITCHEN.
THE ROOM WHERE THE UNCONSCIOUS BODY OF HIGINA DE BALAGUER OSTALÉ WAS FOUND.

3
MASTER BEDROOM.
THE ROOM WHERE THE CORPSE OF LUCIANA BORCINO WAS FOUND.

Above. THE WIDOW LUCIANA BORCINO WAS FOUND HALF BURNED IN A SMOKE-FILLED ROOM.

Below. HER MAID AND DOG WERE ALSO FOUND UNCONCIOUS. THE DOG WAS LATER PROVEN TO HAVE BEEN DRUGGED WITH ANAESTHETIC. ↓

PART TWO.

EMMA CUNNINGHAM + JOHN ECKEL + JOHN J. DWYER + DIEDRICH MAHNKEN
THOMAS YOUNG + HANNAH MARTIN SOUTHWORTH + DANIEL DRISCOLL
DR H. G. MCGONIGAL + FANNIE SHAW + AMEER BEN ALI + MARY LIVINGSTON FLEMING
LIZZIE BORDEN + BELLE GUNNESS + EVA LLOYD + SADIE REIGH + CHARLES RYAN
HERMAN SIEGLER

NORTH
AMERICA.

THOMAS NEILL + CREAM PATRICK EUGENE PRENDERGAST + ADOLPH LUETGERT
HENRY HOWARD HOLMES + JOHANN OTTO HOCH + THOMAS JENNINGS
WILLIAM C. QUANTRILL + THE BENDER FAMILY + HENRY NEWTON BROWN
LAURA FAIR + WILLIAM HENRY THEODORE DURRANT + JAMES C. DUNHAM
CHARLES B. HADLEY

EMMA CUNNINGAM & JOHN ECKEL.
✕ *Dr Harvey Burdell.*

WEAPON. KNIFE.	TYPOLOGY. DOMESTIC.	POLICING. N/A.

31 BOND STREET, LOWER MANHATTAN.

EMMA CUNNINGHAM. JOHN ECKEL.

In 1855, Emma Cunningham (1818–87) took rooms in a large house owned by Dr Harvey Burdell (1811–57), a New York dentist. An attractive widow with four children, Emma started a relationship with Burdell but also with another resident, John Eckel (dates unknown). On the night of 30 January 1857, a scream of 'murder!' was heard from Burdell's house and the next morning one of his servants found him dead in his office. Burdell had been stabbed fifteen times and strangled, most likely by a left-handed assailant. Emma was left-handed and so she was top of the police's list of suspects. Along with Eckel, she was thrown into the New York jail known as the Tombs. Emma produced a marriage certificate that revealed that she and the dentist were married; she now stood to profit from his death as his estate was estimated at around $100,000. However, the police remained suspicious and it was rumoured that Eckel had impersonated Burdell as part of the conspiracy to kill him and steal his fortune. Emma was not content with proving she was the dentist's wife, however, and also claimed to be carrying his child, something that would further cement her entitlement to his wealth.

During her trial, Emma appeared in the dock showing signs of pregnancy, and this undoubtedly helped her. The sight of a pregnant and grieving woman won her the sympathy of the jury and she was acquitted of murder. But the physician who treated her, Dr Uhl (dates unknown), was not convinced she was with child at all. Emma refused all of Uhl's attempts to examine her, and while this was not unusual in the 1850s, it was suspicious in the circumstances. Then, on 27 July, the police (who had decided to watch the Cunningham home) caught a nun bringing a baby to Emma's home in a basket. Emma had apparently bought a child for $1,000! This ended her attempt to benefit from Burdell's fortune and she moved to California. The actual mother of the baby in the basket rented it to P. T. Barnum (1810–91), the sensationalist showman, for $25 a week. Dr Burdell's murder remains unsolved. ∎

Above. JOHN ECKEL SURPRISES DR HARVEY BURDELL AS HE SITS AT HIS DESK.

Above. THE PAIR STRUGGLE AND JOHN ECKEL PRODUCES A KNIFE AND STABS AT THE NEW YORK DENTIST.

Above. DR HARVEY BURDELL IS FATALLY WOUNDED BY EMMA CUNNINGHAM'S LOVER.

Above. JOHN ECKEL LEANS OVER HIS VICTIM; TRACES OF BLOOD CAN BE SEEN SPATTERED ON THE WALLS.

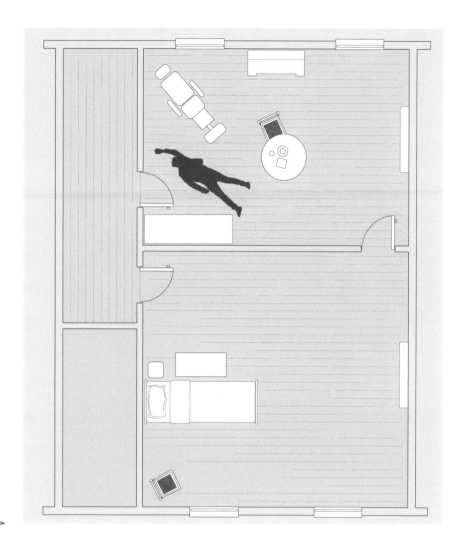

Right. FLOOR PLAN OF
DR HARVEY BURDELL'S
DENTISTRY OFFICE WITHIN
HIS APARTMENT AT 31 BOND
STREET, SHOWING THE
LOCATION OF HIS BODY.

Opposite. FRANK LESLIE'S
ILLUSTRATED NEWSPAPER,
21 FEBRUARY 1857. A
SLIGHTLY SURREAL PORTRAIT
OF DR HARVEY BURDELL IN
HIS COFFIN, SHOWING ONLY
HIS HEAD AND SHOULDERS.

Above. THE ATTIC ROOM WHERE
JOHN ECKEL TRIED TO BURN
HIS CLOTHES FOLLOWING
THE MURDER.

Above. THE OFFICE IN WHICH
DR HARVEY BURDELL WAS
KILLED, SHOWING THE DENTIST'S
DEAD BODY *IN SITU*.

Above. JOHN ECKEL
LOCKED IN A CELL AT
THE TOMBS PRISON.

Above. EMMA CUNNINGHAM
IN JAIL. SHE CLAIMED THAT
SHE WAS PREGNANT WITH
DR HARVEY BURDELL'S CHILD.

USA — NEW YORK CITY.	*4 October 1880.*

JOHN J. DWYER.
× *Thomas H. Jones.*

WEAPON.	TYPOLOGY.	POLICING.
POOL CUE.	BRAWL.	N/A.

ATLANTIC STREET, BROOKLYN.

The killing of Thomas Jones (dates unknown) was a tragic waste of a young life. Jones was celebrating a new job and an impending relocation to San Francisco when John Dwyer (dates unknown) walked into Debrowski's Brooklyn saloon. Dwyer was drunk and belligerent and when the landlord told him he had no whisky to sell him he took his anger out on Jones and his friend George Secor (dates unknown) as they played pool. Seizing a cue, Dwyer struck Jones, knocking him down. As Jones died, Secor fled, with the drunken assailant in pursuit. It took several police to subdue the violent man, who denied any knowledge of what he had done. ∎

Above. THOMAS JONES'S MURDER, ILLUSTRATED IN A CONTEMPORARY NEWSPAPER.

USA — NEW YORK CITY.	*17 April 1883.*

DIEDRICH MAHNKEN.
× *Diedrich Steffens.*

WEAPON.	TYPOLOGY.	POLICING.
PISTOL.	JEALOUSY.	N/A.

PARK AVENUE, BROOKLYN.

Diedrich Mahnken (dates unknown) could never quite shift his conviction that his best friend, Diedrich Steffens (unknown–1883), was having an affair with his wife. She denied it, Steffens denied it and all his neighbours told him it was not true. But on 17 April 1883, Mahnken strode out of his grocery store and shot his friend dead as he crossed the street. It was widely believed that his obsessive jealousy had driven him mad; doctors at the jail where he was confined noted his delusional state and his refusal to eat for fear of being poisoned. Consequently, he was declared insane and committed to the state asylum at Utica, New York. ∎

Above. A NEWSPAPER ILLUSTRATION OF DIEDRICH MAHNKEN SHOOTING HIS FRIEND DIEDRICH STEFFENS IN THE STREET.

USA — NEW YORK CITY.	*23 October 1883.*

THOMAS YOUNG.
✕ *Mrs Young.*

WEAPON. PISTOL.	TYPOLOGY. DOMESTIC.	POLICING. N/A.

95 TOMPKINS AVENUE, BROOKLYN.

Mrs Young (dates unknown) was a beautiful woman and her husband, Thomas (dates unknown), was infatuated with her. Sadly, the former Inland Revenue clerk turned saloon keeper and local politician had a temper matched only by his jealousy. On numerous occasions, the couple argued as Thomas struggled with his distrust of his spouse and she finally left him, returning home to her mother. On 23 October 1883, Thomas called at his mother-in-law's house and demanded to see his wife. As Mrs Young tried to get away from him, he shot her in the abdomen. A neighbour overpowered Thomas until the police took him into custody for murder. ∎

USA — NEW YORK CITY.	*22 November 1889.*

HANNAH MARTIN SOUTHWORTH.
✕ *Stephen L. Pettus.*

WEAPON. PISTOL.	TYPOLOGY. DOMESTIC.	POLICING. N/A.

FULTON STREET, BROOKLYN.

Stephen Pettus (unknown–1889) was murdered in November 1889 as he walked along Fulton Street, New York, in broad daylight. His attacker, Mrs Hannah Martin Southworth (unknown–1890), made no attempt to escape and was charged with the killing. Her defence was insanity, brought on by Pettus's cruelty, but she never faced trial, dying of bronchitis and pneumonia in New York's notorious prison, the Tombs. According to Hannah, Pettus had ruined her, making her pregnant and then forcing her to abort the child. Pettus's friends told a different story: that Hannah was obsessed and could not cope with his rejection. Whatever the truth, the tragedy ultimately claimed two lives. ∎

Above. A CONTEMPORARY NEWSPAPER ILLUSTRATION OF MRS YOUNG'S MURDER BY HER HUSBAND.

Above. AN ILLUSTRATION OF HANNAH MARTIN SOUTHWORTH SHOOTING STEPHEN PETTUS IN THE BACK IN NOVEMBER 1889.

DANIEL DRISCOLL.
× *Bridget "Beezy" Garrity.*

WEAPON. PISTOL.	TYPOLOGY. GANG.	POLICING. BALLISTICS.

HESTER STREET, MANHATTAN.

DANIEL DRISCOLL.

BRIDGET GARRITY.

When Daniel Driscoll (1855–88) set eyes on Bridget Garrity (unknown–1886), he fell head over heels in love and lust. The 18-year-old Bridget (known as 'Beezy') worked for John McCarthy (dates unknown) as a prostitute, and he was also infatuated with her. McCarthy was a member of the Whyos, a New York gang that dominated the Five Points neighbourhood in the 1880s. Driscoll

Above. THE HEADQUARTERS OF THE WHYOS GANG IN BOTTLE ALLEY, THE BOWERY.

Below. MUG SHOTS OF MEMBERS OF THE INFAMOUS WHYOS GANG.

ran the gang with Dan Lyons (1860–88) and claimed Beezy for himself. McCarthy's jealousy led him to attempt to kill his boss. This failed, and Driscoll went to McCarthy's Hester Street brothel to take revenge, with Bridget accompanying him in an effort to broker peace. As the pair scuffled, it was Bridget who was shot and later died, killed by a bullet from Driscoll's revolver. She told the police it was McCarthy; however, he was able to prove he had not fired a shot, and so charges were pressed against Driscoll and he was hanged for manslaughter.

The underworld of gangs, violence, betrayals and allegiances that provides the setting for this murder is described in Herbert Asbury's (1889–1963) colourful history *The Gangs of New York* (1927). This was an attempt to draw historical precedents for the Mafia crime families that dominated New York, Chicago and other US cities in the decades after the First World War. As is often the case with popular 'true crime' history, Asbury's version of the past, while sensationalized and exaggerated, has its roots in fact. The Five Points neighbourhood in Lower Manhattan was notorious for poverty, degradation and crime. It took its name from the intersection of five thoroughfares that converged at Paradise Square. This was a misnomer, as the poor quality of land at the foot of Manhattan meant that the residents of the 'Points' lived in one of the worst slums in the Western world. Out of this swamp of human misery grew several rival gangs, deriving their loyalties from their ethnic origins.

The United States was a nation of immigrants, which fuelled bitter resentment and political tension, particularly between the so-called 'native' white Americans and the large numbers of poor Irish incomers. Gangs clashed over territory, economic resources, crime and politics. From the 1830s, the Bowery Boys were the pre-eminent powerhouse on the street, representing those who opposed Irish immigration. They operated as a political club, intimidating voters and beating up rivals, as well as running criminal activities and engaging in violence and murder. Their key opponents were the Forty Thieves, the Dead Rabbits and, later, the Whyos, which Driscoll

Above. THE SHORT TAIL GANG (NAMED FOR THEIR SHORT COAT-TAILS) PHOTOGRAPHED BY JACOB RIIS IN 1887.

Below. JACOB RIIS'S 'A GROWLER GANG IN SESSION', TAKEN IN 1887.

Above. 'BANDIT'S ROOST' BY JACOB RIIS, 1888, ONE OF THE MOST CRIME-RIDDEN, DANGEROUS PARTS OF NEW YORK CITY.

Below. A GROUP OF YOUNG GANG MEMBERS AT WEST 37TH STREET DOCK, CAPTURED BY JACOB RIIS IN 1887.

commanded. These three gangs all drew their membership from among the large Irish immigrant community to which Beezy Garrity belonged.

The gang violence that blighted New York from the 1820s to the turn of the century involved the murder of hundreds of people, but the murder rate in the city, while higher than in some other US urban areas, was nothing like as out of control as Asbury's colourful 'true crime' history describes. ∎

GANGLAND MANHATTAN.

❶ 1830s–1860s. FIVE POINTS. Territory of the Shirt Tails gang.

❷ 1830s–1860s. 487 MULBERRY STREET, FIVE POINTS. Territory of the Dead Rabbits gang.

❸ 1830s–1860s. THE BOWERY. Territory of the Bowery Boys gang.

❹ 1838. 388 BROADWAY. Edward Coleman (the Forty Thieves). × ANN 'HOT CORN GIRL' COLEMAN.

❺ 1855. STANWIX HALL BAR, BROADWAY. Lewis Baker & Jim Turner. × WILLIAM 'BILL THE BUTCHER' POOLE (BOWERY BOYS).

❻ 1857. BAYARD STREET. Riot between the Dead Rabbits gang and the Bowery Boys gang. × 8 MEN.

❼ 1860s–90s. BOTTLE ALLEY. Headquarters of the Whyos gang.

8 1860s–90s. THE MORGUE TAVERN, MULBERRY AND WORTH STREET.
Favoured drinking establishment of the Whyos gang. × 100.

9 1875. GREENWICH STREET. 'Dandy' Johnny Dolan (Whyos). × JAMES H. NOE.

10 1886. HESTER STREET. Daniel Driscoll (Whyos). × BRIDGET 'BEEZY' GARRITY.

11 1890s. LITTLE NAPES CAFÉ, 59 JONES STREET. Headquarters of the Five Points gang.

12 1903. RIVINGTON STREET. Gun battle between the Five Points gang and Eastman gang.

13 1904. 77 SHERIFF STREET. Harris Stahl (Eastman gang). × RICHIE FITZPATRICK.

UNKNOWN.
✕ *Benjamin Nathan.*

WEAPON.	TYPOLOGY.	POLICING.
BLUDGEON.	PROPERTY CRIME.	N/A.

WEST 23RD STREET, MANHATTAN.

When Benjamin Nathan's (1813–70) body was found bloodied and battered in his New York office, it opened a mystery that remains unsolved. Nathan, a wealthy stockbroker, was bludgeoned to death in what seemed to police to be a burglary gone wrong. A pillar of New York's Sephardic Jewish community, Nathan and four others were in the house that night: Nathan's sons Frederick (1844–unknown) and Washington (1848–unknown), who had seen their father sleeping before they went to bed, Mrs Kelly (dates unknown) the housekeeper and her son William (dates unknown). No one heard or saw anything that night and the police were baffled.

At first, Washington was suspected. He was a reputedly 'dissolute' young man who liked to gamble and drink, and it was well known that he and his father often quarrelled. But under the terms of the will, Washington would not benefit from his father's death, and he was able to provide an alibi. William Kelly, an army deserter, a drunk and a person with criminal links, seemed a better fit for the crime. But nothing pointed to his guilt, and the coroner concluded that Nathan had been killed by 'a person or persons unknown'.

There are rumours that the killing was not properly investigated and that Albert Cardozo (1828–85), Washington's brother-in-law and a Supreme Court judge, protected Washington and his family's reputation from being dragged through the courts. Cardozo quit soon after this, brought low by another scandal. He named his own son Benjamin, after the man murdered in July 1870. ∎

❶ WEST TWENTY-THIRD STREET.
THE STREET WHERE THE BODY OF BENJAMIN NATHAN WAS DISCOVERED IN HIS HOME.

❷ ST JAMES HOTEL ON FIFTH AVENUE.
THE HOTEL WHERE WASHINGTON NATHAN HAD A DRINK ON THE NIGHT OF THE MURDER.

❸ DELMONICO'S, 2 SOUTH WILLIAM STREET.
THE BAR WHERE WASHINGTON NATHAN READ THE PAPERS ON THE NIGHT OF THE MURDER.

❹ EAST FOURTEENTH STREET.
THE BROTHEL WHERE WASHINGTON NATHAN SAW A PROSTITUTE ON THE NIGHT OF THE MURDER.

Above. NEW YORK CITY DETECTIVES SEARCHING THE PROPERTY FOR CLUES.

Above. THE POLICE EXAMINING THE PLUMBING IN THE BATHROOM.

Above. IT WAS SUGGESTED THAT THE KILLER ENTERED THE PROPERTY THROUGH THE LIBRARY WINDOW.

Above. WASHINGTON NATHAN WAS SUSPECTED OF HIS FATHER'S MURDER AND WAS HOUNDED BY THE PRESS.

DR H. G. MCGONIGAL
& FANNIE SHAW.
× *Annie Goodwin.*

WEAPON.	TYPOLOGY.	POLICING.
ABORTION.	ACCIDENT.	N/A.

EAST 103RD STREET, MANHATTAN.

DR H. G. MCGONIGAL.	FANNIE SHAW.	ANNIE GOODWIN.

Annie Goodwin (unknown–1890) was a free-spirited young woman who had caught the eye of more than one man in late 19th-century New York. Her lifestyle disturbed her elder sister Mamie (dates unknown), who confronted her about her relationship with Gus Harrison (dates unknown), a young but wealthy 'man about town'. When Mamie asked Annie to choose between her and Gus, Annie opted for the man she loved and left to stay with her friend Sadie Traphagen (dates unknown).

On 2 July 1890, Annie vanished. Sadie tracked her to an apartment on East 103RD Street owned by Fannie Shaw (dates unknown). Annie was ill and on 14 July Sadie was told that she had died. Shaw told the police that a Dr McGonigal (dates unknown) had 'treated' Annie. Meanwhile, another man was on the scene; Andrew Fanning (dates unknown) said Annie had agreed to marry him. It now seemed that Annie was hedging her bets, having fallen pregnant with Harrison – who refused to marry her – she had an abortion to secure her marriage to Fanning. However, the abortion killed her, and the police now went after McGonigal. They found that he had filed Annie's death under a false name – Jane Wilber – and when 'Jane Wilber' was disinterred, Mamie and Sadie identified the body as Annie's.

McGonigal and Shaw were tried for manslaughter with Harrison cited as an accessory. The doctor, a known abortionist, was convicted and sent to the Tombs prison for seven and a half years. He did not serve the full term, however, being released on bail the following April. ∎

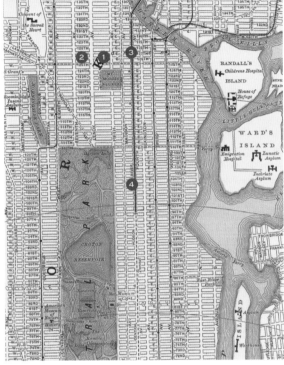

 126TH STREET.
THE STREET WHERE ANNIE LIVED WITH HER SISTER.

 126TH STREET.
THE STREET WHERE ANNIE STAYED WITH HER FRIEND SADIE TRAPHAGEN.

127TH STREET.
JOHN COLLINS'S BOARDING HOUSE WHERE ANNIE GOODWIN STAYED.

EAST 103RD STREET.
FANNIE SHAW'S APARTMENT WHERE ANNIE GOODWIN DIED.

Above. A SKETCH OF GUS HARRISON, ANNIE GOODWIN'S MYSTERIOUS LOVER.

Above. THE SCENE OF THE INQUEST INTO ANNIE GOODWIN'S DEATH.

Above. ILLEGAL ABORTIONIST DR H. G. MCGONIGAL IN THE DOCK.

Above. DR H. G. MCGONIGAL'S HOME.

Above. FANNIE SHAW'S HOME.

Above. THE TRAPHAGEN HOME.

AMEER BEN ALI.
✕ *Carrie Brown.*

WEAPON.	TYPOLOGY.	POLICING.
KNIFE.	RECKLESS ACT.	MORTUARY PHOTOGRAPHY.

EAST RIVER HOTEL, MANHATTAN.

AMEER BEN ALI.   CARRIE BROWN.

When a New York prostitute was found dead and brutally mutilated in a room in the East River Hotel on 24 April 1891, the press immediately drew links to Jack the Ripper. The poor woman was naked from her armpits down, her abdomen had been opened up and she had been strangled. The murder bore all the hallmarks of those committed in east London in 1888, so the press fervently speculated whether the Whitechapel killer could have emigrated to the United States.

The victim was Carrie Brown (1834–91), known to her friends as 'Old Shakespeare' because she liked to regale them with quotes from the playwright when she had been drinking. Carrie had checked into the hotel between 10:30 and 11:00 p.m. on 23 April with a male customer. The hotel's assistant housekeeper, Mary Minter (dates unknown), remembered him and offered a description. She said he was about 32 years old, approximately 170 centimetres (5 ft 8 in.) tall, slim and with 'a long, sharp nose and a heavy moustache of a light colour'. The police never traced this man, but they soon had someone in custody for Carrie's murder.

Ameer Ben Ali (dates unknown), alias 'Frenchy', was an Algerian Arab staying in a room just across from Carrie's. Police found blood on his door frame and arrested him. He was convicted and sentenced to life imprisonment. But the police had the wrong man, and the blood on his door was either planted by detectives or smeared during the investigation. When this came to light, he was released from prison, but by this point Ali had already served eleven years. No one else was prosecuted for the murder of Carrie Brown and the case must have haunted the lead detective, Inspector Byrnes (1842–1910) of the New York Police Department. When asked about the Whitechapel Murders, he had supposedly told journalists that 'it would be impossible for crimes such as "Jack the Ripper" committed in London to occur in New York and the murderer not be found'. Some have suggested that 'Jack' did come to New York and that the killer of Carrie Brown was Georgee (1865–1903), real name Severin Klosowski, a well-established 'Ripper' suspect. If this is true, then the Whitechapel murderer had become a truly transatlantic phenomenon. ∎

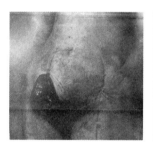
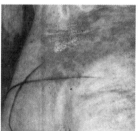

Below. TWO MORTUARY PHOTOS OF CARRIE BROWN. SHE HAD BEEN KILLED AND MUTILATED IN A HOTEL ROOM.

Above. THE EAST RIVER HOTEL IN MANHATTAN, WHERE CARRIE BROWN WAS MURDERED.

Above. ROOM 31, WHERE THE MURDER OCCURRED, ON A PLAN OF THE HOTEL FLOOR.

Above. THE STAIRS LEADING TO THE ROOF OF THE HOTEL.

Above. SKETCHES OF THE MURDER WEAPON AND THE KEY TO ROOM 31.

Right. A STREET SCENE OF
THE WATERFRONT AREA,
WITH THE EAST RIVER
HOTEL – THE SCENE OF
THE MURDER – VISIBLE
IN THE BACKGROUND.

Right. MAP OF LOWER
MANHATTAN SHOWING
THE LOCATION OF THE
EAST RIVER HOTEL,
WHERE CARRIE BROWN
WAS MURDERED.

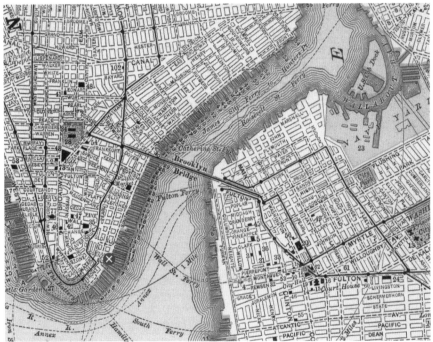

Above. CARRIE
BROWN'S PERSONAL
EFFECTS.

Above. THE SCENE INSIDE ROOM
31 WHERE CARRIE BROWN WAS
STRANGLED BY AN UNKNOWN KILLER.

Above. CARRIE BROWN'S
DEAD BODY AS IT WAS
FOUND BY POLICE.

Above. THE ENTRANCE TO
ROOM 31 WITH A CROSS
CARVED ON THE WALL.

MARY LIVINGSTON FLEMING.
× *Evelina Bliss.*

WEAPON.	TYPOLOGY.	POLICING.
ARSENIC.	PROPERTY CRIME.	TOXICOLOGY.

397 ST NICHOLAS AVENUE, HARLEM.

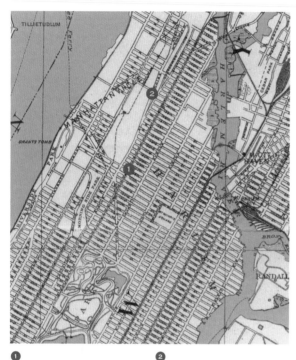

Mary Livingston (dates unknown) was rather too 'modern' by the standards of late 19th-century New York society. By 1895, she had already given birth to three children and was pregnant with a fourth, yet remained unmarried. Moreover, her offspring had three different fathers, which was highly uncommon in the so-called 'Gilded Age' of the 'Big Apple'. Mary called herself 'Mrs Fleming' in an attempt to garner some respectability, but in August she crossed another line when she was arrested for murder. The police were alerted when it was discovered that her mother – the 53-year-old widow Evelina Bliss (unknown–1895) – had been found dead in her Harlem mansion. A chemical analysis of Evelina's stomach and also of the dregs of a clam chowder, brought to the widow by Mary's 10-year-old daughter, revealed the presence of the 'king of poisons': arsenic. The motive was assumed to be financial, with Mary hoping to profit from the widow's will. The press made capital out of Livingston's supposedly immoral character, but the defence played to the public's distaste for the execution of women. Mary, who dressed in mourning for her mother throughout the trial, was duly acquitted. ∎

① THE COLONIAL HOTEL, 125TH STREET AND 8TH AVENUE. THE HOTEL WHERE MARY LIVINGSTON FLEMING LIVED.

② ST NICHOLAS STREET. THE STREET WHERE EVELINA BLISS LIVED AND WAS MURDERED.

Below. HANDPRINTS OF MARY LIVINGSTON FLEMING AND HER DAUGHTER FROM A CONTEMPORARY NEWSPAPER ARTICLE IN WHICH AN EXPERT IN PALMISTRY DECLARED THAT THERE WAS NO CLEAR PREDISPOSITION TO CRIME IN THE FAMILY.

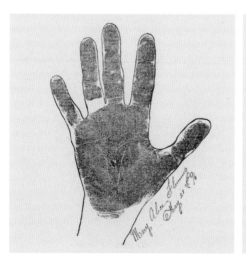
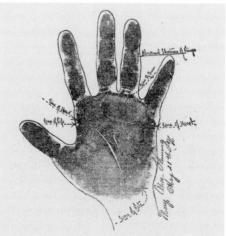
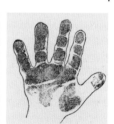

Mrs. Fleming and Types of Women Criminals as Given
by Prof. Lombroso, the Criminologist.

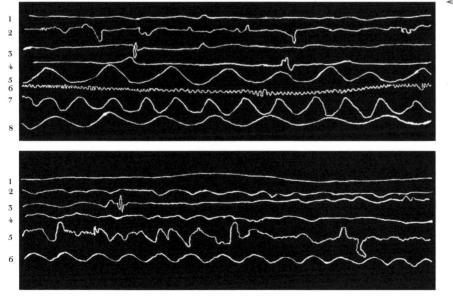

LIZZIE BORDEN.
× *Andrew Borden.* × *Abby Borden.*

WEAPON. AXE.	TYPOLOGY. DOMESTIC.	POLICING. CRIME SCENE PHOTOGRAPHY.

92 SECOND STREET, FALL RIVER.

'Lizzie Borden took an axe
And gave her mother forty whacks.
When she saw what she had done,
She gave her father forty-one.'

So runs a US folk rhyme popularized in the 1890s that, despite some factual inaccuracies, succinctly captures the sensation surrounding one of the Americas' most infamous murder cases.

On 4 August 1892, someone murdered Abby Borden (1828–92) and her husband Andrew (1822–92) at their home in Fall River, Massachusetts. Ever since then, the finger of blame has pointed at Andrew's 32-year-old daughter Lizzie (1860–1927), who may well have been suffering from some form of mental illness. It was Lizzie who found her father's body that morning; he had been struck multiple times (ten to twelve not forty-one) with an axe or hatchet while he dozed on a sofa downstairs. Upstairs, those arriving at the scene found his wife (Lizzie's stepmother) dead in a bedroom. She, too, had been battered with a hatchet, at least seventeen times. The killing was gruesome: Andrew's 'left eye had been dug out', the *Herald* newspaper reported, and his 'face was hacked to pieces'.

Lizzie was chief suspect almost immediately. She had discovered the crime but gave contradictory answers when questioned about her stepmother's movements that day, and where she (Lizzie) was at the time of Abby's death. Lizzie had also tried to buy poison from a local drugstore, which was clearly suspicious. The police investigation was badly botched, however, and undoubtedly led to Lizzie being acquitted when she faced trial in June. The police failed to secure the murder scene, question Lizzie or examine her clothes for traces of blood. They found an axe in the cellar a day or so later, which appeared to have been cleaned and tampered with; Lizzie was also caught destroying a dress that she said was ruined by paint. Key parts of forensic evidence were, therefore, missed by investigators and this, coupled with the fact that Lizzie was deemed to be part of middle-class US society (and so enjoyed the support of wealthier townsfolk), ensured she was found not guilty of the murders.

Lizzie and her sister Emma benefitted directly from the death of their parents, inheriting their father's considerable fortune as he died intestate. Lizzie remained in Fall River but moved to a new property with Emma and changed her name to 'Lisbeth'. She died at the age of 66 leaving an estate valued at $7 million in today's money. Was Lizzie guilty? The case remains unproven, but numerous theories have continued to circulate as to her motives. Was she after the money? Was she a victim of abuse or even incest? Was she criminally insane? The mystery, and the folklore surrounding it, continues. ∎

ANDREW BORDEN.
1822–92.
FATHER.

ABBY BORDEN.
1828–92.
STEPMOTHER.

Above. A LOCK OF ABBY BORDEN'S HAIR AND LIZZIE BORDEN'S AXE.

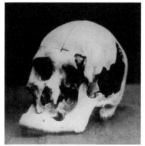

Above. ABBY BORDEN'S SKULL WITH CLEAR EVIDENCE OF TRAUMA TO THE LEFT SIDE.

Above. NEWSPAPER COVERAGE OF THE MURDER TRIAL.

Right. THE BORDEN FAMILY HOME AT FALL RIVER, MASSACHUSETTS: AN ORDINARY HOUSE FOR AN EXTRAORDINARY TRAGEDY.

1

92 SECOND STREET.
THE HOUSE WHERE ANDREW BORDEN AND ABBY BORDEN WERE MURDERED.

2

THE BORDENS' BARN.
THE BARN WHERE LIZZIE BORDEN CLAIMED TO HAVE BEEN DURING THE TIME OF THE MURDERS.

3

90 SECOND STREET.
THE HOUSE WHERE ADELAIDE B. CHURCHILL LIVED, WHO LIZZIE BORDEN FETCHED AFTER DISCOVERING HER FATHER, AND WHO TESTIFIED AT THE TRIAL.

4

94 SECOND STREET.
THE HOUSE WHERE MICHAEL AND CAROLINE KELLY LIVED. CAROLINE KELLY WAS ONE OF THE LAST PEOPLE TO SEE ANDREW BORDEN ALIVE AND TESTIFIED AT LIZZIE BORDEN'S TRIAL.

5

DR SEABURY BOWEN'S HOUSE.
THE HOUSE WHERE DR SEABURY BOWEN LIVED, WHO WAS THE FIRST TO EXAMINE THE BODIES AND TESTIFIED AT THE TRIAL.

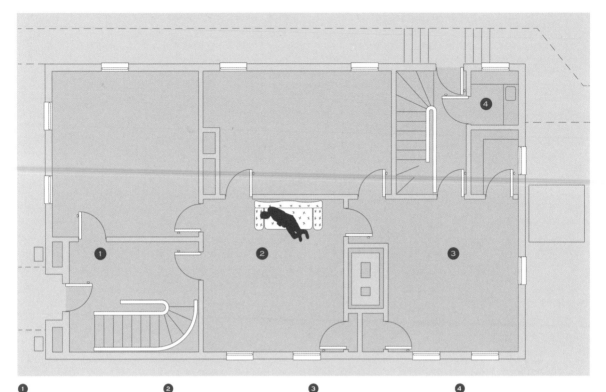

❶ FRONT ENTRY.
THE ENTRANCE TO THE
BORDENS' HOUSE.

❷ SITTING ROOM.
THE ROOM WHERE ANDREW
BORDEN'S BODY WAS FOUND.

❸ KITCHEN.
THE ROOM WHERE LIZZIE
BORDEN BURNED HER DRESS.

❹ SINK ROOM.
THE ROOM WHERE THE
MAID WASHED THE DISHES.

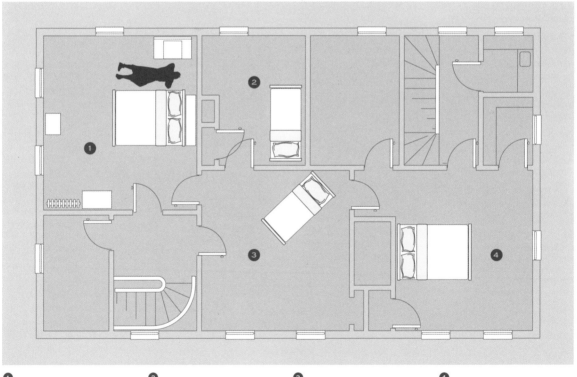

❶ GUEST BEDROOM.
THE ROOM WHERE ABBY
BORDEN'S BODY WAS FOUND.

❷ BEDROOM.
THE ROOM WHERE EMMA
BORDEN SLEPT.

❸ BEDROOM.
THE ROOM WHERE LIZZIE
BORDEN SLEPT.

❹ MASTER BEDROOM.
THE ROOM WHERE ANDREW
AND ABBY BORDEN SLEPT.

Right. THE FIRST OF TWO CRIME SCENE
PHOTOGRAPHS SHOWING ABBY BORDEN
AS THE POLICE FOUND HER.

Right. THE SECOND CRIME SCENE
PHOTOGRAPH SHOWING ABBY BORDEN
LYING DEAD IN BETWEEN A BED
AND A CHEST OF DRAWERS.

Right. A CRIME SCENE PHOTOGRAPH
SHOWING ANDREW BORDEN ON THE
SOFA WHERE HE HAD BEEN SLEEPING
WHEN HE WAS ATTACKED AND KILLED.

Right. A SECOND CRIME SCENE PHOTOGRAPH
OF ANDREW BORDEN'S BODY ON THE SOFA.
THE WOUNDS FROM THE TEN TO TWELVE
HITS HE RECEIVED FROM THE AXE
ARE VISIBLE.

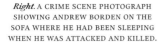

BELLE GUNNESS.
× *40.*

WEAPON. VARIOUS.	TYPOLOGY. PROPERTY CRIME.	POLICING. CRIME SCENE PHOTOGRAPHY.

GUNNESS FARM, MACLUNG ROAD, LA PORTE.

On the morning of 28 April 1908, a huge fire consumed the home of Belle Gunness (1859–1908) and her family in La Porte, Indiana. In the immediate aftermath, a man was seen running from the burning homestead and was later arrested. Ray Lamphere (1870–1909) had been hired as a farmhand by Belle, a wealthy widow who lived there with her children. Investigators found the charred bodies of the children along with the headless corpse of a woman. It was assumed Lamphere had killed Belle and then fired the house. Earlier that spring, Belle had instructed her lawyer to draw up a will, telling him that her employee was dangerously mad and that she was afraid 'that fool Lamphere is going to kill me and burn my house'.

Belle Gunness (née Storset) had arrived in the United States from Norway in 1881. Over the course of the next thirty-seven years, she murdered perhaps as many as forty people, profiting directly from the insurance she had taken out on their lives. Her early victims were her first husband, Mads Sorensen (1853–94), and two of their four children, Alex, (unknown–1898) and Caroline (unknown–1896). Mads and Belle ran a confectionery shop, which also burnt down. Belle used the money from the insurance payouts (around $8,500) to buy the farmstead in La Porte.

Killing for insurance money was a well-established ploy by the late 1800s, one that was hard to prove until forensic science became more sophisticated in the early 1900s. In 1873, Mary Ann Cotton (1832–73) had gone to the gallows at Durham Prison for poisoning around twenty-one people, including two of her husbands and several children. It was an infamous case from England and perhaps Belle had read about it in the newspapers.

In April 1902, Belle married Peter Gunness (1872–1902), a local butcher and widower. He had two daughters for Belle to care for, along with her own children. Soon after the wedding, one child died, in mysterious circumstances. Peter harboured doubts about his new wife and sent the other daughter to stay with relatives. He was right to be worried, because by December 1902 he, too, was dead, apparently killed in a bizarre accident when a meat grinder fell on his head. It was no accident of course; Belle had delivered the fatal blow and then claimed $3,000 to $4,000 on the insurance. Her foster daughter, Jennie (1890–1906), knew the truth, however, whispering to her school chums, 'My mama killed my papa... Don't tell a soul.' Despite the coroners noticing some signs of strychnine poisoning, no hard evidence could be found against Belle and accidental death was the verdict.

Next, Belle settled on a new scheme to make money, profiting from the lonely hearts columns of the newspapers. Using the early 20th century's version of dating apps, Belle advertised herself as a lonely widow looking for a suitable (and well-off) husband. Dozens of men answered the call, and

① 1894. × *Mads Sorensen.* *Poisoned with strychnine.*	② 1902. × *Peter Gunness.* *Bludgeoned with meat grinder.*	③ 1908. × *Lucy Sorensen.* *Burnt in farmhouse.*	④ 1908. × *Myrtle Sorensen.* *Burnt in farmhouse.*	⑤ 1908. × *Philip Gunness.* *Burnt in farmhouse.*	⑥ 1906. × *Jennie Olsen.* *Bludgeoned.*	⑦ 1908. × *Andrew Helgelien.* *Bludgeoned & dismembered.*

Above. A CONTEMPORARY PHOTOGRAPH OF THE GUNNESS FARM; THE BURNT-DOWN FARMHOUSE IS NOT VISIBLE HERE.

Below. THE GUNNESS FARM AND THE PONY THAT BELONGED TO THE GUNNESS CHILDREN.

Above. WEST VIEW OF THE GUNNESS FARM, SHOWING THE CROWDS OF PEOPLE WHO VISITED AFTER THE MURDERS.

Below. SOUTH VIEW OF THE FARM. PARTS OF THE BODIES OF FORTY OR MORE VICTIMS WERE FOUND BURIED AROUND THE FARM.

the Gunness farmhouse saw a steady stream of male visitors, many or most of whom were never seen again. They arrived with hopes of love and pockets of cash only to be poisoned or smashed over the head with Belle's meat cleaver.

One man survived his visit to La Porte. George Anderson had agreed to wed Belle and to pay off her mortgage. Late one night, he woke up to find Belle peering over him, a candle in her hand and a sinister expression on her face. When she realized he was awake, she ran out of the room. Anderson did not wait for an explanation but fled as fast as he could. He was lucky, but very many others were not. After the farm burnt down in April 1908, the plot was excavated. On the first day, five bodies were discovered, and six more on the second day.

After that, the police apparently 'stopped counting'. There were 'torsos and hands, arms hacked from the shoulders down, masses of human bone wrapped in loose flesh that dripped like jelly', all bundled in burlap sacks and buried in crude shallow graves near the pig pens or by the nearby lake. Identification was difficult, but those who can be confirmed were Andrew Helgelien, Ole Budsberg, Thomas Lindboe, Henry Gurholdt, Olaf Svenherud, John Moe, Olaf Lindbloom and Belle's daughter Jennie (who told her classmates the truth about her stepfather's death). It seemed that Belle paid for her crimes, killed and decapitated by her farm hand Lamphere. However, doubts remain as to whether Belle escaped and faked her own death; DNA testing in 2008 proved inconclusive. ∎

⑧
1908 (discovered).
× *Ole B. Budsberg.*
Bludgeoned &
dismembered.

⑨
1908 (discovered).
× *Henry Gurholdt.*
Bludgeoned &
dismembered.

⑩
1908 (discovered).
× *John Moe.*
Bludgeoned &
dismembered.

⑪
1908 (discovered).
× *Thomas Lindboe.*
Bludgeoned &
dismembered.

⑫
1908 (discovered).
× *Olaf Svenherud.*
Bludgeoned &
dismembered.

⑬
1908 (discovered).
× *Olaf Lindbloom.*
Bludgeoned &
dismembered.

⑭ – ㊵
Body parts
unearthed equating
to a possible 27
further victims.

BONES AND BODY PARTS
FOUND BURIED ON
THE FARM.

A CRATE FULL OF BONES
AND BODY PARTS FOUND
BURIED ON THE FARM.

RINGS FOUND IN THE RUINS
OF THE GUNNESS FARM. ONE
MARKED 'S.B. MAY 28, 1907'.

BRIDGEWORK IDENTIFIED
AS BELONGING TO
BELLE GUNNESS.

THE REMAINS OF ANDREW
HELGELIEN WHERE THEY
WERE FOUND BURIED.

THE SKULL OF ONE
OF GUNNESS'S UNKNOWN
VICTIMS.

SKULLS AND OTHER BODY
PARTS FOUND BY POLICE
WHILE SEARCHING THE FARM.

THE DECAPITATED HEAD
OF ONE OF THE
VICTIMS.

INVESTIGATORS SEARCH THE
BASEMENT OF THE BURNT-
DOWN FARMHOUSE.

SHOVELS USED TO EXCAVATE
THE GUNNESS FARM, IN THE
BURNT-OUT CELLAR.

MEN USING SHOVELS AND
FORKS TO SEARCH FOR
BODIES BY THE LAKE.

AN INVESTIGATOR STANDING
IN THE BURNT-OUT REMAINS
OF THE FARMHOUSE.

A FORMER MINER WAS HIRED
TO BUILD A SLUICE IN ORDER
TO SIFT THROUGH THE DEBRIS.

THE AREA OF THE FARM
WHERE NINE BODIES WERE
FOUND BURIED.

THE INVESTIGATION OF THE
SITE DREW LARGE CROWDS
OF ONLOOKERS.

THE MAKESHIFT MORGUE
WITH DOZENS OF CURIOUS
SIGHTSEERS OUTSIDE.

THE BURNT SHELL OF THE
GUNNESS FARMHOUSE, WITH
SPECTATORS AROUND IT.

THE AREA OF THE GUNNESS
FARM WHERE TEN BODIES
WERE FOUND BURIED.

THE SHALLOW GRAVE WHERE
FOUR VICTIMS WERE FOUND
BURIED TOGETHER.

AN INVESTIGATOR MAKING
NOTES WHILE SEARCHING
THE MASS GRAVE.

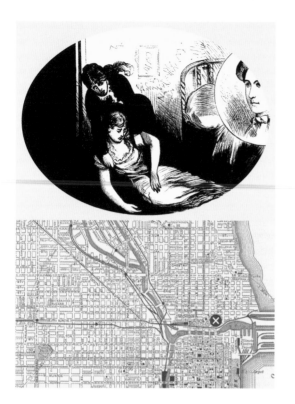

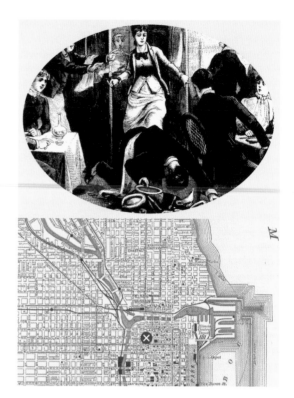

USA—CHICAGO.	*November 1880.*

EVA LLOYD.
✕ *Dora Clarence.*

WEAPON. BLUDGEON.	TYPOLOGY. ACCIDENT.	POLICING. N/A.

396 STATE STREET, NEAR NORTH SIDE.

When Eva Lloyd's (dates unknown) fellow residents entered her room on State Street, Chicago, the smell was overpowering. Eva had vanished several days earlier and the landlady was keen to rent out her room, despite having her deposit. When the closet door was opened, the decomposing body of an undressed woman fell out. She had been bludgeoned beyond recognition. The victim was Dora Clarence (unknown–1880) who, like her assumed killer Eva, was one of the city's many prostitutes. Eva was already in jail, locked up for drunkenness, and said she had found Dora dead after a night's heavy drinking with her. The jury ruled it accidental death. ∎

USA—CHICAGO.	*7 December 1883.*

SADIE REIGH.
✕ *Patrick Kinsley.*

WEAPON. PISTOL.	TYPOLOGY. RECKLESS ACT.	POLICING. N/A.

BRIGG'S HOUSE HOTEL, CORNER OF WELLS STREET & RANDOLPH STREET, THE LOOP.

It must have been a shock to diners at the Brigg's House Hotel in Chicago when a young woman strode into the room and shot the head waiter, Patrick Kinsley (unknown–1883), where he stood. She was arrested and put in jail while the case against her was investigated. Her name was Sadie Reigh (dates unknown), a pantry girl who had fallen for another employee called Delts (dates unknown). Kinsley apparently harboured 'an unnatural affection' for Delts and so spread rumours to besmirch Reigh's character. At first, she determined to sue him for defamation but opted to kill him instead. She pleaded guilty to manslaughter and served just eighteen months. ∎

Above. A NEWSPAPER ILLUSTRATION OF DORA CLARENCE'S MURDER BY EVA LLOYD.

Above. PATRICK KINSLEY IS SHOT BY SADIE REIGH, AS ILLUSTRATED IN A CONTEMPORARY NEWSPAPER.

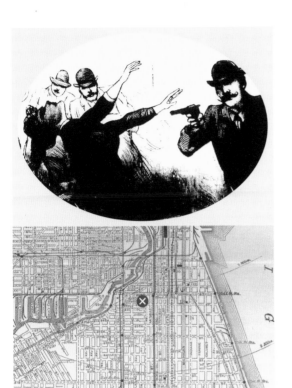

USA — CHICAGO.	*14 November 1892.*

CHARLES RYAN.
✕ *Susie Hess.*
✕ *Frank Whittaker.* ✕ *Himself.*

WEAPON. PISTOL.	TYPOLOGY. JEALOUSY.	POLICING. N/A.

THE LEVEE DISTRICT.

USA — CHICAGO.	*20 November 1892.*

HERMAN SIEGLER.
✕ *Caroline Siels.*

WEAPON. SHOTGUN.	TYPOLOGY. INSANITY.	POLICING. N/A.

FULTON STREET, NEAR WEST SIDE.

Charles Ryan (unknown–1892) was a regular at Frank Whittaker's (unknown–1892) brothel in Chicago's red light district. It was a new venture for Whittaker, but he was an experienced brothel keeper, having run a similar house in New York. Ryan was a gambler, but at Whittaker's place he had fallen for one of the girls, Susie Hess (unknown–1892), a blue-eyed beauty who played him for all she could get. The pair argued on 14 November 1892 and Whittaker suggested a drink to calm everyone down. Ryan was not so easily pacified and shot first Hess, then Whittaker, before turning the gun on himself. ∎

Herman Siegler (dates unknown) was a troubled soul, suffering from depression and prone to dark thoughts that only he understood. On 20 November 1892, as his mother-in-law Caroline Siels (unknown–1892) greeted him on the stairs of their home he blew off her head with a shotgun. When her husband, Heinrich (unknown–1892), raced to the scene, he shot him, too, injuring his own wife Emilia in the process. A crowd of worshippers from the local evangelical church surrounded the house and the police exchanged shots before Siegler was overpowered. His signed confession stated that God had told him Caroline was a witch and that he had to kill her. ∎

Above. A NEWSPAPER ILLUSTRATION OF THE MOMENT CHARLES RYAN SHOT SUSIE HESS.

Above. A CONTEMPORARY SKETCH SHOWING CAROLINE SIELS'S DEAD BODY, WITH HERMAN SIEGLER HOLDING A SMOKING GUN.

DR THOMAS NEILL CREAM.
× 5. +

WEAPON. STRYCHNINE.	TYPOLOGY. VARIOUS.	POLICING. N/A.

CHICAGO & LONDON.

Thomas Neill Cream's (1850–92) arrogance was evident throughout his life, in which he killed five women and performed numerous illegal abortions within sixteen years. However, his sense of infallibility was eventually to be his downfall. Cream studied medicine, qualifying as a doctor in Montreal in 1876. In the same year, he married his first wife, Flora Brooks (unknown–1877), but not before he had nearly killed her performing a failed abortion. When Flora's father found out, a shotgun wedding followed. Cream left Flora and Canada, moving to Scotland to continue his studies. Returning to Canada, he started practising abortions, a branch of medicine that, while illegal, was lucrative. When a chambermaid was found dead on his premises, Cream was suspected but not prosecuted; unnerved, he moved to Chicago.

Here, he established himself as an abortionist operating in the red light district, serving working girls who treated pregnancy as an occupational hazard. Again, he narrowly avoided arrest and prosecution when a client died. Then, in June 1881, he poisoned the husband of Julia Stott (dates unknown). Cream had been making money from selling an elixir, a supposed cure for epilepsy. Daniel Stott (unknown–1881) discovered that Cream was sleeping with his wife and, perhaps at Julia's instigation, Cream added strychnine to Stott's medicine. Cream tried to blame the pharmacist who prepared the medicine and demanded Stott's

buried body be exhumed to demonstrate he had not died of epilepsy. The district attorney agreed and poisoning was revealed. Cream went to prison for life, a fate entirely caused by his own sense of invulnerability. Locked up in Joliet Prison, he could no longer practise his callous brand of medicine. However, Chicago's justice system was corrupt and Cream's brother was able to bribe officials to let him out early. Cream served just ten years for the murder of Daniel Stott and, released for 'good behaviour', he went north to collect some inheritance money before sailing for England to start a new life where he was not known.

It did not take him long to pick up where he had left off stateside. On 13 October 1891, just under a week after docking at Liverpool, Cream met a 19-year-old prostitute in Lambeth, London: three days later, she died. Nellie Donworth (1872–91) had been poisoned with strychnine and Cream followed that killing with another on 20 October. He met Matilda Clover (unknown–1891), gave her poison and left her to die. It seems likely that Cream's latent misogyny was brought to the surface by his experience in Chicago with Julia Stott. He clearly blamed her for his arrest and imprisonment, and his desire to take vengeance on the women he encountered subsequently led to the deaths of Matilda and Nellie and then two more young women, Alice Marsh (1871–92) and Emma Shrivell (1874–92), whom he killed in April 1892.

Opposite below. ILLUSTRATED POLICE NEWS, 22 OCTOBER 1892. DR THOMAS NEILL CREAM AT HIS TRIAL.

Left. A SERIES OF SKETCHES FROM THE *ILLUSTRATED POLICE NEWS*, DEPICTING SCENES FROM THE NEILL CASE.

Right. SENSATIONAL PRESS COVERAGE OF THE 'LAMBETH POISONING MYSTERY', AS THE PRESS DUBBED IT, SHOWING DR THOMAS NEILL CREAM'S VICTIMS.

There was nothing to tie Cream to any of these murders; all the victims were London prostitutes and 'stranger' murders were the hardest to solve (as the detectives hunting Jack the Ripper found to their cost). Cream's arrogance finally undermined him, though, this time fatally. He tried to frame two local doctors for the murders, writing to the police with information about them. The police became suspicious because he named Clover, whom they believed died of natural causes. Cream then met a New York policeman in London and showed him round the murder sites. The cop told a fellow London officer and Cream was arrested. On 21 October 1892, Cream was convicted of Clover's murder and sentenced to death. He was hanged on 16 November, hoisted by his own petard.

Cream has been put forward as a possible suspect in the Whitechapel Murders of 1888. He was certainly a misogynist who killed prostitutes, but it was a report of the event of his hanging that has led some people to believe he was Jack the Ripper. According to the hangman, as Cream fell to his death he cried out, 'I am Jack...'. Sadly, nobody else present that morning, and most notably Sir Henry Smith, Commissioner of the City Police, heard him. Smith makes no mention of the incident in his autobiography. Moreover, we know that in 1888 Cream was in prison in Chicago and, despite attempts to suggest that Cream had a 'doppelganger' who served his sentence for him, it seems highly unlikely that he could be in two places at once. ∎

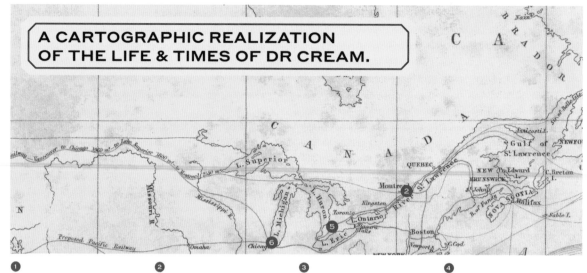

A CARTOGRAPHIC REALIZATION OF THE LIFE & TIMES OF DR CREAM.

❶
GLASGOW, SCOTLAND.
THE CITY WHERE DR THOMAS
NEILL CREAM WAS BORN.

❷
MONTREAL, CANADA.
THE CITY WHERE DR THOMAS
NEILL CREAM ATTENDED
MCGILL UNIVERSITY.

❸
LONDON, ENGLAND.
THE CITY WHERE DR THOMAS
NEILL CREAM STUDIED
AT ST THOMAS'S HOSPITAL.

❹
EDINBURGH, SCOTLAND.
THE CITY WHERE DR THOMAS
NEILL CREAM COMPLETED
HIS STUDIES AT THE ROYAL
COLLEGE OF PHYSICIANS.

EDINBURGH, SCOTLAND.

❶
THE ROYAL COLLEGE OF
PHYSICIANS, EDINBURGH,
SCOTLAND.
THE INSTITUTION WHERE
DR THOMAS NEILL CREAM
COMPLETED HIS STUDIES.

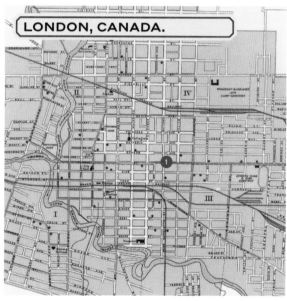

LONDON, CANADA.

❶
DUNDAS STREET, LONDON,
ONTARIO, CANADA.
THE LOCATION WHERE KATE
GARDENER WAS FOUND DEAD IN
A WOODSHED BEHIND DR THOMAS
NEILL CREAM'S RESIDENCE.

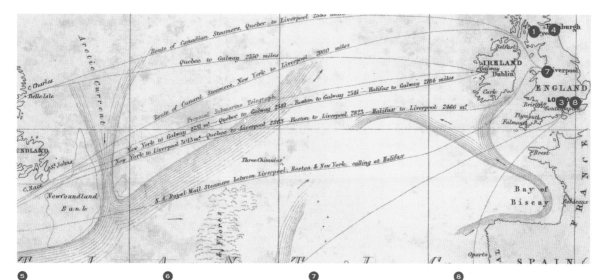

5
LONDON, ONTARIO, CANADA.
THE CITY DR THOMAS NEILL
CREAM MOVED TO FOLLOWING
THE COMPLETION OF HIS STUDIES.

6
CHICAGO, USA.
THE CITY WHERE DR THOMAS
NEILL CREAM SET UP AS
AN ABORTIONIST, AND WAS
SUBSEQUENTLY IMPRISONED
FOR TEN YEARS.

7
LIVERPOOL, ENGLAND.
THE CITY WHERE DR THOMAS
NEILL CREAM DOCKED IN
ENGLAND IN 1891.

8
LONDON, ENGLAND.
THE CITY WHERE DR THOMAS
NEILL CREAM MURDERED
MULTIPLE WOMEN, AND
WAS ARRESTED AND HANGED.

LONDON, ENGLAND.

1
434 WEST MADISON STREET,
CHICAGO, USA.
THE BUILDING WHERE DR THOMAS
NEILL CREAM LIVED AND SET UP
HIS MEDICAL PRACTICE.

2
1056 MADISON STREET,
CHICAGO, USA.
THE BUILDING WHERE
THE PROSTITUTE MARY ANNE
FAULKNER DIED FOLLOWING
DR THOMAS NEILL CREAM'S
TREATMENT.

3
BUCK AND RAYNER'S PHARMACY,
CHICAGO USA.
THE CHEMIST WHERE JULIA STOTT
PURCHASED THE MEDICINE FOR
HER HUSBAND THAT DR THOMAS
NEILL CREAM FATALLY ALTERED.

1
103 LAMBETH PALACE ROAD,
LONDON, ENGLAND.
THE HOUSE IN WHICH DR THOMAS
NEILL CREAM STAYED.

3
WATERLOO ROAD,
LONDON, ENGLAND.
THE ROAD WHERE NELLIE
DONWORTH MET DR THOMAS
NEILL CREAM THE NIGHT SHE
WAS MURDERED.

5
118 STAMFORD STREET,
LONDON, ENGLAND.
THE BUILDING WHERE DR THOMAS
NEILL CREAM MURDERED ALICE
MARSH AND EMMA SHRIVELL.

2
PRIEST'S CHEMIST,
22 PARLIAMENT STREET,
LONDON, ENGLAND.
THE CHEMIST WHERE DR THOMAS
NEILL CREAM PURCHASED POISON.

4
27 LAMBETH ROAD,
LONDON, ENGLAND.
THE BUILDING WHERE MATILDA
CLOVER LIVED, AND WHERE
SHE WAS MURDERED.

6
NEWGATE PRISON,
LONDON, ENGLAND.
THE PRISON WHERE
DR THOMAS NEILL CREAM
WAS HANGED.

PATRICK EUGENE PRENDERGAST.
× *Mayor Carter Harrison, Sr.*

WEAPON. REVOLVER.	TYPOLOGY. POLITICAL.	POLICING. N/A.

231 ASHLAND BOULEVARD, WEST TOWN.

PATRICK EUGENE PRENDERGAST.

MAYOR CARTER HARRISON, SR.

The murder of Mayor Carter Henry Harrison (1825–93) profoundly affected 1890s America. The mayor, a popular politician, tipped for the highest office, was killed in his home by a 'madman'. The killing shook a nation coming to terms with rapid industrialization and urbanization and still recovering from the assassination of President Garfield (1831–81) in 1881. Political assassination was on everyone's mind, so perhaps the mayor should have been more on his guard when Patrick Eugene Prendergast (1868–94) called at his home on 28 October 1893. The Irish-born newspaper distributor, who believed the mayor had betrayed a non-existent promise to promote him, shot him four times as he sat in his chair resting after a long day of political engagements. Prendergast surrendered to the police and was tried for murder. His defence pleaded insanity, but, while witnesses testified to his obsessive personality, a clear insanity diagnosis was absent. The prosecution noted he had carried a revolver with one chamber left empty: a rational decision in the days before safety catches were standard. Convicted of murder, he was hanged on 13 July 1894. ∎

Above. THE HARRISON MANSION ON ASHLAND BOULEVARD, CHICAGO, WHERE THE MAYOR WAS SHOT AND KILLED.

Left. MAP SHOWING THE LOCATION OF ASHLAND BOULEVARD, WHERE MAYOR CARTER HARRISON WAS SHOT DEAD IN HIS OWN HOME.

Right. THE *CHICAGO TRIBUNE*'S SOMEWHAT INACCURATE RECONSTRUCTION OF MAYOR CARTER HARRISON'S MURDER. HE WAS ACTUALLY SHOT WHILE SITTING DOWN.

ADOLPH LUETGERT.
✕ *Louisa Bicknese.*

WEAPON. UNKNOWN.	TYPOLOGY. DOMESTIC.	POLICING. FORENSIC ANTHROPOLOGY.

601 DIVERSEY STREET, PARK WEST.

ADOLPH LUETGERT. | LOUISA BICKNESE.

Adolph Luetgert (1845–99) appeared to have made a success of life in the United States. He had moved there in the 1870s from Germany, and after a stint as a saloon keeper founded a prosperous sausage company. By 1897, however, his trappings of wealth obscured the reality that the so-called 'sausage king' was struggling. His relationship with his wife Louisa (1855–97) was undermined by his philandering, and he had accumulated large debts. Then, in May, Louisa disappeared. He told his children that she had gone to visit her family, and later that she had left him. Neither account was true. In fact, Luetgert had murdered his wife and disposed of her in his sausage factory, dissolving her body in a vat of lye (sodium hydroxide). Police found traces of human bones and Louisa's jewelry in the factory furnaces, and Luetgert's protestations that the bones belonged to animals were refuted by a forensic anthropologist, the first time such an expert witness was used. The trial was widely covered by the press, who even attempted to listen in on the jury's deliberations, another first for US justice. Luetgert ended his life in Joliet Prison, dying of heart disease in 1899. ▪

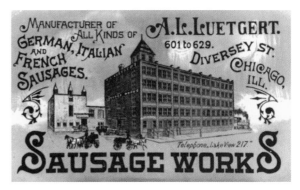

Above. ADVERTISEMENT FOR THE SAUSAGE WORKS, THE FACTORY OWNED BY THE 'SAUSAGE KING' ADOLPH LUETGERT.

Left above. BONE FRAGMENTS FOUND IN THE FACTORY FURNACES AND IDENTIFIED AS HUMAN BY A POLICE EXPERT.

Left below. THE BOILER ROOM IN ADOLPH LUETGERT'S FACTORY, WHERE IT IS CLAIMED HE DISPOSED OF HIS WIFE'S BODY BY DISSOLVING IT IN SODIUM HYDROXIDE.

Right. MAP SHOWING THE LOCATION OF ADOLPH LUETGERT'S SAUSAGE FACTORY ON DIVERSEY STREET, WHERE THE MURDER TOOK PLACE.

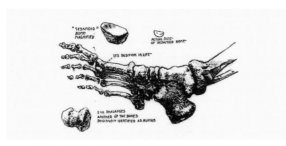

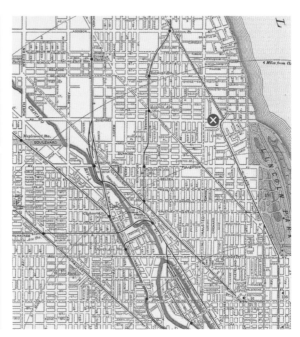

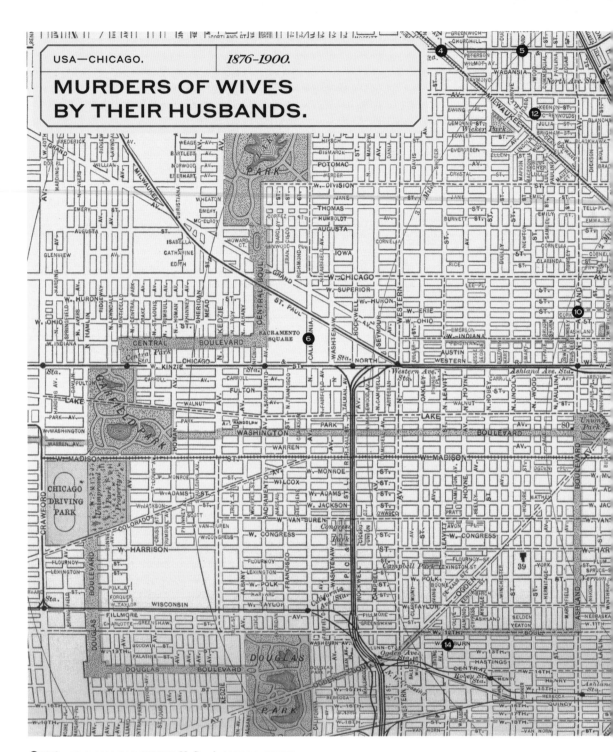

MURDERS OF WIVES
BY THEIR HUSBANDS.

1 1876. 473 W. MADISON STREET. **Mr Guerin.** × MRS A. GUERIN.

2 1882. 487 W. MADISON STREET. **James McNamara.** × JOHANNA MCNAMARA.

3 1883. 564 N. HALSTED STREET. **Adolph Ehrke.** × MARGARET EHRKE.

4 1884. MILWAUKEE AVENUE AND LEAVITT STREET. **Peter Dentler.** × WILHELMINA DENTLER.

5 1887. 642 MILWAUKEE AVENUE. **August Krakow.** × EMILIE KRAKOW.

6 1889. 3735 CALIFORNIA AVENUE. **Charles F. Harder.** × HELEN HARDER.

7 1889. ADAMS STREET. **Mr Bradley.** × MRS BRADLEY.

8 1890. 536 SEDGEWICK STREET. **Les Klein.** × LOUISE KLEIN.

9 1893. 131 VAN BUREN STREET. **Frank Eck.** × FRANCES ECK.

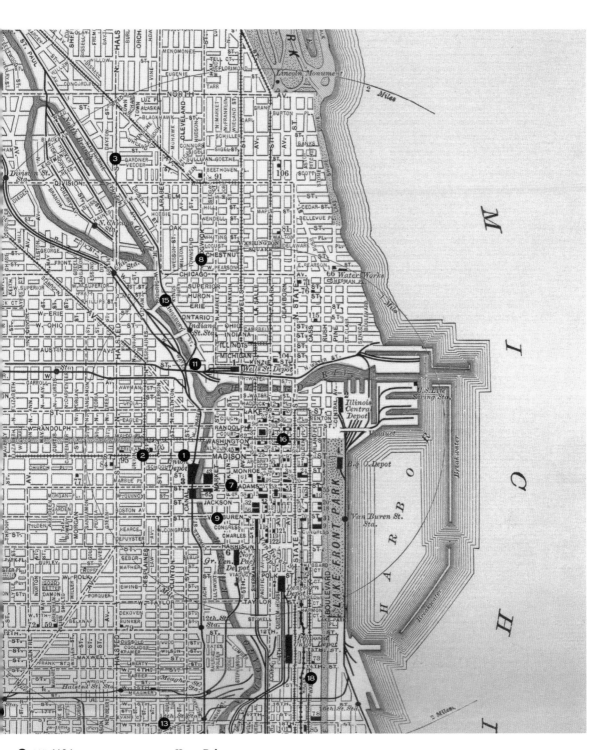

🔟 1893. 1604 N. ASHLAND AVENUE. **Henry Dahme.** ✕ LOUISE DAHME.

⑪ 1894. KINZIE STREET BRIDGE. **Frank Kurz.** ✕ ELLA KURZ.

⑫ 1895. 641 N. WOOD STREET. **Jacob Miller.** ✕ RACHEL MILLER.

⑬ 1897. 922 W. 18TH STREET. **Albert Doylai.** ✕ MARY DOYLAI.

⑭ 1897. 376 WASHBURN AVENUE. **Frank Kocton.** ✕ MARY KOCTON.

⑮ 1898. 543 LARRABEE STREET. **Charles Lachner.** ✕ MARY LACHNER.

⑯ 1899. 110 DEARBORN AVENUE. **Thomas Houlihan.** ✕ LIZZIE HOULIHAN.

⑰ 1900. 824 ALLPORT STREET. **Charles Babor.** ✕ MRS BABOR.

⑱ 1900. 1335 WABASH AVENUE. **Joseph O'Neill.** ✕ MAUDE O'NEILL.

HENRY HOWARD HOLMES.
× 4. +

WEAPON.	TYPOLOGY.	POLICING.
VARIOUS.	PROPERTY CRIME.	N/A.

63RD STREET, ENGLEWOOD & ACROSS THE USA.

The story of Dr Henry Howard Holmes (1861–96), real name Herman Webster Mudgett, is one of the most bizarre and sensational ones in the history of serial murder. According to legend, Holmes killed anything from 16 to 200 men, women and children between 1885 and his execution in 1896. What we know about Holmes is limited, at least in terms of the murders he is supposed to have committed, and this is almost certainly because Holmes was a compulsive liar.

Born in New Hampshire in 1861, Holmes moved to Chicago sometime around 1885 and established himself in business, first taking over ownership of a pharmacy before buying a large plot of land opposite it. Here, he built a three-storey 'hotel' (later dubbed the 'Castle') in order to profit from visitors to the much-anticipated 1893 'World's Columbian Exposition' international trade fair. Holmes was a skilled conman and insured the premises and its contents multiple times in order to profit from fires he then started. He also defrauded local businessmen by ordering furniture, which he never paid for. When they came to investigate him, they could find no trace of the goods. Later investigations, however, revealed that the 'hotel' (which never operated as such) was mostly a sham building with hidden rooms and false doors, most of which were probably designed by Holmes to allow him to hide the furniture and goods he fraudulently obtained. As suspicions about Holmes's sharp business practices grew, he left Chicago with his long-term associate Benjamin Pitezel (1856–94), whom he had persuaded to help him execute an elaborate insurance fraud. It was arranged that Holmes would fake Pitezel's death and the pair would benefit from the $10,000 life insurance payout. In reality, Holmes murdered Pitezel and tried to make it look like a scientific accident. He then travelled around the United States with both Pitezel's widow and his own wife (whom he had married bigamously), keeping each in the dark about his actions. As they moved about, Holmes systematically murdered Pitezel's three children, because the eldest had discovered his secret. He was finally captured by a Pinkerton detective and held for a horse theft in Texas.

While he was in prison, investigations in Toronto, Indianapolis and at the Castle in Chicago

Above. THE 'SURGING SEA OF HUMANITY' ARRIVING FOR THE WORLD'S COLUMBIAN EXPOSITION IN CHICAGO, 1893.

Above. THE INFAMOUS 'MURDER HOTEL' THAT H. H. HOLMES BUILT ON 63RD STREET, CHICAGO.

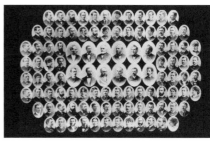

caused prosecutors to revise their opinion of the man they had in custody. Using unsent letters written by the Pitezel children, Detective Frank P. Geyer (1853–1918) had traced Holmes's journey across America and discovered the remains of the three murdered children. Instead of a serial fraudster, they now realized they had a serial murderer on their hands. Holmes went before a judge and jury in Philadelphia solely for the murder of Benjamin Pitezel, but he later made a dramatic confession in which he claimed to have killed twenty-seven people. Excavations at the Castle (now dubbed the 'Murder Hotel') unearthed some evidence of buried bodies but not in the numbers that Holmes claimed. That he killed Pitezel and his three children seems clear, and at least six other people who went missing at the Castle were almost certainly murdered by Holmes. But at least three of the people he confessed to killing were still alive, one of whom made an impassioned statement to that effect to the newspapers.

It seems that the reality of Holmes was very quickly conflated with the mythology of the man. Much of what we think we know has been gleaned from fairly spurious newspaper reports that printed detailed floor plans of the Castle suggesting that Holmes had built mini-gas chambers, a 'dummy elevator for lowering bodies' to the basement and his own crematorium. These details and the speculation that Holmes had constructed a purpose-built 'Murder Hotel' may have been the work of contemporary journalists and later pulp fiction writers. All the evidence was destroyed in 1895, when the Castle burnt down. Holmes was, by all accounts, attractive, charming and credible, and it appears likely that he was able to inveigle several women into his home before murdering them when they became surplus to requirements. Among these were Julia Conner, née Smyth, and her daughter Pearl, Emeline Cigrande, Edna Van Tassel, and Minnie and Nannie Williams. In his confession, Holmes is alleged to have said: 'I was born with the devil in me. I could not help the fact that I was a murderer, no more than the poet can help the inspiration to sing – I was born with the "Evil One" standing as my sponsor beside the bed where I was ushered into the world, and he has been with me since.' Even this may be a myth. ∎

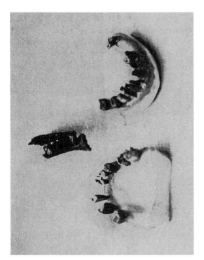

Above. THE BURNT TEETH OF HOWARD PITEZEL. H. H. HOLMES MADE HIS DEATH LOOK LIKE AN ACCIDENT.

Above. THE SHOVEL USED BY H. H. HOLMES TO BURY ALICE AND NELLIE PITEZEL IN TORONTO.

Above. MOYAMENSING PRISON, WHERE H. H. HOLMES WAS IMPRISONED, AND LATER HANGED ON 7 MAY 1896.

THE WORLD'S FAIR HOTEL.

SECOND FLOOR [THIS PAGE].
THIRD FLOOR [OPPOSITE].

63RD STREET, ENGLEWOOD.

ASPHYXIATION CHAMBER.
Holmes claimed to have killed several of his victims by asphyxiation with gas, including Pearl and Julia Conner, Elizabeth Perr, Sarah Cook and Mary Havercamp.

LABORATORY.
Holmes was alleged to have stripped some of his victims of their flesh in order to sell their skeletons to medical practitioners.

SECRET CHAMBER.
In his confession Holmes claimed to have murdered a 'Rogers' here using chloroform, and Robert Latimer using gas asphyxiation.

BATHROOM.
In this room there was a trap door in the floor, 120 × 60 cm (4 × 2 ft). Below were narrow stairs leading into another secret chamber, from which stairs led to a tin shop on Wallace Street.

CLOSED ROOM.
This was one of the largest rooms in the hotel, at about 365 × 244 cm (12 × 8 ft). There was no furniture in it and the air was stifling when the detectives entered; there was no visible means of ventilation. At one end of the chamber there was found near the ceiling a chute which ran up a few feet and then opened into the dummy elevator shaft.

RECEPTION ROOM.
Holmes claimed Charles Cole was killed here by an accomplice using a piece of gas pipe while being 'engaged in conversation' by Holmes.

KEY TO SECOND FLOOR.

1. LABORATORIES.
2. TRAP DOOR [FROM THIRD FLOOR].
3. TRAP DOOR [FROM THIRD FLOOR].
4. BATHROOM WITH HIDDEN STAIRS TO BASEMENT.
5. SECRET HIDING PLACE.
6. CHUTE FROM ROOF TO BASEMENT.
7. BATHROOM.

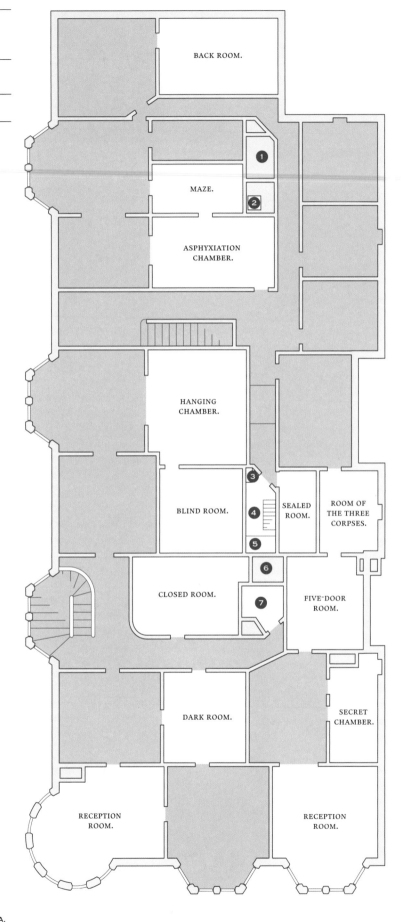

MINNIE WILLIAMS'S ROOM.

Minnie Williams lived with Holmes in the World's Fair Hotel as his secretary and likely mistress. She disappeared, and Holmes claimed to have poisoned her in Momence, Illinois, as a fire at the hotel meant he could not use his usual methods.

OFFICE.

Holmes claimed to have murdered Dr Russell here by striking him with a chair following a quarrel over rent payment.

OFFICE VAULT.

Inside Holmes's office was a sealed vault in which he could gas victims or simply leave them to die. It featured a steel lining and asbestos covering to deaden sound. Nobody but Holmes could open this safe, which was large enough for people to stand inside. He claimed to have killed domestic servant Lizzie, Emeline Cigrand, Nannie Williams and an unnamed woman here.

BASEMENT.

Holmes claimed Edna Van Tassel was poisoned and buried in the basement, and Mr Warner was incinerated in a kiln in the basement.

OTHER.

Holmes claimed he poisoned both Anna Betz and Gertrude Conner, although they did not die within the hotel walls. An unnamed man visiting the World's Fair was also alleged to have been killed while staying in the hotel.

NOTES.

Holmes was only convicted of killing Benjamin Pitezel and his children, but while in prison he wrote a sensational confession claiming to have killed a total of 27 people, many in his Chicago 'Murder Hotel', the World's Fair Hotel. Most of these subsequently proved to be fabrication. However, this claim, along with the police reports of the investigation of the hotel, created a storm in the press.

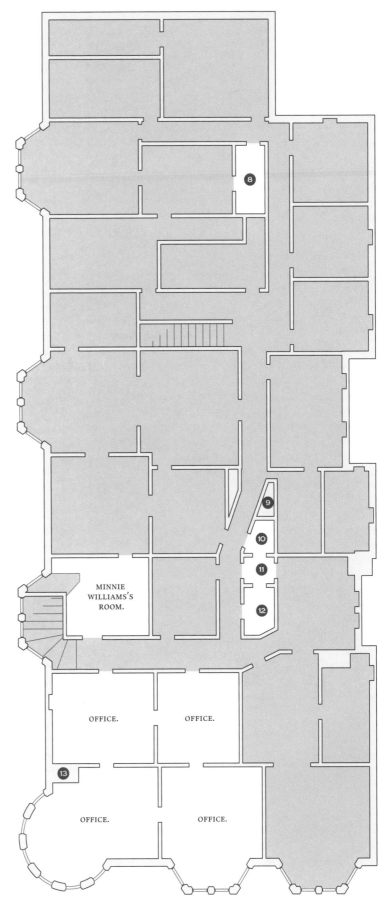

KEY TO THIRD FLOOR.

8 LABORATORY.
9 STORAGE.
10 STORAGE.
11 STORAGE.
12 BATHROOM.
13 OFFICE VAULT.

1

THE WORLD'S FAIR
HOTEL 63RD STREET,
ENGLEWOOD, CHICAGO, IL.
THE LOCATION OF THE
'MURDER CASTLE' RUN
BY H. H. HOLMES.

2

1316 CALLOWHILL STREET,
PHILADELPHIA, PA.
THE HOUSE IN WHICH
H. H. HOLMES MURDERED
BENJAMIN PITEZEL.

3

305 POPLAR STREET,
CINCINNATI, OH.
A HOUSE IN WHICH
H. H. HOLMES INTENDED
TO MURDER ALICE, NELLIE
AND HOWARD PITEZEL.

4

241 JULIAN AVENUE,
IRVINGTON, INDIANAPOLIS, IN.
THE HOUSE IN WHICH
H. H. HOLMES MURDERED
HOWARD PITEZEL.

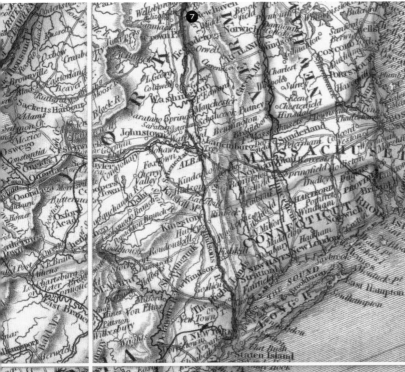

CARRIE ALICE
CANNING PITEZEL.
1859–1929.
WIFE OF ACCOMPLICE.
SURVIVED.

BENJAMIN FREELON
PITEZEL.
1856–94.
FRIEND & ACCOMPLICE.
1316 CALLOWHILL STREET,
PHILADELPHIA, PA.

HOWARD ROBERT PITEZEL.
1886–94.
SON OF ACCOMPLICE.
241 JULIAN AVENUE,
IRVINGTON, IN.

ETTA 'ALICE' PITEZEL.
1879–94.
**YOUNGEST DAUGHTER
OF ACCOMPLICE.**
16 ST VINCENT STREET,
TORONTO, ON, CANADA.

❺
241 EAST FOREST AVENUE,
DETROIT, MI.
A HOUSE IN WHICH
H. H. HOLMES INTENDED
TO MURDER ALICE AND
NELLIE PITEZEL.

❻
16 ST VINCENT STREET,
TORONTO, ON, CANADA.
THE HOUSE IN WHICH
H. H. HOLMES MURDERED
ALICE AND NELLIE PITEZEL.

❼
26 WINOOSKI AVENUE,
BURLINGTON, VT, CANADA.
A HOUSE IN WHICH
H. H. HOLMES INTENDED
TO MURDER CARRIE, DESSA
AND HORTON PITEZEL.

ROSA NELL
'NELLIE' PITEZEL.
1884–94.
**DAUGHTER
OF ACCOMPLICE.**
16 ST VINCENT STREET,
TORONTO, ON, CANADA.

JOHANN OTTO HOCH.
× *Marie Walcker.*

WEAPON.	TYPOLOGY.	POLICING.
ARSENIC.	PROPERTY CRIME.	TOXICOLOGY.

6225 UNION AVENUE, ENGLEWOOD.

John Schmidt (1855–1906) emigrated to the United States for the opportunities it presented. For Schmidt, better known as Johann Hoch or the 'Bluebeard murderer', these 'opportunities' were vulnerable women. In the thirteen years between 1892 and 1905, Hoch is believed to have bigamously married and then killed more than fifty women. His method was to befriend 'marriageable widows or divorced women with money', slowly poison them with arsenic and then benefit from their wills or insurance schemes.

His first victim was probably Caroline Hoch, whom he had married in April 1895. After her death, Hoch (calling himself Jacob Huff) staged a fake suicide. He pretended to drown himself in the Ohio River, when in reality he was dumping his victim's internal organs, something detectives did not discover until they exhumed Caroline's body to test for poisons years later. It was only when Hoch got careless following the murder of Marie Walcker (unknown–1905) in Chicago that the police managed to catch him, tracking him down to rooms in New York. He protested his innocence right up to the morning of his execution. ∎

Above. THREE OF THE MANY WIVES OF THE BIGAMIST JOHANN HOCH; THESE ALL SURVIVED HIM.

Below. MRS EMELIE FISHER HOCH, PHOTOGRAPHED OUTSIDE THE COURTHOUSE AT THE TRIAL OF JOHANN HOCH IN 1905.

① NEW YORK CITY, NY.
JOHANN HOCH WAS ALLEGED TO HAVE MURDERED TWO WOMEN, AND SWINDLED MORE, HERE.

② CHICAGO, IL.
JOHANN HOCH WAS ALLEGED TO HAVE MURDERED SEVEN WOMEN, AND SWINDLED MORE, HERE.

③ MILWAUKEE, WI.
JOHANN HOCH WAS ALLEGED TO HAVE MURDERED FOUR WOMEN, AND SWINDLED MORE, HERE.

④ WHEELING, WV.
JOHANN HOCH WAS ALLEGED TO HAVE MURDERED A WOMAN HERE.

⑨ JERSEY CITY, NJ.
JOHANN HOCH WAS ALLEGED TO HAVE MARRIED AND SWINDLED A WOMAN HERE.

⑩ BUFFALO, NY.
JOHANN HOCH WAS ALLEGED TO HAVE MURDERED A WOMAN HERE.

⑪ NORFOLK, VA.
JOHANN HOCH WAS ALLEGED TO HAVE MURDERED A WOMAN HERE.

⑫ COLUMBUS, OH.
JOHANN HOCH WAS ALLEGED TO HAVE MARRIED AND SWINDLED A WOMAN HERE.

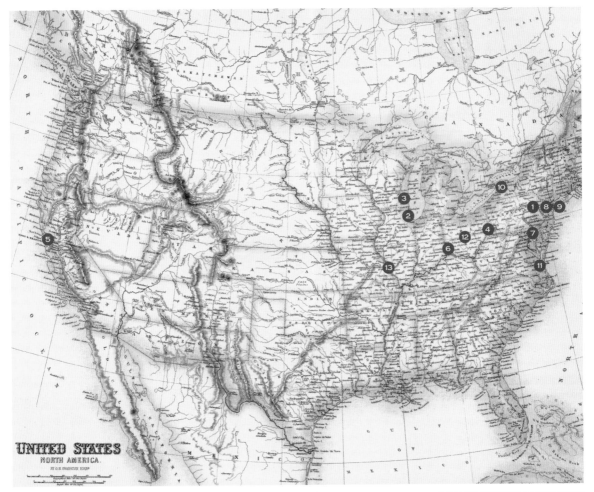

Above. JOHANN HOCH (ARROWED)
ENTERING A POLICE WAGON IN NEW
YORK FOR HIS RETURN TO CHICAGO
TO FACE PROSECUTION FOR MURDER.

Above. JOHANN HOCH IS LED INTO
THE COURT BUILDING TO FACE
TRIAL FOR HIS LIFE.

Above. A COURT PHOTOGRAPH OF JOHANN HOCH
(CENTRE) AT HIS MURDER TRIAL.

5

SAN FRANCISCO, CA.
JOHANN HOCH WAS ALLEGED TO
HAVE MURDERED FIVE WOMEN,
AND SWINDLED MORE, HERE.

6

CINCINNATI, OH.
JOHANN HOCH WAS ALLEGED TO
HAVE MURDERED ONE WOMAN,
AND SWINDLED MORE, HERE.

7

BALTIMORE, MD.
JOHANN HOCH WAS ALLEGED
TO HAVE MURDERED A WOMAN,
AND SWINDLED MORE, HERE.

8

WILLIAMSBURG, NY.
JOHANN HOCH IS ALLEGED
TO HAVE MARRIED AND
SWINDLED A WOMAN HERE.

13

ST LOUIS, MO.
JOHANN HOCH IS ALLEGED TO
HAVE MARRIED AND SWINDLED
A WOMAN HERE.

THOMAS JENNINGS.
× *Clarence B. Hiller.*

WEAPON.	TYPOLOGY.	POLICING.
PISTOL.	PROPERTY CRIME.	FINGERPRINTING.

WEST 104TH STREET, WASHINGTON HEIGHTS.

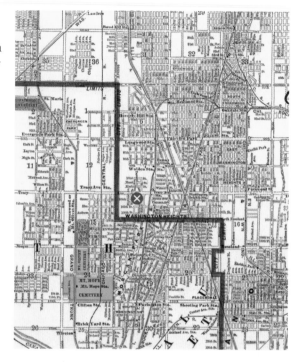

'When Thomas Jennings, a paroled convict on burglary bent, left the marks of his fingers on the freshly painted porch of the Hiller residence early on the morning of 19 September [1910], he unknowingly wrote his own death sentence as plainly as if he had signed that sentence in his own handwriting,' wrote the *Chicago Examiner* in November 1910.

Jennings (unknown–1912) had broken into Clarence Hiller's (unknown–1910) home, disturbing his wife and family while they slept. Alerted by his daughter's screams, Hiller confronted Jennings and was shot dead as they grappled. Arrested by police in the aftermath, Jennings gave a false name (Jones), but when his fingerprints were taken they matched prints left at the scene of the crime. This was the first occasion on which fingerprint evidence secured a conviction in a murder case in the United States. It was a major breakthrough for the Chicago Bureau of Identification, which had adopted Alphonse Bertillon's (1853–1914) pioneering system. Jennings spent two years on death row, before being hanged on 16 February 1912. ∎

Below. THOMAS JENNINGS'S FINGERPRINTS.

Below. THOMAS JENNINGS (AKA BOB JONES), PHOTOGRAPHED IN 1910.

Above. MAP SHOWING THE LOCATION OF 104TH STREET, WHERE THOMAS JENNINGS MURDERED CLARENCE HILLER.

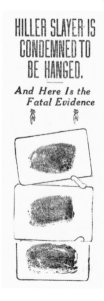

HILLER SLAYER IS CONDEMNED TO BE HANGED.

And Here Is the Fatal Evidence

1 THE FRONT DOOR.
THE POINT AT WHICH THOMAS
JENNINGS ENTERED THE HILLER
RESIDENCE, LEAVING HIS
FINGERPRINTS ON THE
FRONT DOOR.

2 THE UPSTAIRS LANDING.
THE LOCATION OF THE STRUGGLE
BETWEEN THOMAS JENNINGS
AND CLARENCE HILLER, AFTER
CLARENCE HILLER WAS AWOKEN
BY HIS DAUGHTER'S SCREAMS.

3 THE FOOT OF THE STAIRS.
THE LOCATION WHERE THOMAS
JENNINGS SHOT CLARENCE
HILLER.

4 WINDOW.
THE WINDOW THROUGH
WHICH THOMAS JENNINGS
MADE HIS ESCAPE.

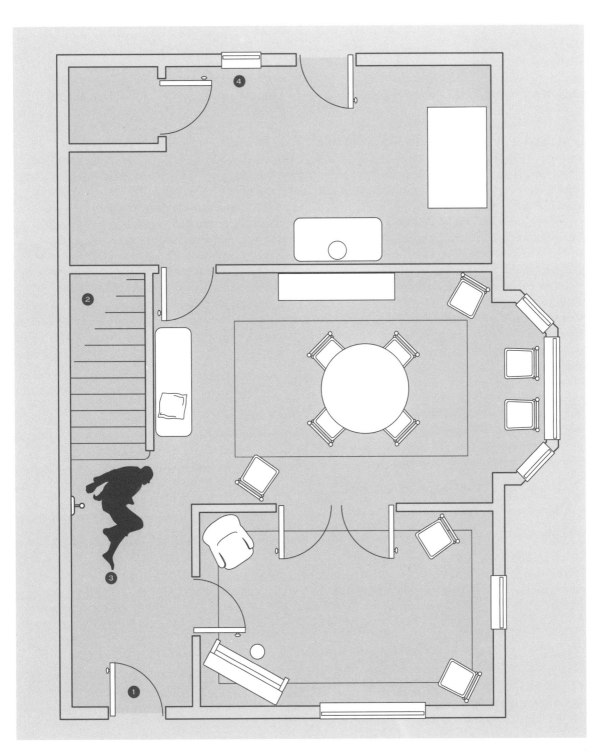

WILLIAM C. QUANTRILL.
× *40.* +

WEAPON. FIREPOWER.	TYPOLOGY. POLITICAL.	POLICING. N/A.

LAWRENCE, DOUGLAS COUNTY.

In August 1863, the United States was at war with itself. The Civil War between the Confederate south and the Union north had raged for nearly two and a half years, dividing families and friends. For many, the war – with slavery at its heart – was ideological, while for others it presented opportunities for revenge, criminality and personal gain. One such individual was William Quantrill (1837–65), a Confederate guerrilla leader who provided inspiration for several post-war Wild West outlaws, including Frank (1843–1915) and Jesse (1847–82) James who served with him. Quantrill's 'raiders' delighted in hunting escaped slaves and attacking Union patrols and camps, and so by 1863 he had been commissioned as a captain in the Confederate army.

Quantrill had previously lived in the town of Lawrence in Kansas, a place synonymous with abolitionism. It was also the centre for the pro-Union vigilante Jayhawkers, who, like Quantrill's men, raided the plantations and homes of their enemies. In August 1863, prompted by the death of several female Confederate prisoners held in jail at Kansas City, Quantrill and 350 raiders set off to attack Lawrence. With their ranks swollen by Confederate recruits and assorted volunteers,

around 450 of them hit the town on 21 August. In a furious and violent raid, Quantrill's men 'began a three-hour orgy of killing', one that left 150 dead and many more wounded, many just young lads. Although the raiders were careful not to kill or abuse any women in Lawrence, scant regard was paid to anyone else as they set fire to occupied buildings, robbed businesses and destroyed all the newspaper offices in the town. Only one of the attackers was killed: a lapsed Baptist preacher who passed out after drinking himself stupid was captured and publicly stoned to death as his naked body was drawn through the town by a freed slave on horseback. In the aftermath, Quantrill led his men south to Texas to wait out the furious reaction of the Union's own vigilantes who went in search of those responsible. He died in 1865 in Kentucky, from wounds sustained in a later raid. ∎

> *Below.* THE 1,588 SURVIVORS OF THE LAWRENCE MASSACRE PHOTOGRAPHED ON THE MAIN STREET; 150 OR MORE LOCALS DIED IN WILLIAM C. QUANTRILL'S RAID. ↓

① MILLER HOUSE.
THE HOUSE WHERE THE RAIDERS KILLED THEIR FIRST VICTIM.

② 11TH STREET.
FROM HERE THE RAIDERS SENT AN OBSERVATION SQUAD TO MOUNT OREAD.

③ NEW HAMPSHIRE STREET.
ON THIS STREET SEVENTEEN MEN WERE KILLED BY THE RAIDERS.

④ ELDRIDGE HOUSE.
THE HOUSE WAS PLUNDERED AND BURNT BY THE RAIDERS.

⑤ A WOODEN BRIDGE.
THE RAIDERS USED THE BRIDGE TO CROSS INTO WEST LAWRENCE.

⑥ 7TH STREET.
FOUR PROMINENT CITIZENS WERE SHOT BY THE RAIDERS ON THIS STREET.

⑦ 743 INDIANA STREET.
A BOARDING HOUSE WAS SPARED BY THE RAIDERS ON THIS STREET.

⑧ OHIO STREET.
THE STREET WHERE MR BELL LIVED, WHO WAS MURDERED BY RAIDERS.

⑨ VANTAGE POINT.
FROM HERE THE RAIDERS' SCOUTS COULD SURVEY LAWRENCE CITY.

⑩ THE GOSS HOUSE, 21ST STREET.
A HOUSE WHERE CITIZENS HID DURING THE RAID.

⑪ PIONEER CEMETERY.
THE CEMETERY WHERE THE VICTIMS WERE FIRST BURIED.

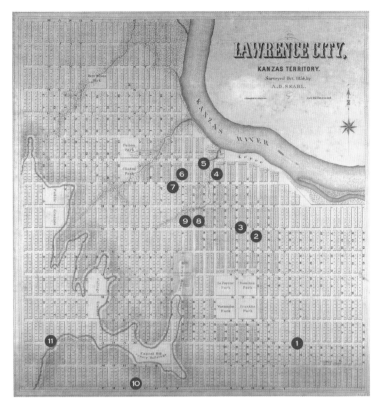

Right. ELDRIDGE HOUSE IN LAWRENCE WAS LOOTED AND BURNT BY THE RAIDERS.

THE BENDER FAMILY.
× *20.* +

WEAPON. KNIFE & HAMMER.	TYPOLOGY. PROPERTY CRIME.	POLICING. MANHUNT.

THE BENDER FARM, CHERRYVILLE.

JOHN BENDER, SR.

ELVIRA BENDER.

JOHN BENDER, JR.

KATE BENDER.

Between 1861 and 1865, the United States tore itself apart as brother fought brother in an epic struggle to determine the future of the Union. A new America now emerged as settlers moved west to seek new land and opportunities. Under the Homestead Acts, any citizen could acquire land they were intent on improving, effectively granting them licence to take Native American land. Postbellum Kansas became home to many Civil War veterans, seeking peace and prosperity after the horrors of war. In 1870, it also became home to the Bender family, European immigrants who settled close to the growing community of Cherryville and brought a new horror with them. John (dates unknown) and Elvira Bender (dates unknown) spoke little English, relying mostly on their grown-up children – Kate (dates unknown) and John (dates unknown) – to communicate with local people. Despite being seen as outsiders, the Benders soon established their homestead – a small one-room cabin, divided by a simple wagon cloth – as a crude stop-off point for travellers heading through Kansas.

Then, in the spring of 1873, Dr William Henry York (unknown–1873) arrived at the cabin seeking a bed for the night. He was heading back to the town of Independence but he never arrived.

There had already been dark rumours in the neighbourhood about the Bender cabin and the disappearance of guests there, but until March 1873, no one seems to have been prepared to investigate. Dr York was well connected, though, and his brothers, one a colonel in the US Army, the other a Kansas state senator, organized a search.

The Benders were soon implicated in York's disappearance and Elvira reacted badly to this, screaming abuse at the men who came to the cabin to investigate. A few weeks later, it was noticed that the homestead had been abandoned; the Benders had fled. The building was searched, and several buried bodies were discovered. It seemed clear that the Benders had lulled their guests with food and drink before knocking them unconscious and cutting their throats. As a guest sat with his back to the wagon cloth, one of the men would hit him with a hammer and drag the body to the cellar to be finished off by Kate or Elvira.

None of the Benders were ever successfully prosecuted for the murder of Dr York or any of the other nineteen people the family were collectively suspected of murdering. There are many myths about the Benders: two women, believed to be Kate and Elvira, were tried at Oswego, Kansas, in 1890, but there was insufficient proof to convict them. Another story claims that a posse tracked down the family and summarily executed them, throwing their bodies into a river. Alternatively, the Benders were killed by vigilantes and buried in an unmarked grave. No one has ever claimed the reward offered for their capture, and the Benders' plot is said to be haunted to this day. ∎

Above. A KNIFE FOUND ON THE BENDERS' PROPERTY DURING THE INVESTIGATION.

Above. A SIDE VIEW OF THE BENDERS' CABIN ON THE ROAD OUTSIDE CHERRYVILLE.

Centre. THE FRONT VIEW OF THE BENDER INN, WITH SEVERAL LOCAL PEOPLE PRESENT FOLLOWING THE FAMILY'S FLIGHT.

Below. EXCAVATING THE BENDER LAND AS INVESTIGATORS SEARCH FOR BODIES.

Opposite. THE THREE HAMMERS USED BY THE BENDERS TO MURDER THEIR GUESTS.

Photographed by Julius Plootz
May 9th 187

McCortys Grave.

Old Well. Sconces Grave.

Browns Grave.

McKinneys Grave.

Darks Grave.

Soncher and
Little girls grave.

South West View

G. K. Gamble
Photographer
Parsons. Kan

Right. MAP SHOWING THE
LOCATION OF THE BODIES
FOUND ON THE BENDER FARM.

 JOHN GEARY.

 W. F. MCCROTTY.

③ JOHN NEWTON LONGCOR &
HIS BABY GIRL.

④ JOHNNY BOYLE.

⑤ BEN BROWN.

⑥ HARRY MCKENZIE.

⑦ DR YORK.

⑧ FIVE UNIDENTIFIED BODIES
FOUND IN DRUM CREEK.

⑨ TWO UNIDENTIFIED BODIES
FOUND IN THE PRAIRIE.

⑩ TWO UNIDENTIFIED BODIES &
ASSORTED BODY PARTS ALSO
FOUND IN THE ORCHARD.

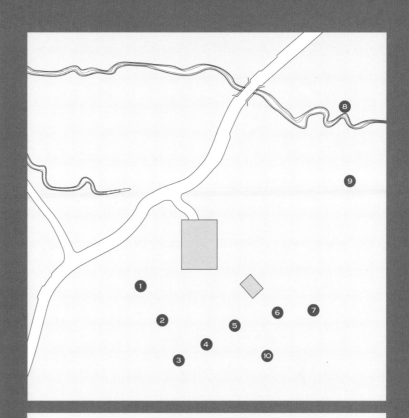

Right. FLOOR PLAN OF
THE BENDER CABIN.

✗
THE SPOT JOHN BENDER SR.
STOOD BEHIND THE CANVAS SHEET
TO STRIKE HIS VICTIMS.

✗
THE SEAT VISITORS TO THE
BENDER CABIN TOOK BEFORE
BEING KILLED FROM BEHIND.

Opposite above. INVESTIGATORS
POSE FOR A PHOTOGRAPH BEHIND
THE GRAVES OF SEVERAL VICTIMS.

Opposite below. A PHOTOGRAPH BY
G. R. GAMBLE SHOWING SEVERAL
GRAVES WHERE THE BENDERS'
VICTIMS COULD BE IDENTIFIED.

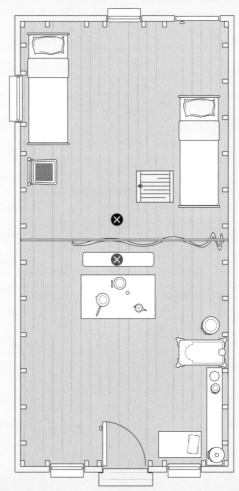

HENRY NEWTON BROWN.
× *E. W. Payne.* × *George Geppert.*

WEAPON.	TYPOLOGY.	POLICING.
REVOLVER.	PROPERTY CRIME.	POSSE.

MEDICINE LODGE, BARBER COUNTY.

When the citizens of Caldwell, Kansas, appointed Henry Newton Brown (1857–84) as their marshal, they believed they had secured one of the fastest gunmen around. Caldwell, a frontier cattle town like Dodge City, was dangerously lawless. It took many months, but Brown's ruthless approach to law and order transformed the place into a relatively quiet backwater.

Marshal Brown may have been genuine in his desire to clean up Caldwell, but he was less than transparent about his personal history. As a member of John Tunstall's (1853–78) 'Regulators', Brown had fought alongside Billy the Kid (1859–81) in the Lincoln County War in New Mexico. He later switched sides, serving as a lawman in Texas, but did not last long there, drifting through various places before ending up in Caldwell.

Brown comes down through history and folklore as a complex character: part Wild West outlaw anti-hero, part violent and self-interested chancer. In April 1884, Brown left Caldwell in the company of his assistant, Ben Wheeler (unknown–1884), and two cowboys: William Smith (unknown–1884) and John Wesley (unknown–1884). It seems that Brown had reverted to his old outlaw ways and decided to pull off a large heist. The gang rode to Medicine Lodge in Barber County, just west of Wichita. There, they tried to rob a local bank, but the raid went spectacularly wrong. The bank had just opened when the men arrived; they walked into the bank and demanded money. The president of the bank, E. W. Payne (unknown–1884), was shot as he reached for his revolver, and despite throwing up his hands in surrender the chief cashier George Geppert (unknown–1884) was also shot. However, he managed to pull the door of the vault shut behind him before he expired.

Brown and his men fled the scene with a local posse in hot pursuit. They were cornered in a box canyon and, after a fierce fire fight that reportedly lasted two hours, were captured and dragged back to Medicine Lodge to face the fury of the enraged inhabitants. In the Wild West, the chance of a fair trial was a distant hope for men like Brown and Wheeler, and the quartet faced the very real prospect of being lynched by the mob. Brown wrote a long letter to his wife admitting his attempt to rob the bank but denying murder. In reality, we do not know who shot whom but Brown had a long history of killing, even if some of his victims were killed when he was a marshal.

Brown did not want to die on the end of a rope, though, and when the citizens of Medicine Lodge broke into the county jail to string the robbers up, Brown and his men tried to force their way out. Three of the men were wounded but survived long enough to be hanged. Brown escaped the noose but only because he was almost cut in half by the blast of a shotgun fired at point-blank range. With that, the story of Henry Brown, poacher turned gamekeeper, ended in a suitably 'Western' style. ∎

① CALDWELL. THE TOWN IN WHICH HENRY NEWTON BROWN SERVED AS MARSHAL.

② MEDICINE LODGE. THE TOWN IN WHICH THE BANK ROBBERY TOOK PLACE.

Right. ASSISTANT MARSHAL'S BADGE FROM CALDWELL, KANSAS. HENRY NEWTON BROWN WAS APPOINTED MARSHAL AFTER HAVING FIRST SERVED AS ASSISTANT MARSHAL FOR FIVE MONTHS.

Right. BEN WHEELER'S SINGLE-ACTION COLT REVOLVER, POSSIBLY USED IN THE BANK HEIST.

Right. A HANGMAN'S NOOSE FROM MEDICINE LODGE, OF THE TYPE USED TO DESPATCH OUTLAWS LIKE WILLIAM SMITH AND BEN WHEELER.

Above. A CROWDED STREET IN CALDWELL WHERE HENRY NEWTON BROWN SERVED AS MARSHAL.

Above. THE BANK IN MEDICINE LODGE THAT HENRY NEWTON BROWN'S GANG ATTEMPTED TO ROB.

Above. AN INTERIOR SHOT OF THE BANK, FEATURING A TELLER AND ANOTHER MEMBER OF STAFF.

Above. THE SITE OF THE GUNFIGHT BETWEEN HENRY NEWTON BROWN'S GANG AND THE POSSE.

Above. THE HEAVILY ARMED POSSE THAT HUNTED DOWN
HENRY NEWTON BROWN AND HIS GANG.

Below. THE INTERIOR OF THE MEDICINE LODGE BANK,
WITH A CUSTOMER STANDING BY THE TELLER'S WINDOW.

Above. THE MEDICINE POSSE SHOWING OFF THEIR CHAINED
AND BOUND CAPTIVES, INCLUDING HENRY NEWTON BROWN.

Below. THE MEDICINE VALLEY BANK WHERE THE ILL-FATED
ROBBERY ATTEMPT TOOK PLACE.

LAURA FAIR.
✕ *Alexander Parker Crittenden.*

WEAPON.	TYPOLOGY.	POLICING.
PISTOL.	DOMESTIC.	N/A.

SAN FRANCISCO FERRY, OAKLAND.

A criminal psychologist familiar with Laura Fair's (1837–1919) life history would probably have warned the authorities that she was a potentially dangerous individual. In 1859, she had married her third husband, Colonel W. B. Fair (unknown–1861), having been widowed and divorced previously. The colonel only lasted two years, killing himself in 1861. During the Civil War, she attempted to shoot a Northern soldier, but missed. She also took aim at a man who insulted her. He too survived, but the pattern was set. She had another short-lived marriage in 1870 before she met Alexander Crittenden (1816–70), a San Francisco lawyer. He and Laura became close and she hoped for another wedding, but Crittenden was already married; he had just neglected to tell her. When he went to meet his wife and family as they returned from a trip, Fair rushed up to him, produced a pistol and shot him in the chest. Initially, Fair was convicted and sentenced to death, but at a second trial she was acquitted on fairly self-evident grounds of emotional instability. ∎

Below. TWO VIEWS OF THE *EL CAPITAIN* STEAMER BOAT THAT ALEXANDER CRITTENDEN WAS TRAVELLING ON WHEN LAURA FAIR SHOT HIM.

1
SHASTA, CA.
THE TOWN WHERE LAURA MET AND MARRIED HER THIRD HUSBAND, WILLIAM FAIR.

2
SAN FRANCISCO, CA.
THE CITY WILLIAM AND LAURA FAIR MOVED TO, AND WHERE WILLIAM COMMITTED SUICIDE.

3
SACRAMENTO, CA.
THE CITY LAURA FAIR AND HER MOTHER MOVED TO AND SET UP A BOARDING HOUSE.

4
VIRGINIA CITY, NV.
THE CITY WHERE LAURA FAIR SET UP A NEW BOARDING HOUSE AND MET ALEXANDER CRITTENDEN.

5
SAN FRANCISCO, CA.
THE CITY WHERE LAURA FAIR CONTINUED HER AFFAIR WITH ALEXANDER CRITTENDEN.

6
OAKLAND, CA.
THE CITY WHERE LAURA FAIR MURDERED ALEXANDER CRITTENDEN.

UNKNOWN.
× *8.*

WEAPON. GUNPOWDER.	TYPOLOGY. POLITICAL.	POLICING. N/A.

CURTIN BOARDING HOUSE, MAIN STREET, THE EAST CUT.

At midnight on 24 September 1893, a small suitcase containing explosives was detonated outside Johnny Curtin's (dates unknown) boarding house on Main Street. The explosion left six people dead and several others wounded, two of whom eventually succumbed to their injuries. Among the dead was Curtin's son, who had discovered the valise and shouted to warn his mates. The 'outrage' was immediately blamed on sailors who had been striking since 1891 after bosses had imposed a 25 per cent pay cut. One sailor, John Tyrell (dates unknown), was arrested and tried but cleared of any guilt. In the aftermath of the blast, the Sailor's Union of the Pacific offered a $1,000 reward for information leading to the conviction of the actual culprit. They suggested the bomb had been placed by ship owners themselves, to undermine the sailors' dispute, or by their allies, the 'crimps and boarding masters' who worked the San Francisco seafront. The union's head, Andrew Furuseth (1854–1938), wrote that 'like a clap of thunder from the clear sky came the dynamite outrage setting the whole city against us', adding, 'We are innocent.' ∎

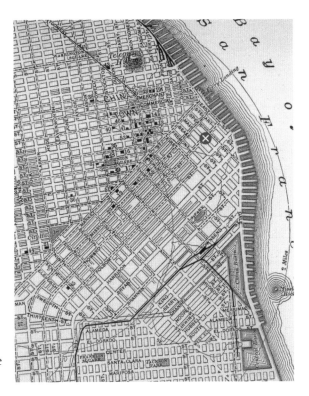

Above. MAP SHOWING THE LOCATION ON MAIN STREET OF JOHNNY CURTIN'S BOARDING HOUSE WHERE THE EXPLOSION TOOK PLACE.

Left. A NEWSPAPER SKETCH OF THE DAMAGE CAUSED BY THE BOMB IN JOHNNY CURTIN'S BOARDING HOUSE.

Right. THE 'DEADLY ENGINES OF THE AUTHORS OF THE EXPLOSION': NITROGLYCERIN, IGNITION CAPS AND FUSES.

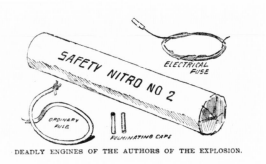

DEADLY ENGINES OF THE AUTHORS OF THE EXPLOSION.

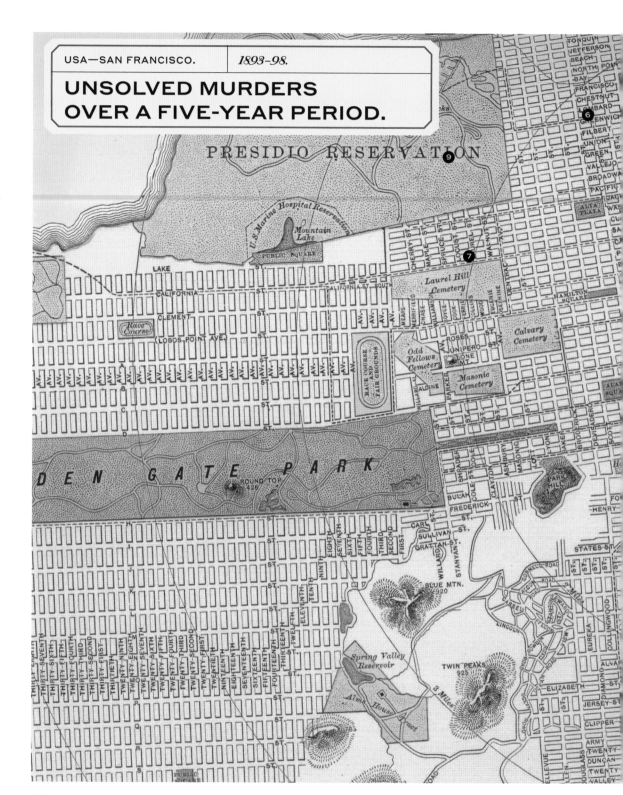

UNSOLVED MURDERS OVER A FIVE-YEAR PERIOD.

❶ 1893. CURTIN'S BOARDING HOUSE, MAIN STREET. Unknown. × EIGHT MEN.

❷ 1894. DRUGSTORE, ST NICHOLAS HOTEL, LARKIN STREET. Unknown. × EUGENE WARE.

❸ 1895. CHINATOWN. Unknown. × J. B. FOREMAN.

❹ 1895. LODGING HOUSE, 1017 ELLIS STREET. Unknown. × ELLEN HARRINGTON.

❺ 1895. EAST STREET. Unknown. × ROBERT MOREHEAD.

❻ 1895. GROCERY STORE, GREENWICH STREET. Unknown. × A. NEVILLE.

❼ 1895. LAUREL HILL. Unknown. × JENNIE MATTHEWS.

8 1895. FOLSOM STREET. Unknown. × CHARLES KOELING.

9 1895. MORTON STREET. Unknown. × MAY MCDERMOTT.

10 1895. ST MARY STREET. Unknown. × BERTHA PARADIS.

11 1896. FOURTH STREET. Unknown. × JOSEPH MANNING.

12 1897. CHINATOWN. Unknown. × LITTLE PETE.

13 1898. KEARNEY STREET. Unknown. × J. H. DOW.

14 1898. 310 WASHINGTON STREET. Unknown. × JEONG YING CHOW.

WILLIAM HENRY THEODORE DURRANT.
× *Blanche Lamont.* × *Minnie Williams.*

WEAPON.	TYPOLOGY.	POLICING.
KNIFE.	SEXUAL.	EARLY FORENSICS.

EMMANUEL BAPTIST CHURCH, 21ST STREET, MISSION DISTRICT.

| WILLIAM HENRY DURRANT. | BLANCHE LAMONT. | MINNIE WILLIAMS. |

In early April 1895, 21-year-old Blanche Lamont (1873–95) disappeared. The young Montana student had moved to San Francisco in 1894 to train to be a teacher. There she met William Henry Theodore Durrant (1871–98), the handsome leader of the Christian Endeavor Society at the nearby Baptist church. Durrant was studying medicine, and he and Blanche developed a romantic connection. He soon proposed but Blanche rejected him, not believing him to be serious. She proved correct, because she quickly discovered he had been seeing someone else and ended the relationship. In fact, Durrant, despite his social awkwardness, was rarely short of female company and had been dating another young churchgoer, Minnie Williams (1873–95), while seeing Blanche. However, on 3 April 1895, Durrant and Blanche were seemingly reconciled and were seen together in good spirits on a San Francisco cable car. One parishioner later saw the pair enter the Emmanuel Baptist church, but saw neither of them leave. This was the last time Blanche was seen alive and Durrant joined in the frantic search for her.

On 13 April, members of the Emmanuel Baptist church congregation made a shocking discovery. The body of a young woman was found lying in a closet in the library: she had been strangled and her underwear had been roughly shoved into her throat with a stick. The girl had been stabbed and horribly mutilated, with cuts to her face and arms. The slashes to her wrists were so deep that her hands were almost cut away. She had also been raped. This was a brutal act, displaying anger and sexual frustration on a shocking scale. Initial fears that this was Blanche Lamont were dismissed when the identity of the cadaver was confirmed as Minnie Williams, Durrant's sometime paramour. He now became the chief suspect and as police searched the church for more clues they found another body, in the belfry. In contrast to the brutal treatment of Williams's body, this time the killer had carefully positioned the corpse so that it was laid out like a statue, calm and at rest. This *was* Blanche, and she had been stripped naked, with her arms folded neatly across her chest. She, too, had been raped and strangled but was otherwise unblemished.

That same day, her mother received a parcel in the post containing three rings that belonged to her daughter. The police traced them to a San Francisco pawnshop where the owner gave a detailed description of a man who had tried to sell them; the description matched Durrant.

Durrant was a poor witness in his own defence. Medical and police forensic evidence was heard that connected him to the crime, and his own testimony was evasive and full of contradictions. It took the jury less than five minutes to convict him (although for form's sake they delayed their return for a little longer, finishing their cigars before delivering their verdict). Durrant – the 'demon of the belfry' – went to his death on 7 January 1898. He protested his innocence to the last, but it seems pretty clear that this man, who had been rejected by the woman that he had determined to marry, had exacted a terrible and unforgivable revenge on both her and another entirely innocent young woman. ∎

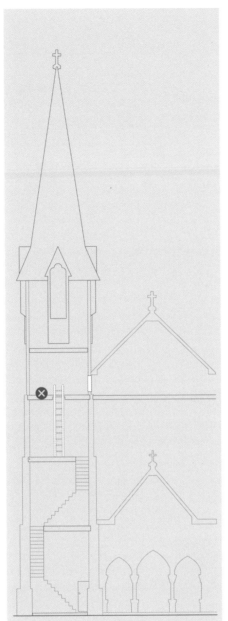

Left. CROSS SECTION OF THE CHURCH BELFRY SHOWING WHERE BLANCHE LAMONT'S BODY WAS FOUND.

Right. MUG SHOT OF DURRANT IN HIS OWN CLOTHES (ABOVE) AND IN HIS PRISON UNIFORM (BELOW).

Opposite left. THE EXTERIOR OF EMMANUEL BAPTIST CHURCH, SAN FRANCISCO.

Opposite centre. THE INTERIOR OF EMMANUEL BAPTIST CHURCH, SAN FRANCISCO.

Opposite right. BLOOD SPATTERS ON THE WALL WHERE MINNIE WILLIAMS WAS DISCOVERED.

Below left. THE BELFRY STEPS WHERE BLANCHE LAMONT'S BODY WAS POSED BY THE KILLER.

Below centre. THE CHURCH SUNDAY SCHOOL ROOMS.

Below right. EVIDENCE USED AT THE TRIAL TO SHOW THAT SOMEONE RIDING A CABLE CAR MAY BE RECOGNIZED BY SOMEONE ON THE PAVEMENT.

JAMES C. DUNHAM.
× *6.*

WEAPON.	TYPOLOGY.	POLICING.
GUN & AXE.	RECKLESS ACT.	N/A.

MCGLINCY RANCH, CAMPBELL, SANTA CLARA.

On 27 May 1896, neighbours raced towards the sound of gunshots emanating from Colonel Richard McGlincy's (1840–96) ranch on the outskirts of Campbell in Santa Clara County, California. There, they found the colonel dead in his own front yard before discovering his wife, Ada (1843–96), stepdaughter, Hattie Dunham (1871–96), and stepson, James Wells (1874–96), alongside two servants, Minnie Shesler (1868–96) and Robert Briscoe (1846–96): they had all been either shot or hacked to death with an axe. The only McGlincy to be spared was Hattie's infant son, Percy. Another survivor, George Schaeble (dates unknown), a ranch hand, had taken cover in the barn and thus avoided the massacre.

Suspicion immediately fell on James Dunham (dates unknown), the colonel's son-in-law who was seen riding away on his brother-in-law's saddleless horse. The county sheriff's investigation worked to put together the case against Dunham, even though he was still on the run.

The law student had picked up a bicycle tyre from a shop on the day of the murders and his behaviour had not given the storekeeper any cause for concern. Dunham was known to have a temper, however, something he had supposedly inherited from his mother. Could this explain why he had butchered six people, three of them women, in such a horrific manner, seemingly without any reason? Dunham had killed and mutilated his mother's chickens when he was 31. Then, in 1893, he had attacked a co-worker on a farm at Chico, nearly killing him. After he was sacked for this assault, he declared he wished he had killed the man and apparently boasted that he could easily have made it look like an accident.

After the McGlincy massacre, several people spoke of Dunham as 'a man [with a] violent and ungovernable temper'. Schaeble reported an angry row between Dunham and the servant girl, Minnie Shesler, on the day of the murders. Those who knew the family and knew Dunham suggested that the McGlincys treated him 'something terrible' and that Hattie's mother (Ada) was hoping to force a divorce. It may even have been the case that Dunham simply intended to confront the family and take Hattie away, but things went badly wrong – he lost his temper and went berserk – meaning the killing of his wife was a tragic accident. Regardless of motive, it seemed clear to everyone that Dunham was responsible for the killings. However, he remained at large despite a substantial reward being offered and a posse being dispatched to hunt him down. A wanted poster was circulated with a photograph and description, and both the horse he took and his abandoned bicycle was uncovered near the McGlincy ranch, but no one was ever caught and prosecuted. Dunham had withdrawn all the funds from his bank account, perhaps as much as $20,000, and vanished, never to be seen again. ∎

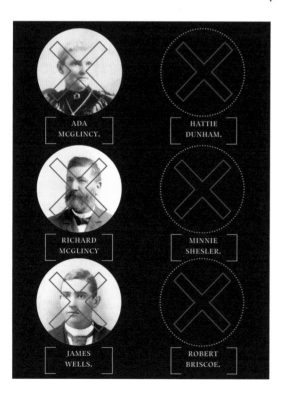

Below. THE SIX VICTIMS OF JAMES C. DUNHAM, KILLED ON THE MCGLINCY RANCH.

ADA MCGLINCY.

HATTIE DUNHAM.

RICHARD MCGLINCY.

MINNIE SHESLER.

JAMES WELLS.

ROBERT BRISCOE.

Right. THE MCGLINCY RANCH.
GEORGE SCHAEBLE HID IN
THE BARN ON THE RIGHT AND
SURVIVED THE MASSACRE.

Right. MAP SHOWING THE
LOCATION OF THE MCGLINCY
RANCH IN CAMPBELL,
SANTA CLARA.

 THE MCGLINCY RESIDENCE.
THE HOUSE WHERE THE
MCGLINCYS LIVED, AND WHERE
THE FIRST FIVE VICTIMS
WERE KILLED.

 THE BARN.
THE BARN FROM WHICH GEORGE
SCHAEBLE WATCHED THE MURDER
OF COLONEL MCGLINCY.

 THE CABIN.
THE CABIN WHERE COLONEL
MCGLINCY TRIED TO SEEK REFUGE.

④ THE FARMYARD.
THE PLACE IN THE YARD WHERE
COLONEL MCGLINCY'S MURDERED
BODY WAS FOUND.

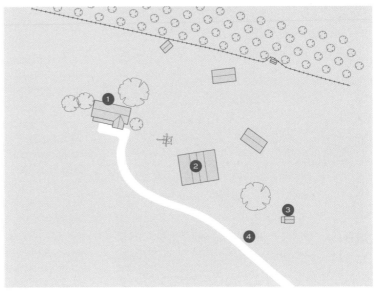

CHARLES B. HADLEY.
× *Nora Fuller.*

WEAPON.	TYPOLOGY.	POLICING.
UNKNOWN.	SEXUAL.	GRAPHOLOGY.

2211 SUTTER STREET, WESTERN ADDITION.

The killing of 15-year-old Nora Fuller (1887–1902) remains unsolved to this day. In January 1902, Nora (born Eleanor Parline) disappeared after supposedly going for a job interview at the Popular Restaurant on Geary Street, San Francisco. Her naked body, strangled and demonstrating signs of rape, was discovered ten days later in an empty apartment at 2211 Sutter Street, close to the home of her best friend Madge Graham (dates unknown). Nora had apparently gone to meet a man named John Bennett, who had advertised the position f a nanny. Nora, or someone sounding like Nora, had phoned home to say the man she had met wanted her to start work immediately, at a building nearby at 1500 Geary Street. Nora's 12-year-old brother had answered the call.

When he conveyed his sister's message, their mother called out for her to come home directly, adding whatever the job was it could wait until the following week. The caller agreed, but sounded distressed and nervous. That was the last time anyone heard from Nora.

Madge told the police that Nora had been seeing a man named Bennett in secret and the advert was probably part of their secret liaison, an elaborate ruse to allow the couple to meet away from the prying eyes of her family. There was no business at 1500 Geary Street anyway, and the mystery deepened as the police made a more thorough search of the crime scene. At Sutter Street, detectives found evidence linking the property to a person named C. B. Hawkins. Moreover, a furniture company had recently delivered a mattress to the address, ordered by a Mr C. B. Hawkins. C. B. Hadley (dates unknown) was a journalist working for the *Examiner* and he disappeared soon after the murder was discovered. Could he, Hawkins and Bennett be the same person? The police, led by Detective Charles Cody (dates unknown), clearly believed it was possible. A comparison of Hadley's handwriting with that of the mysterious Mr Hawkins revealed a match. Unfortunately, despite their efforts, the police never caught Hadley and it is rumoured that he committed suicide.

Hadley was not the only person in the frame, however. Hugh Grant (dates unknown), a San Francisco lawyer, was well known to have courted Nora, despite her mother's objections. Grant had bought Nora an expensive new dress and she was said to be afraid of him. There was no evidence to tie him to the murder, however. In fact, one of the features of this case was the large number of innocent men whose names and reputations were dragged through the mud as the police and newspapers linked them to the murder. In all of this, the role of Madge Graham has to be considered. She lived close to the murder site; she knew of Nora's movements. Was she involved in her death? Sadly, we are unlikely to ever know the truth. ∎

Below. MAP SHOWING 2211 SUTTER STREET, WHERE NORA FULLER'S BODY WAS DISCOVERED.

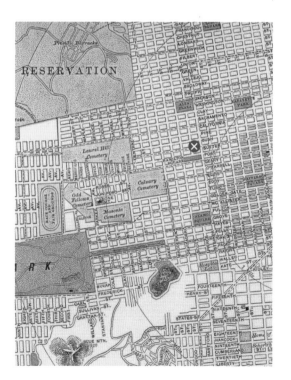

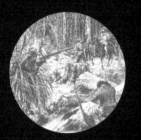

PART THREE.

ISABELLA O'BRIEN + THOMAS MEREDITH SHERIDAN + JOHN MAKIN
SARAH MAKIN + JIMMY GOVERNOR

AUSTRALIA.

NED KELLY + FREDERICK BAILEY DEEMING
FRANCES KNORR + MARTHA NEEDLE

AUSTRALIA — NSW.	*Autumn 1870.*

ISABELLA O'BRIEN.
× *Daniel O'Brien.*

WEAPON. DROWNING.	TYPOLOGY. INFANTICIDE.	POLICING. N/A.

MURRUMBIDGEE RIVER, WAGGA WAGGA.

In April 1871, Isabella O'Brien (1852–c. 1871) was put on trial at the Wagga Wagga Circuit Court accused of killing her young son Daniel (1869–70). In the late autumn of the previous year, Isabella had been seen sitting by the river, with her two sons, William (aged 4) and Daniel (aged 2). A concerned passer-by, James Bruce (dates unknown), had warned her that her boys were in danger of falling in and drowning, but she waved him away dismissively. Some weeks later, the decomposing body of a child was found in the river and Isabella was arrested. She claimed she had sent the boy away to live with a family upriver, but there was no trace of them. Her common-law partner testified that she had always struggled to cope with her two offspring and the jury decided she deliberately murdered the youngest. When the judge sentenced her to death, giving her 'no hope of mercy', Isabella hardly reacted at all. ∎

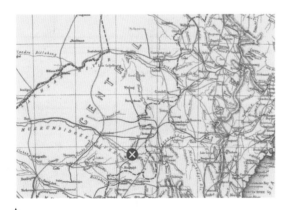

Above. MAP SHOWING WAGGA WAGGA, WHERE ISABELLA O'BRIEN KILLED HER SON DANIEL O'BRIEN.

AUSTRALIA — NSW.	*September 1895.*

THOMAS MEREDITH SHERIDAN.
× *Jessie Amelia Nicholls.*

WEAPON. ABORTION.	TYPOLOGY. ACCIDENT.	POLICING. N/A.

DUKE STREET, WOOLLOOMOOLOO BAY, SYDNEY.

When police raided the premises of the British Medical Institute in Sydney in September 1895, they uncovered an illegal abortion practice. They had been prompted by the discovery of the mutilated body of a young woman dumped at Woolloomooloo Bay days earlier. She was identified as Jessie Amelia Nicholls (1872–95), a farmer's daughter from Windsor near Parramatta, who had fallen pregnant and gone to the city to avoid shaming her family. Jessie had turned to a man calling himself 'Dr' Thomas Meredith Sheridan (1853–96), who performed abortions. However, Jessie died during the operation and Sheridan co-opted his housekeeper and a sailor named Seawell (dates unknown) to help get rid of her body. Sheridan was tried for Jessie's murder with Seawell as an accessory. The housekeeper, Mrs Chapman (dates unknown), avoided prosecution by co-operating with the police, whereas Sheridan was hanged in January 1896. ∎

Above. MAP SHOWING DUKE STREET, SYDNEY, WHERE THOMAS MEREDITH SHERIDAN KILLED JESSIE AMELIA NICHOLLS.

No. 6191   Name *Thomas Meredith Sheridan*

Date when Portrait was taken, 28 / 9 / 18 95

Native place *Sydney*
Year of birth *1853*
Arrived in { Ship
Colony { Year *86*
Trade or occupation } *Chemist*
previous to conviction }
Religion *R. Cath.*
Education, degree of *R & W*
Height *5* feet *8 3/4* inches.
Weight { On committal *146*
in lbs. { On discharge
Colour of hair *Brown*
Colour of eyes *Grey*
Marks or special features :— *Scars*
on centre of forehead
& bridge of nose.
Sabre and cupping
Scars under left
breast —

(No. of previous Portrait *3303*).

Convicted in the first instance with *William Bell & Edward D. Bae*
" " second " *John Seawell*

PREVIOUS CONVICTIONS.

Where and When.			Offence.	Sentence.
Syd CC	*19 + 25 Mch*	*'85*	*Procuring Abortion — 2 chgs*	*1st 10 years ps* *2nd 10 years ps* *5 years of the 2nd to be accumulative with the 1st (Ds from pinatta 28 Oct 92)*
Syd CC	*20 nov*	*'95*	*Murder*	*Death*
			Executed 7th January 1896	

Above. THOMAS MEREDITH SHERIDAN'S PRISON RECORD,
NOTING HIS EXECUTION ON 7 JANUARY 1896.

JOHN MAKIN & SARAH MAKIN.
✕ *Horace Murray.* ✕ *12.*

WEAPON.	TYPOLOGY.	POLICING.
UNKNOWN.	INFANTICIDE.	N/A.

BURREN STREET, MACDONALDTOWN. GEORGE STREET, REDFERN.
ALDERSON STREET, REDFERN. LEVEY STREET, CHIPPENDALE.

JOHN MAKIN.   SARAH MAKIN.

Prior to 1892 and the passage of the Children's Protection Act, the care of illegitimate children was a market open to corruption and murder. The practice of 'baby farming' – the care of children for money – was common enough in Australia and Britain and so it was not unusual for John (1845–93) and Sarah (1845–1918) Makin to adopt it.

The couple struggled financially after an accident left John unable to continue his work as a drayman. Moving around New South Wales, they took in dozens of children from desperate mothers, such as 18-year-old Amber Murray (1874–unknown). She agreed to pay the Makins 10s a week to care for her baby, Horace. Every time Amber tried to see her son, she was put off with excuses and then, when she decided to turn up at the Makins' home anyway, she discovered that they had disappeared, apparently taking her little boy with them.

In October 1892, a drainage worker undertaking underground clearance work at Burren Street, Macdonaldtown, New South Wales, found the remains of two small children. Police investigators traced the property (and the dead children) to the Makins, who were arrested. Further digging at the Makins' homes not only revealed yet more bodies but also exposed a baby-farming scandal in New South Wales. The Makins were convicted of Horace's murder on evidence given in court by their daughters, Clarice (aged 16) and Daisy (aged 11), who testified to seeing children in their parents' care, children who had subsequently vanished. In total, the Makins were believed to be responsible for twelve other murders, but the killing of Horace was enough to bring about a conviction. John was sentenced to death, but his wife was spared, being recommended to mercy by the jury. Sarah spent nineteen years in prison for her crime.

The crime had one positive outcome: it prompted the authorities to pass legislation to protect children from any future attempts by murderous couples such as the Makins to exploit the desperation of young women like Amber Murray. ∎

1

BURREN STREET,
MACDONALDTOWN.
SEVEN MURDERED BABIES
WERE FOUND HERE.

2

GEORGE STREET, REDFERN.
THREE MURDERED BABIES
WERE FOUND HERE.

3

ALDERSON STREET, REDFERN.
TWO MURDERED BABIES
WERE FOUND HERE.

4

LEVEY STREET, CHIPPENDALE.
ONE MURDERED BABY WAS
FOUND HERE.

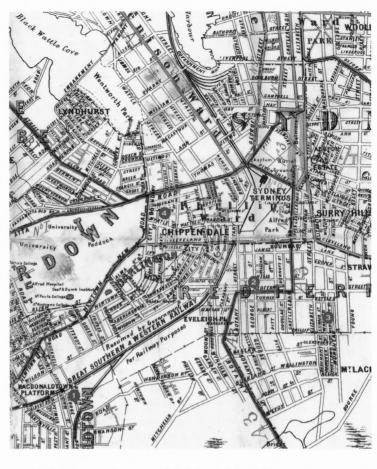

Right. PLAN OF THE BACKYARD
OF THE MAKINS' RESIDENCE
AT BURREN STREET,
MACDONALDTOWN, SHOWING
WHERE THE SEVEN BODIES
OF BABIES WERE FOUND.

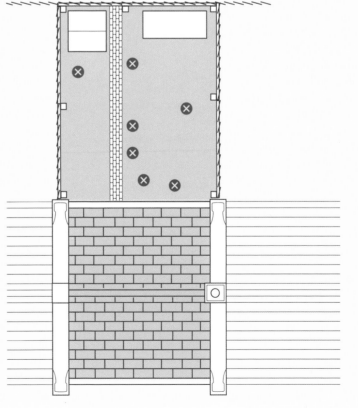

Opposite left. JOHN MAKIN'S
PRISON RECORD. IT NOTES
HIS EXECUTION ON
18 AUGUST 1893.

Opposite right. SARAH MAKIN'S
PRISON RECORD DETAILING
THE DEATH SENTENCE THAT
WAS COMMUTED TO LIFE
IMPRISONMENT.

JIMMY GOVERNOR.
× 9.

WEAPON.	TYPOLOGY.	POLICING.
TOMAHAWK & *NULLA NULLA*.	RECKLESS ACT.	MANHUNT.

BREELONG, GILGANDRA.

JIMMY GOVERNOR.

The tragedy at Breelong in New South Wales in April 1900 had its roots in prejudice and racism. Jimmy Governor (1875–1901) was an indigenous Australian who had married a 16-year-old white girl named Ethel Page (1882–1945). Jimmy and his brother Joe (1877–1900), along with other family members, were working at John Mawbey's (1849–1900) farm at Breelong. Mrs Mawbey (unknown–1900) told Ethel exactly what she thought of interracial marriages, suggesting 'that any white woman who married a black fellow ought to be shot'. Jimmy's anger got the better of him. He assaulted Sarah Mawbey, brutally killing her and three of her children as well as their schoolteacher, Helen Kerz (unknown–1900), using a tomahawk and a traditional aboriginal *nulla nulla* stick. Jimmy, his brother Joe and their friend Jack Underwood fled and a manhunt, the largest in Australian history, ensued.

The Governor brothers turned to bushranging, drawing support from the indigenous inhabitants who shared their anger at the way they had been treated. The trio went on a rampage of robbery and murder, terrorizing the Hunter Valley as they settled old scores. Alexander McKay (unknown–1900) was killed near Ulan on 23 July before the gang murdered Elizabeth O'Brien (unknown–1900) and her infant child at Poggie. Two days later, they killed Kieran Fitzpatrick (unknown–1900). Their rampage created an atmosphere of terror across the areas that they visited. Such was the fear of attack from the three bushrangers that settlers moved out of their homesteads at any news that they were nearby, and women and children were brought together in towns for better protection. As the fugitives continued their violent spree uncaught, public pressure to have them captured steadily mounted.

As a result, they were declared outlaws, which meant they could be shot on sight. Eventually Jack Underwood was captured, Jimmy was shot and wounded, allowing him to be captured a couple of weeks later, and Joe Governor was shot and instantly killed. Both Jack and Jimmy were hanged. ∎

 BREELONG.
THE TOWN WHERE THE MAWBEY FAMILY LIVED, AND WHERE THEY WERE MURDERED ON 20 JULY 1900.

2 DENISON TOWN.
THE TOWN WHERE JACK UNDERWOOD WAS ARRESTED.

3 ULAN.
THE TOWN WHERE ALEXANDER MCKAY WAS MURDERED ON 23 JULY 1900.

4 POGGIE.
THE TOWN WHERE ELIZABETH O'BRIEN AND HER 18-MONTH-OLD SON WERE MURDERED ON 24 JULY 1900.

5 WOLAR.
THE TOWN WHERE KIERAN FITZPATRICK WAS MURDERED ON 26 JULY 1900.

6 FORBES RIVER.
THE RIVER WHERE JIMMY GOVERNOR WAS SHOT AND WOUNDED ON 13 OCTOBER 1900.

7 BOBIN CREEK.
THE CREEK WHERE JIMMY WAS CAPTURED ON 27 OCTOBER 1900.

8 MOUNT ROYAL, SINGLETON.
THE AREA WHERE JOE GOVERNOR WAS SHOT AND KILLED ON 31 OCTOBER 1900.

NUMEROUS ROUTES TAKEN BY POLICE TRACKING THE KILLERS.

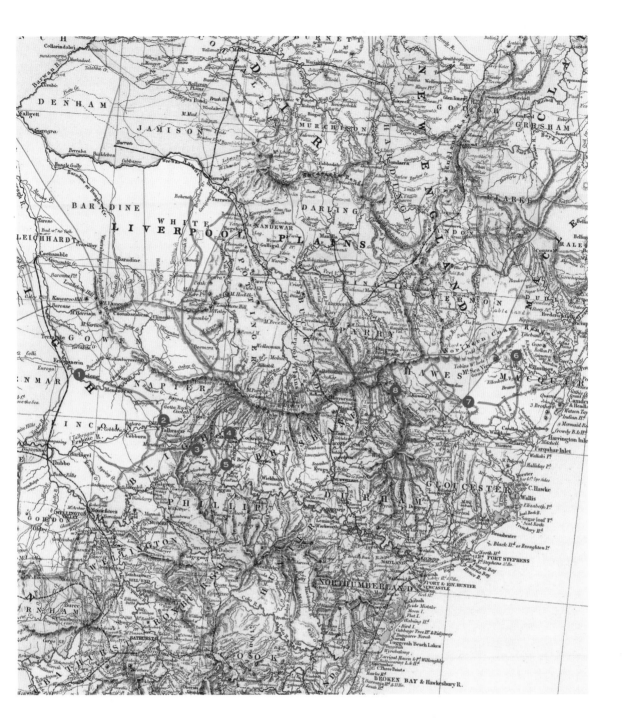

John and Sarah
Mawbey.

Above. The posse that tracked the
Governors and their allies
across the bush.

Above. Joe
Governor's
body.

Above. A post-mortem photograph
of Joe Governor, following
his death in a shoot-out.

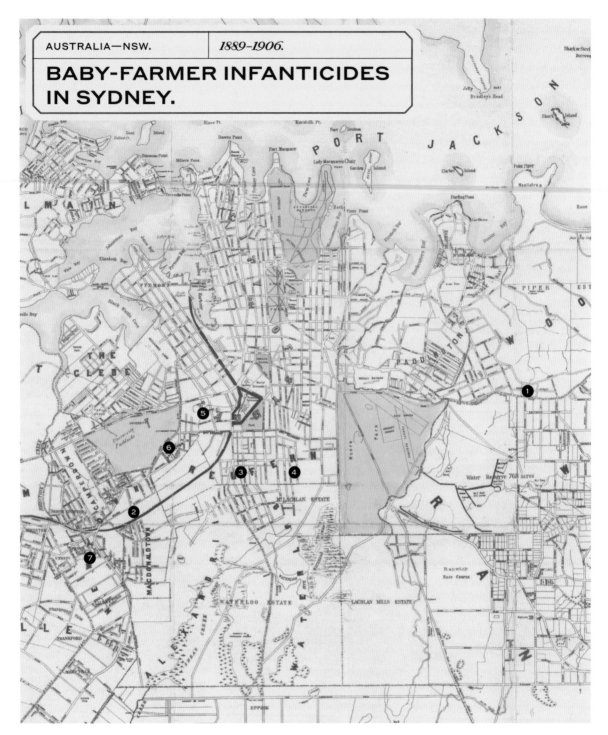

BABY-FARMER INFANTICIDES IN SYDNEY.

① 1889. 10 VERNON STREET, WOOLAHRA. Ellen Batts. ✕ LIZZIE COHEN.

② 1892. BURREN STREET, MACDONALDTOWN. John Makin & Sarah Makin. ✕ SEVEN UNNAMED INFANTS.

③ 1892. GEORGE STREET, REDFERN. John Makin & Sarah Makin. ✕ THREE UNNAMED INFANTS.

④ 1892. ALDERSON STREET, REDFERN. John Makin & Sarah Makin. ✕ TWO UNNAMED INFANTS.

⑤ 1892. LEVEY STREET, CHIPPENDALE. John Makin & Sarah Makin. ✕ ONE UNNAMED INFANT.

⑥ 1898. DARLINGTON. Katie De Lawrie. ABANDONED AT LEAST EIGHT INFANTS.

⑦ 1906. NEWTOWN. Elizabeth Scholes, Grace Saru & Eliza Ann Kennedy. MULTIPLE INFANTS.

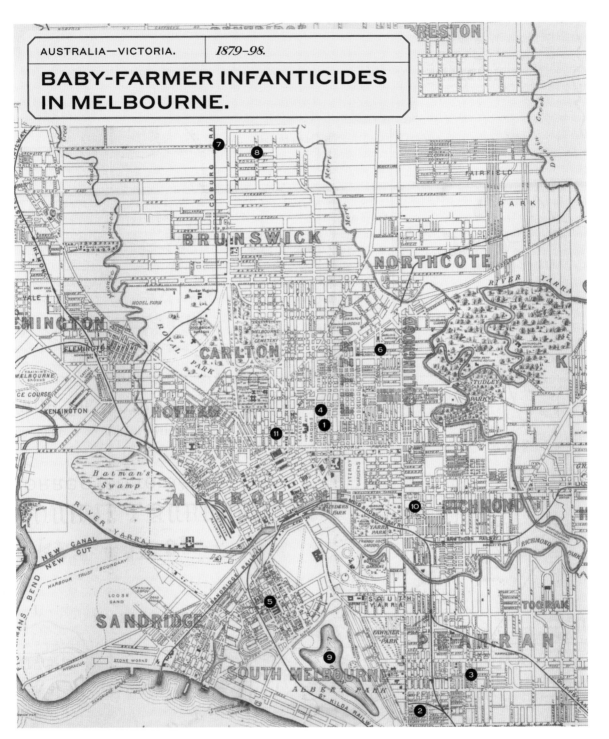

BABY-FARMER INFANTICIDES IN MELBOURNE.

❶ 1879. 2 JAMES STREET, FITZROY. **Mrs Evans.** × FIVE UNNAMED CHILDREN.

❷ 1887. 59 PEEL STREET, WINDSOR. **Ellen Gardiner.** × UNNAMED INFANT (10 WEEKS OLD). × UNNAMED INFANT (3 WEEKS OLD).

❸ 1888. YORK STREET, SOUTH YARRA. **Mrs Tatt.** × UNNAMED INFANT (*c.* 10 MONTHS OLD).

❹ 1889. KING WILLIAM STREET, FITZROY. **Emma Parry.** × JESSIE THORP.

❺ 1889. 64 DORCAS STREET, SOUTH MELBOURNE. **Mrs Grant.** × UNNAMED INFANT.

❻ 1890. GOLD STREET, COLLINGWOOD. **Mrs White.** × UNNAMED INFANT.

❼ 1891–93. 26 MORELAND ROAD, BRUNSWICK. **Francis Knorr.** × TWO UNNAMED INFANTS.

❽ 1891–93. DAVIES STREET, BRUNSWICK. **Francis Knorr.** × UNNAMED INFANT.

❾ 1892. LAGOON, PORT MELBOURNE. **Unknown.** × TWO UNNAMED INFANTS.

❿ 1897. 86 ROWENA PARADE, RICHMOND. **Ellen Mary Fuller.** × UNNAMED INFANT.

⓫ 1898. CARDIGAN STREET, CARLTON. **Nurse Meade.** × UNNAMED INFANT (7 WEEKS OLD).

NED KELLY.
× *Thomas Lonigan.* × 2.

WEAPON.	TYPOLOGY.	POLICING.
GUN.	GANG.	N/A.

STRINGYBARK CREEK.

Unpacking the truth from the myth that surrounds Australia's most infamous criminal is difficult. Edward (Ned) Kelly (1855–80) was the son of a transported convict. In April 1878, a policeman named Fitzpatrick turned up at the Kelly homestead with a warrant to arrest Ned's brother Dan (1861–80) for horse theft. The Kelly brothers were petty criminals, in and out of jail for a host of minor offences, and had cultivated the image and belief that they were the victims of police persecution. This escalated when Fitzpatrick was shot and cited Ned as the culprit (something he denied). Dan and Ned vanished into the bush and the authorities locked up Mrs Kelly and two others for the attempt on the officer's life. On 25 October, Ned and Dan, along with accomplices John Byrne (1856–80) and Steve Hart (1859–80), surprised a police patrol at Stringybark Creek and three officers died. The Victorian state now outlawed all the members of the Kelly Gang, removing any necessity to capture them alive, and the real legend of Ned Kelly was born.

Ned and his gang then began a series of outlandish criminal exploits: holding up a sheep station, robbing banks and taking over a police station before escaping dressed as officers. The police put a huge bounty on their heads, but Ned wrote an 8,000-word letter of justification of his actions, cementing his anti-hero status in the minds of Australians then and since.

The gang's epic criminal escapade came to a sorry end at a railway hotel at Glenrowan on 29 June 1880. The Kelly Gang had intended to stop a police train bringing a large force from Melbourne to capture them. However, the plan failed and the gang found themselves surrounded by armed police as they sheltered in the hotel with the owner and about sixty other hostages. They had made crude armour, which they mistakenly thought would protect them from the police bullets. The police opened fire and a furious gunfight followed, in which Ned and Dan were wounded and Byrne was killed. At dawn, Ned emerged at the rear o f the police positions, strolling out of the mist in his heavy armour and iconic helmet, shooting at the officers until they brought him down by aiming at his legs. Firing continued until the hotel was set on fire and burnt to the ground.

Hart and Dan Kelly committed suicide by poison and so only Ned could be put on trial for the gang's exploits. He was convicted of the murder of police constable Thomas Lonigan (1844–78) in the ambush at Stringybark Creek. There were calls for mercy, but these went unheeded by the government. Kelly was hanged at Melbourne Gaol on 11 November 1880, reportedly telling the hangman 'such is life'. Kelly was a bushranger, a thief and a killer, but thanks to his 'Jerilderie Letter' he has passed into folklore as a political revolutionary rather than merely a violent criminal. ∎

Above. NED KELLY AND HIS GANG AMBUSH AND KILL THREE POLICE OFFICERS SENT TO ARREST THEM.

Above. NED KELLY APPEARS OUT OF THE MIST, WEARING THE BODY ARMOUR THAT HELPED CEMENT HIS ICONIC IMAGE.

Above. THE POLICE SHOOT AT NED KELLY'S UNPROTECTED LEGS, BRINGING HIM DOWN DESPITE HIS ARMOUR.

Right. NED KELLY IN CHAINS AT MELBOURNE GAOL; HE REMAINS AUSTRALIA'S MOST INFAMOUS AND ENIGMATIC OUTLAW.

Above. A WOUNDED KELLY IS BROUGHT BACK TO MELBOURNE TO FACE TRIAL FOR HIS CRIMES.

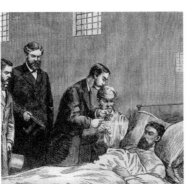

Above. NED KELLY RECOVERS IN THE PRISON HOSPITAL FROM THE WOUNDS HE SUSTAINED IN THE SHOOT-OUT.

Above. NED KELLY IS TRIED AT MELBOURNE IN 1880; HIS ACCOMPLICES TOOK POISON TO AVOID SUCH A FATE.

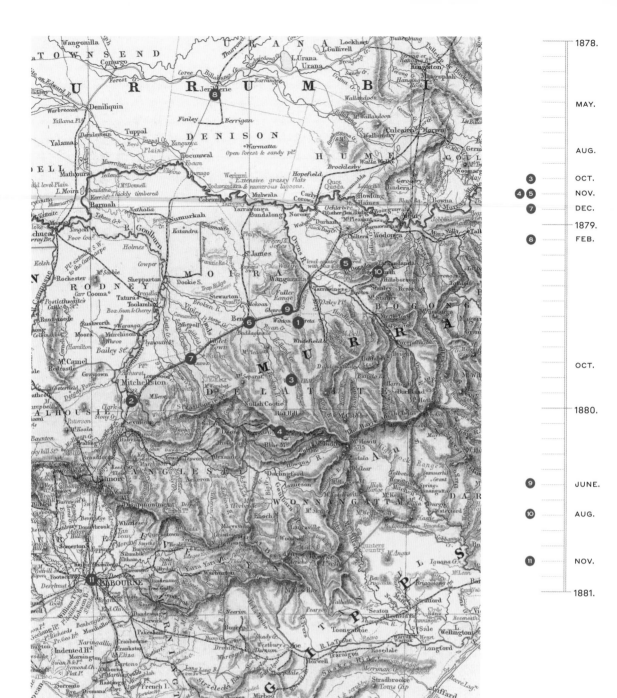

1878.

MAY.

AUG.

OCT.

NOV.

DEC.

1879.

FEB.

OCT.

1880.

JUNE.

AUG.

NOV.

1881.

1 GRETA.
THE TOWN WHERE THE KELLY FAMILY LIVED FROM 1867.

2 AVENEL.
THE TOWN WHERE NED KELLY RESCUED A BOY FROM DROWNING IN 1865.

3 STRINGYBARK CREEK.
THE PLACE WHERE THE KELLY GANG KILLED THREE POLICEMEN IN 1878.

4 MANSFIELD COURTHOUSE.
THE COURTHOUSE WHERE THE KELLY GANG WERE DECLARED OUTLAWS IN 1878.

5 THE WOOLSHED VALLEY.
THE AREA WHERE THE KELLY GANG HID IN THE 'KELLY CAVES' IN 1878.

6 BENALLA.
THE LOCATION OF THE POLICE HQ WHEN HUNTING NED KELLY.

7 EUROA.
THE TOWN WHERE THE KELLY GANG ROBBED THE EUROA NATIONAL BANK IN 1878.

8 JERILDERIE.
THE TOWN WHERE NED KELLY DELIVERED HIS 'JERILDERIE LETTER' FOR PUBLICATION IN 1879.

9 GLENROWAN.
THE TOWN WHERE NED KELLY WAS CAPTURED BY THE POLICE IN 1880.

10 BEECHWORTH
THE TOWN WHERE NED KELLY WAS JAILED BEFORE HIS MURDER TRIAL.

11 MELBOURNE GAOL, MELBOURNE.
THE JAIL WHERE NED KELLY WAS EXECUTED IN 1880.

Right. THE WANGARATTA POLICE POSE FOR A PHOTOGRAPH FOLLOWING THE SUCCESSFUL CAPTURE OF NED KELLY.

Right. ARMOUR BELONGING TO THE KELLY GANG AND NED KELLY'S RIFLE, AS DISPLAYED BY THE POLICE.

Right. THE SPOT WHERE NED KELLY WAS FINALLY CAPTURED AFTER HE WAS OVERWHELMED BY POLICE FIRE.

FREDERICK BAILEY DEEMING.
× *6.*

WEAPON.	TYPOLOGY.	POLICING.
AXE & KNIFE.	DOMESTIC.	N/A.

DINHAM VILLA, RAINHILL, ENGLAND.
ANDREW STREET, WINDSOR, MELBOURNE.

'Mad Fred' Deeming (1853–92) was an emotionally unstable man who earned the dubious accolade of being featured among the many candidates for the elusive Jack the Ripper. In other respects, Deeming was a fairly ordinary killer. He was born in Leicestershire in 1853, but by the age of 16 was living at Birkenhead, near Liverpool. He was very close to his mother, and her death in 1873 had a profound effect on him. Leaving Liverpool, he travelled the world as a ship's steward and on one voyage suffered a violent brain seizure from which he never fully recovered. Deeming would later say that he heard voices urging him to kill.

In truth, Deeming was a fraudster – thieving and cheating for money – who moved frequently to avoid his criminality catching up with him. In 1882, he married Marie James (unknown–1891), who bore him four children. He continued to travel, swindling money here and there, turning up in Australia, Cape Town, South Africa, and Hull, England, where he committed a fraud that led to his arrest and imprisonment. Released in July 1891, Deeming (now using the name Williams) started an extramarital affair with a woman named Emily Mather (unknown–1891) and, after renting a house in Rainhill, Merseyside, for his existing family, left with her for Australia, settling in the Melbourne suburb of Windsor. When Emily disappeared in December 1891, Deeming told neighbours she had gone away on business, before vanishing himself. He had used the same explanation for his wife and family's supposed departure from the Rainhill home earlier in the year.

The truth was much darker: he had murdered them all. When his Melbourne landlady's concerns brought the police to his property, they soon discovered Emily's remains buried under the hearthstone. They alerted police in Liverpool who dug up Marie and her four children at the house in Rainhill. Deeming was arrested and tried in Melbourne on 25 April. Convicted of Emily's murder, he went to the gallows on 23 May. He is supposed to have told fellow inmates that he was Jack the Ripper but there is no credible evidence for this, despite a contemporary ditty that ran:

'Ta-ra-da-boom-di-ay,
This is a happy day,
An East End holiday,
Jack the Ripper's gone away.' ∎

Left. THE FRONT COVER OF A SENSATIONAL ACCOUNT OF FREDERICK BAILEY DEEMING'S LIFE AND CRIMES, PUBLISHED IN 1892, THE YEAR HE WAS HANGED.

Right. A COMPARISON OF A SKETCH OF FREDERICK BAILEY DEEMING (RIGHT) WITH A SKETCH OF A SUSPECT IN THE WHITECHAPEL MURDERS CASE FROM AN 1888 DRAWING IN THE *ILLUSTRATED POLICE NEWS.*

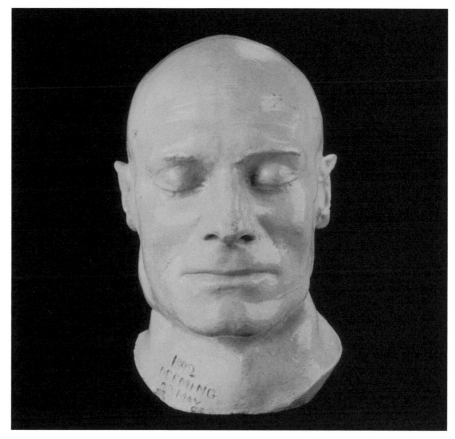

Below. ILLUSTRATED POLICE NEWS, 2 APRIL 1892. A DRAMATIC SUMMARY OF FREDERICK BAILEY DEEMING'S MURDERS.

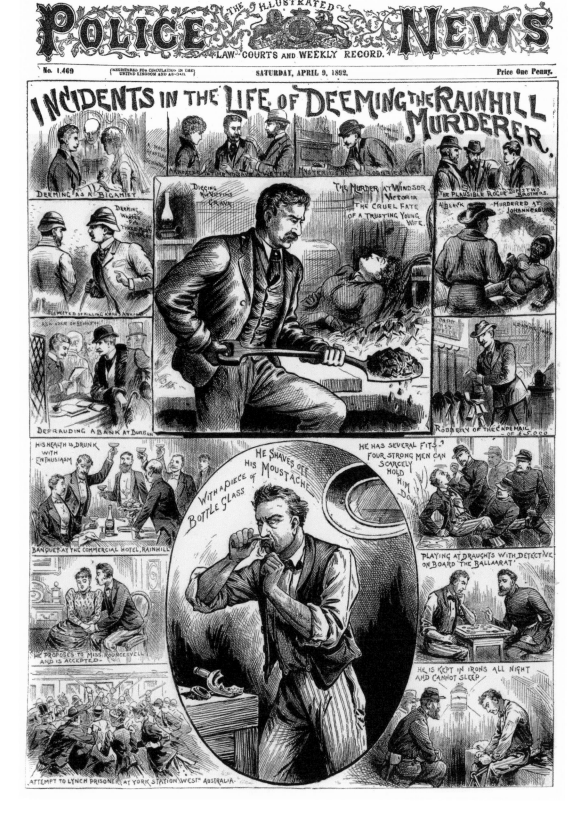

FRANCES KNORR.
× 3. +

WEAPON. UNKNOWN.	TYPOLOGY. INFANTICIDE.	POLICING. N/A.

26 MORELAND ROAD, MELBOURNE. DAVIES STREET, MELBOURNE.

When Frances Knorr's (1868–94) husband was sent to prison for selling goods he had obtained fraudulently, it removed Frances's financial support at a stroke and threatened to plunge her into poverty. Pregnant and with at least one other child already, she chose to set out on a path that would eventually lead her to the gallows.

In 1892, Australia was experiencing an economic depression and work was hard to come by. So instead, Frances opted to go into business herself and set up as a child minder, a useful service to offer to parents when both might need to retain jobs. However, Frances was not caring for the babies she took in; she was murdering some and selling others to childless couples who asked few questions. Two of the babies she buried in the garden of her home in Moreland Road, Melbourne, where they were discovered by an incoming tenant after Frances returned to Sydney following her husband's release from jail. Another dead child was discovered at Davies Street where Frances had also lived. She was executed on 15 January 1894 after making a full confession. ∎

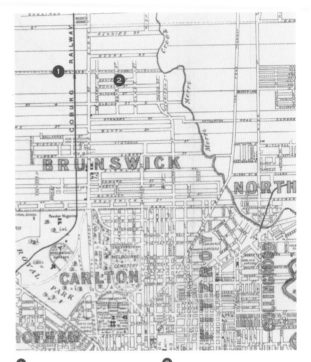

1 26 MORELAND ROAD, BRUNSWICK. THE HOUSE WHERE TWO MURDERED BABIES WERE FOUND.

2 DAVIES STREET, BRUNSWICK. THE HOUSE WHERE ONE MURDERED BABY WAS FOUND.

Below. MORELAND ROAD, WHERE FRANCES KNORR OPERATED A BABY-FARMING BUSINESS IN THE 1890S.

MARTHA NEEDLE.
× 5.

WEAPON.	TYPOLOGY.	POLICING.
ARSENIC.	DOMESTIC.	N/A.

137 BRIDGE ROAD, MELBOURNE.

In June 1894, Herman Juncken (dates unknown) fell ill after eating a meal prepared by Martha Needle (1863–94) at her Melbourne lodging house. He recovered, but succumbed again after eating the breakfast Martha made him. His physician, Dr Boyd, suspecting foul play, sent a sample for analysis. It tested positive for arsenic and the doctor decided to set a trap. Alerting the police, he arranged for them to arrive just as Martha was serving Herman tea from a pot that contained enough poison to kill five adults.

The subsequent police inquiry discovered that not only had Martha murdered Herman's brother Louis (dates unknown) – for opposing her engagement to Otto (dates unknown), their other brother – she had also poisoned her first husband and their three children. Detectives had all the bodies exhumed and tested, which revealed the presence of arsenic. Martha's motive was unclear; she had profited from death insurance on two of her children but had spent this on their graves, and there was no obvious motive for killing Louis. She was hanged for her crimes, but maintained her innocence to the last. ∎

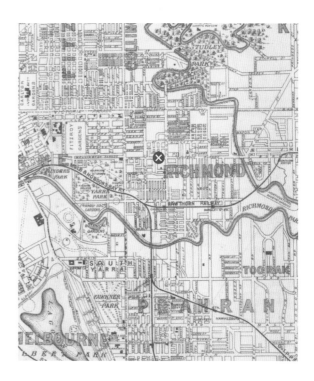

Above. MAP SHOWING THE LOCATION OF 137 BRIDGE ROAD, WHERE MARTHA NEEDLE MURDERED LOUIS JUNCKEN.

Left. MARTHA NEEDLE IN A PHOTOGRAPHER'S STUDIO, GIVING NO SIGN OF THE MURDERER SHE WOULD BECOME.

Right. TWO OF MARTHA'S CHILDREN POSE FOR A PHOTOGRAPH; THEY WERE KILLED FOR THE INSURANCE MONEY.

A CRIMINOLOGY MATRIX. [1/3]

PERTAINING TO EVERY MURDER EXAMINED IN THIS BOOK.

MURDERER.	ENVIRONMENT.	GENDER.	WEAPON.	TYPOLOGY.	PROFILE.
ALLAIN, Louis.	Urban.	Male.	PISTOL.	DOMESTIC.	Single.
ANASTAY, Louis.	Urban.	Male.	KNIFE.	PROPERTY CRIME.	Single.
ÁVILA, Dolores.*	Urban.	Female.	KNIFE.	PROPERTY CRIME.	Single.
BASSOT, Henri.*	Urban.	Male.	STRANGULATION.	PROPERTY CRIME.	Single.
BEN ALI, Ameer.	Urban.	Male.	KNIFE.	RECKLESS ACT.	Single.
BERCHTOLD, Johann.	Urban.	Male.	STRANGULATION.	PROPERTY CRIME.	Single.
BERECZ, János.*	Urban.	Male.	STRANGULATION.	PROPERTY CRIME.	Single.
BOMPARD, Gabrielle.*	Urban.	Female.	PULLEY.	PROPERTY CRIME.	Single.
BORDEN, Lizzie.	Rural.	Female.	AXE.	DOMESTIC.	Single.
CENERI, Pietro.	Urban.	Male.	GUN.	GANG.	Single.
CHAUFFEURS OF DRÔME.	Rural.	Male.	FIRE.	PROPERTY CRIME.	Serial.
CODEBO.*	Urban.	Male.	BLOWS.	PROPERTY CRIME.	Single.
COGNEVAUX, Louis.	Urban.	Male.	KNIFE.	JEALOUSY.	Single.
CORDER, William.	Rural.	Male.	PISTOL.	DOMESTIC.	Single.
CREAM, Thomas Neill.	Urban.	Male.	STRYCHNINE.	VARIOUS.	Serial.
CRIPPEN, Hawley Harvey.	Urban.	Male.	POISON.	DOMESTIC.	Single.
CRIPPS, Thomas William.	Urban.	Male.	KNIFE.	DOMESTIC.	Single.
CUNNINGHAM, Emma.*	Urban.	Female.	KNIFE.	DOMESTIC.	Single.
DE BALAGUER, Higinia Ostalé.*	Urban.	Female.	KNIFE.	PROPERTY CRIME.	Single.
DEEMING, Frederick Bailey.	Urban.	Male.	AXE & KNIFE.	DOMESTIC.	Serial.
DOLEŽAL, Otakar.*	Urban.	Male.	KNIFE.	POLITICAL.	Single.
DRAGOUN, František.*	Urban.	Male.	KNIFE.	POLITICAL.	Single.
DRISCOLL, Daniel.	Urban.	Male.	PISTOL.	GANG.	Single.
DUMOLLARD, Martin.*	Rural.	Male.	BLOWS.	PROPERTY CRIME.	Serial.
DUNHAM, James C.	Rural.	Male.	GUN & AXE.	RECKLESS ACT.	Single.
DURRANT, William H. T.	Urban.	Male.	KNIFE.	SEXUAL.	Serial.
DWYER, John J.	Urban.	Male.	POOL CUE.	BRAWL.	Single.
ECKEL, John.*	Urban.	Male.	KNIFE.	DOMESTIC.	Single.
EYRAUD, Michel.*	Urban.	Male.	PULLEY.	PROPERTY CRIME.	Single.
FÄHDING, Jakob.*	Rural.	Male.	SWORD.	GANG.	Serial.
FAIR, Laura.	Urban.	Female.	PISTOL.	DOMESTIC.	Single.
FLANNAGAN, Catherine.*	Urban.	Female.	ARSENIC.	PROPERTY CRIME.	Single.
FLEMING, Mary Livingston.	Urban.	Female.	ARSENIC.	PROPERTY CRIME.	Single.
FRANKS, Wilfred Moritz.	Urban.	Male.	DAGGER.	ACCIDENT.	Single.
GALLETLY, George.	Urban.	Male.	KNIFE.	GANG.	Single.
GAUMET, Annet.*	Urban.	Male.	WINE BOTTLE.	PROPERTY CRIME.	Single.
GAY, Anthelme.*	Urban.	Male.	STRANGULATION.	PROPERTY CRIME.	Single.
GIRIAT, Victorine.*	Urban.	Female.	STRANGULATION.	PROPERTY CRIME.	Single.
GOVERNOR, Jimmy.	Rural.	Male.	TOMAHAWK	RECKLESS ACT.	Serial.
GRÁZL, Jan Jiří.*	Rural.	Male.	SWORD.	GANG.	Serial.
GRENETIER, Victor.	Urban.	Male.	KNIFE.	DOMESTIC.	Single.

POLICING.	RESULT.	SENTENCE.	YEAR.	LOCATION.	PAGE.	
N/A.	N/A.	N/A.	1894.	France, AUVERGNE.	92.	
N/A.	Arrested.	Guillotined.	1891.	France, PARIS.	70.	
Toxicology.	Arrested.	Garrotted.	1888.	Spain, MADRID.	129.	
Bertillonage.	Arrested.	Imprisoned.	1903.	France, AUVERGNE.	95.	
Mortuary photography.	Arrested.	Imprisoned.	1891.	USA, NEW YORK.	142–3.	
Photography.	Arrested.	Life imprisoned.	1896.	Germany, BAVARIA.	103.	
Early forensics.	Arrested.	Hanged.	1883.	Hungary, BUDAPEST.	114.	
Pathology.	Arrested.	Imprisoned.	1889.	France, PARIS.	66–7.	
Crime scene photography.	Arrested.	Acquitted.	1892.	USA, MASSACHUSETTS.	146–9.	
Major court case.	Arrested.	Life imprisoned.	1861.	Italy, EMILIA ROMAGNA.	124–5.	
N/A.	Arrested.	Guillotined.	1905–08.	France, AUVERGNE.	96–9.	
Bertillonage.	Arrested.	Unknown.	1901.	France, PARIS.	72.	
N/A.	Killed.	N/A.	1892.	France, PARIS.	71.	
Bow Street Runners.	Arrested.	Hanged.	1827.	England, SUFFOLK.	50–1.	
N/A.	Arrested.	Hanged.	1881–92.	USA, CHICAGO.	156–9.	
Radiotelegraphy.	Arrested.	Hanged.	1910.	England, LONDON.	46–9.	
N/A.	Arrested.	Imprisoned.	1896.	England, LONDON.	42.	
N/A.	Arrested.	Acquitted.	1857.	USA, NEW YORK.	132–3.	
Toxicology.	Arrested.	Garrotted.	1888.	Spain, MADRID.	129.	
N/A.	Arrested.	Hanged.	1891.	Australia, VICTORIA.	208–11.	
N/A.	Arrested.	Imprisoned.	1893.	Bohemia, PRAGUE.	118.	
N/A.	Arrested.	Imprisoned.	1893.	Bohemia, PRAGUE.	118.	
Ballistics.	Arrested.	Hanged.	1886.	USA, NEW YORK.	136–7.	
Photography.	Arrested.	Guillotined.	1855–61.	France, AUVERGNE.	82–3.	
N/A.	Uncaught.	N/A.	1896.	USA, SAN FRANCISCO.	190–1.	
Early forensics.	Arrested.	Hanged.	1895.	USA, SAN FRANCISCO.	188–9.	
N/A.	Arrested.	Imprisoned.	1880.	USA, NEW YORK.	134.	
N/A.	Arrested.	Not tried.	1857.	USA, NEW YORK.	132–3.	
Pathology.	Arrested.	Guillotined.	1889.	France, PARIS.	66–7.	
N/A.	Arrested.	Hanged.	1800–15.	Austria, VIENNA.	106–7.	
N/A.	Arrested.	Acquitted.	1870.	USA, SAN FRANCISCO.	184.	
Toxicology.	Arrested.	Hanged.	1883.	England, LIVERPOOL.	52.	
Toxicology.	Arrested.	Acquitted.	1895.	USA, NEW YORK.	144–5.	
N/A.	Arrested.	Dismissed.	1896.	England, LONDON.	43.	
N/A.	Arrested.	Life imprisoned.	1888.	England, LONDON.	33.	
Lacassagne.	Arrested.	Guillotined.	1898.	France, AUVERGNE.	94.	
Bertillonage.	Arrested.	Imprisoned.	1904.	France, PARIS.	78–9.	
Bertillonage.	Arrested.	Imprisoned.	1903.	France, AUVERGNE.	95.	
Manhunt.	Arrested.	Hanged.	1900.	Australia, NSW.	200–1.	
N/A.	Arrested.	Hanged.	1800–15.	Austria, VIENNA.	106–7.	
N/A.	N/A.	N/A.	1893.	France, AUVERGNE.	92.	

Asterisk [*] denotes criminals working with an accomplice. Serial killers have murdered more than one person and on separate occasions.

MURDERER.	ENVIRONMENT.	GENDER.	WEAPON.	TYPOLOGY.	PROFILE.
GREULING, Frederick.	Urban.	Male.	REVOLVER.	RECKLESS ACT.	Single.
GUMP, Ferdinand.	Rural.	Male.	GUN.	GANG.	Serial.
GUNNESS, Belle.	Rural.	Female.	VARIOUS.	PROPERTY CRIME.	Serial.
HADLEY, Charles B.	Urban.	Male.	UNKNOWN.	SEXUAL.	Single.
HIGGINS, Margaret.*	Urban.	Female.	ARSENIC.	PROPERTY CRIME.	Single.
HILSNER, Leopold.	Rural.	Male.	KNIFE.	RECKLESS ACT.	Single.
HOCH, Johann Otto.	Urban.	Male.	ARSENIC.	PROPERTY CRIME.	Serial.
HOLMES, Henry Howard.	Urban.	Male.	VARIOUS.	PROPERTY CRIME.	Serial.
JACK THE RIPPER.	Urban.	Male.	KNIFE.	SEXUAL.	Serial.
JENNINGS, Thomas.	Urban.	Male.	PISTOL.	PROPERTY CRIME.	Single.
KELLY, Ned.	Rural.	Male.	GUN.	GANG.	Single.
KIESGEN.*	Urban.	Male.	KNIFE.	PROPERTY CRIME.	Single.
KISS, Béla.	Urban.	Male.	STRANGULATION.	PROPERTY CRIME.	Serial.
KNEISSL, Mathias.	Rural.	Male.	GUN.	GANG.	Single.
KNORR, Frances.	Urban.	Female.	UNKNOWN.	INFANTICIDE.	Serial.
KŘÍŽ, Josef.*	Urban.	Male.	KNIFE.	POLITICAL.	Single.
LIABEUF, Jean-Jacques.	Urban.	Male.	KNIFE.	POLITICAL.	Single.
LIPSKI, Israel.	Urban.	Male.	NITRIC ACID.	DOMESTIC.	Single.
LLOYD, Eva.	Urban.	Female.	BLUDGEON.	ACCIDENT.	Single.
LUETGERT, Adolph.	Urban.	Male.	UNKNOWN.	DOMESTIC.	Single.
MAHNKEN, Diedrich.	Urban.	Male.	PISTOL.	JEALOUSY.	Single.
MAKIN, John.*	Urban.	Male.	UNKNOWN.	INFANTICIDE.	Serial.
MAKIN, Sarah.*	Urban.	Female.	UNKNOWN.	INFANTICIDE.	Serial.
MANNING, Frederick.*	Urban.	Male.	PISTOL.	PROPERTY CRIME.	Single.
MANNING, Maria.*	Urban.	Female.	PISTOL.	PROPERTY CRIME.	Single.
MAPLETON, Percy Lefroy.	Urban.	Male.	PISTOL & KNIFE.	PROPERTY CRIME.	Single.
MARINA, Antonio.*	Urban.	Male.	STRANGULATION.	PROPERTY CRIME.	Single.
MARINA, Clara.*	Urban.	Female.	STRANGULATION.	PROPERTY CRIME.	Single.
MARIOTTI, François.	Urban.	Male.	PISTOL.	DOMESTIC.	Single.
MARTIN, Paul Jules.	Urban.	Male.	STRANGULATION.	PROPERTY CRIME.	Single.
MARTINET, Marie-Anne.*	Rural.	Female.	BLOWS.	PROPERTY CRIME.	Serial.
MAYBRICK, Florence.	Urban.	Female.	ARSENIC.	DOMESTIC.	Single.
MCGONIGAL, Dr H. G.*	Urban.	Male.	ABORTION.	ACCIDENT.	Single.
MEREDITH, Thomas Sheridan.	Urban.	Male.	ABORTION.	ACCIDENT.	Single.
MORROT, Jules.*	Urban.	Male.	STRANGULATION.	PROPERTY CRIME.	Single.
MURRI, Tullio.	Urban.	Male.	KNIFE.	DOMESTIC.	Single.
NEEDLE, Martha	Urban	Female.	ARSENIC.	DOMESTIC.	Serial.
NEWTON BROWN, Henry.	Rural.	Male.	REVOLVER.	PROPERTY CRIME.	Single.
NOUGUIER, Evariste.*	Urban.	Male.	WINE BOTTLE.	PROPERTY CRIME.	Single.
O'BRIEN, Isabella.	Rural.	Female.	DROWNING.	INFANTICIDE.	Single.
PAGÈS, Victor.*	Urban.	Male.	STRANGULATION.	PROPERTY CRIME.	Single.

POLICING.	RESULT.	SENTENCE.	YEAR.	LOCATION.	PAGE.	
Bertillonage.	Arrested.	Imprisoned.	1903	France, PARIS.	77.	
Photography.	Arrested.	Died in prison.	1872–73.	Germany, BAVARIA.	100–1.	
Crime scene photography.	Uncaught.	N/A.	1884–1908.	USA, INDIANA.	150–3.	
Graphology.	Uncaught.	N/A.	1902.	USA, SAN FRANCISCO.	192–3.	
Toxicology.	Arrested.	Hanged.	1883.	England, LIVERPOOL.	52.	
N/A.	Arrested.	Imprisoned.	1899.	Bohemia, POLNÁ.	119.	
Toxicology.	Arrested.	Hanged.	1895–1905.	USA, CHICAGO.	170–1.	
N/A.	Arrested.	Hanged.	1894.	USA, CHICAGO.	164–9.	
Criminal profiling.	Uncaught.	N/A.	1888–91.	England, LONDON.	34–9.	
Fingerprinting.	Arrested.	Hanged.	1910.	USA, CHICAGO.	172–3.	
N/A.	Arrested.	Hanged.	1878.	Australia, VICTORIA.	204–7.	
N/A.	Arrested.	Life imprisoned.	1896.	France, PARIS.	71.	
N/A.	Uncaught.	N/A.	c. 1903–14.	Hungary, BUDAPEST.	115.	
N/A.	Arrested.	Executed.	1900.	Germany, BAVARIA.	104–5.	
N/A.	Arrested.	Hanged.	1891–93.	Australia, VICTORIA.	212.	
N/A.	Arrested.	Imprisoned.	1893.	Bohemia, PRAGUE.	118.	
Bertillonage.	Arrested.	Guillotined.	1910.	France, PARIS.	80–1.	
Toxicology.	Arrested.	Hanged.	1887.	England, LONDON.	32.	
N/A.	Arrested.	Acquitted.	1880.	USA, CHICAGO.	154.	
Forensic anthropology.	Arrested.	Imprisoned.	1897.	USA, CHICAGO.	161.	
N/A.	Arrested.	Sectioned.	1883.	USA, NEW YORK.	134.	
N/A.	Arrested.	Hanged.	1892.	Australia, NSW.	198–9.	
N/A.	Arrested.	Imprisoned.	1892.	Australia, NSW.	198–9.	
N/A.	Arrested.	Hanged.	1849.	England, LONDON.	22–3.	
N/A.	Arrested.	Hanged.	1849.	England, LONDON.	22–3.	
Composite Portrait	Arrested.	Hanged.	1881.	England, LONDON.	28–31.	
N/A.	Arrested.	Garrotted.	1849.	Spain, MADRID.	128.	
N/A.	Arrested.	Garrotted.	1849.	Spain, MADRID.	128.	
N/A.	Arrested.	N/A.	1896.	France, AUVERGNE.	93.	
Bertillonage.	Arrested.	Life imprisoned.	1903.	France, PARIS.	76.	
Photography.	Arrested.	Imprisoned.	1855–61.	France, AUVERGNE.	82–3.	
Toxicology.	Arrested.	Imprisoned.	1889.	England, LIVERPOOL.	54–5.	
N/A.	Arrested.	Imprisoned.	1890.	USA, NEW YORK.	141.	
N/A.	Arrested.	Hanged.	1895.	Australia, NSW.	196–7.	
Bertillonage.	Arrested.	Imprisoned.	1904.	France, PARIS.	78–9.	
Lombroso.	Arrested.	Imprisoned.	1902.	Italy, EMILIA ROMAGNA.	126–7.	
N/A.	Arrested.	Hanged.	1894.	Australia, VICTORIA.	213.	
Posse.	Killed.	N/A.	1884.	USA, KANSAS.	180–3.	
Lacassagne.	Arrested.	Guillotined.	1898.	France, AUVERGNE.	94.	
N/A.	Arrested.	Hanged.	1870.	Australia, NSW.	196.	
Bertillonage.	Arrested.	Imprisoned.	1904.	France, PARIS.	78–9.	

MURDERER.	ENVIRONMENT.	GENDER.	WEAPON.	TYPOLOGY.	PROFILE.
PARRY, Lewis.	Urban.	Male.	BEATING.	DOMESTIC.	Single.
PEARCEY, Mary.	Urban.	Female.	POKER & KNIFE.	JEALOUSY.	Single.
PELLONI, Stefano.	Rural.	Male.	GUN.	GANG.	Serial.
PIERSON, Célestin-Nicolas.*	Urban.	Male.	STRANGULATION.	PROPERTY CRIME.	Single.
PIETTE, Marie.*	Urban.	Female.	HUNTING KNIFE.	PROPERTY CRIME.	Single.
PILLOT.*	Urban.	Male.	BLOWS.	PROPERTY CRIME.	Single.
PITÉLI, Mihály Oláh.*	Urban.	Male.	STRANGULATION.	PROPERTY CRIME.	Single.
PRENDERGAST, Patrick E.	Urban.	Male.	REVOLVER.	POLITICAL.	Single.
PRITCHARD, Edward W.	Urban.	Male.	ANTIMONY.	PROPERTY CRIME.	Single.
PROSPERI, Gaetano.	Rural.	Male.	GUN.	GANG.	Single.
QUANTRILL, William C.	Rural.	Male.	FIREPOWER.	POLITICAL.	Single.
REIGH, Sadie.	Urban.	Female.	PISTOL.	RECKLESS ACT.	Single.
REYMOND, Claire.	Urban.	Female.	KNIFE.	JEALOUSY.	Single.
RICHETTO, Luigi Giovanni.	Urban.	Male.	KNIFE.	PROPERTY CRIME.	Serial.
RYAN, Charles.	Urban.	Male.	PISTOL.	JEALOUSY.	Single.
SCHEFFER, Paul.*	Urban.	Male.	STRANGULATION.	PROPERTY CRIME.	Single.
SCHENK, Hugo.	Rural.	Male.	VARIOUS.	PROPERTY CRIME.	Serial.
SCHOSTERITZ, Simon.	Urban.	Male.	KNIFE.	SEXUAL.	Serial.
SCOTTI DI CARLO, Andrea.	Urban.	Male.	KNIFE.	RECKLESS ACT.	Single.
SHAW, Fannie.*	Urban.	Female.	ABORTION.	ACCIDENT.	Single.
SIEGLER, Herman.	Urban.	Male.	SHOTGUN.	INSANITY.	Single.
SLATER, Oscar.	Urban.	Male.	HAMMER.	PROPERTY CRIME.	Single.
SMITH, Madeleine.	Urban.	Female.	ARSENIC.	DOMESTIC.	Single.
SOUTHWORTH, Hannah M.	Urban.	Female.	PISTOL.	DOMESTIC.	Single.
SPANGA, Pál.*	Urban.	Male.	STRANGULATION.	PROPERTY CRIME.	Single.
STANGEL, Ignaz.*	Rural.	Male.	SWORD.	GANG.	Serial.
STRATTON, Albert.*	Urban.	Male.	KNIFE.	PROPERTY CRIME.	Single.
STRATTON, Alfred.*	Urban.	Male.	KNIFE.	PROPERTY CRIME.	Single.
THE BENDER FAMILY.	Rural.	Both.	KNIFE & HAMMER.	PROPERTY CRIME.	Serial.
THIBŒF, Henri.*	Urban.	Male.	HUNTING KNIFE.	PROPERTY CRIME.	Single.
TRUEL.*	Urban.	Male.	KNIFE.	PROPERTY CRIME.	Single.
UNKNOWN.	Urban.	Unknown.	SUFFOCATION.	PROPERTY CRIME.	Single.
UNKNOWN.	Urban.	Unknown.	STRANGULATION.	PROPERTY CRIME.	Single.
UNKNOWN.	Rural.	Unknown.	DROWNING.	ASSASSINATION.	Single.
UNKNOWN.	Urban.	Unknown.	BLUDGEON.	PROPERTY CRIME.	Single.
UNKNOWN.	Urban.	Unknown.	GUNPOWDER.	POLITICAL.	Single.
VACHER, Joseph.	Rural.	Male.	KNIFE & TEETH.	SEXUAL.	Serial.
VAN NOORWEGHE, Paul.*	Urban.	Male.	STRANGULATION.	PROPERTY CRIME.	Single.
WEBSTER, Kate.	Urban.	Female.	STRANGULATION.	PROPERTY CRIME.	Single.
WILLIAMS, John.	Urban.	Male.	MAUL.	RECKLESS ACT.	Serial.
YOUNG, Thomas.	Urban.	Male.	PISTOL.	DOMESTIC.	Single.

POLICING.	RESULT.	SENTENCE.	YEAR.	LOCATION.	PAGE.
N/A.	Arrested.	Life imprisoned.	1883.	England, LIVERPOOL.	53.
Forensics.	Arrested.	Hanged.	1890	England, LONDON.	40–1.
N/A.	Killed.	N/A.	c. 1840–51.	Italy, EMILIA ROMAGNA.	120.
Bertillonage.	Arrested.	Imprisoned.	1904.	France, PARIS.	78–9.
Bertillonage.	Arrested.	Acquitted.	1902.	France, PARIS.	73.
Bertillonage.	Arrested.	Unknown.	1901.	France, PARIS.	72.
Early forensics.	Arrested.	Hanged.	1883.	Hungary, BUDAPEST.	114.
N/A.	Arrested.	Hanged.	1893.	USA, CHICAGO.	160.
Toxicology.	Arrested.	Hanged.	1865.	Scotland, GLASGOW.	60–1.
N/A.	Arrested.	Guillotined.	1861.	Italy, EMILIA ROMAGNA.	121.
N/A.	Uncaught.	N/A.	1863.	USA, KANSAS.	174–5.
N/A.	Arrested.	Imprisoned.	1883.	USA, CHICAGO.	154.
N/A.	Arrested.	Acquitted.	1892.	France, PARIS.	70.
Lacassagne.	Arrested.	Life imprisoned.	1898–99.	France, AUVERGNE.	93.
N/A.	Suicide.	N/A.	1892.	USA, CHICAGO.	155.
Bertillonage.	Arrested.	N/A.	1903.	France, PARIS.	75.
N/A.	Arrested.	Hanged.	1883.	Austria, VIENNA.	108–11.
Suspect image circulated.	Arrested.	N/A.	1898.	Austria, VIENNA.	112–13.
N/A.	Arrested.	Life imprisoned.	1893.	England, LONDON.	42.
N/A.	Arrested.	N/A.	1890.	USA, NEW YORK.	141.
N/A.	Arrested.	N/A.	1892.	USA, CHICAGO.	155.
Identity parade.	Arrested.	Imprisoned.	1908.	Scotland, GLASGOW.	62–5.
Toxicology.	Arrested.	Not proven.	1857.	Scotland, GLASGOW.	58–9.
N/A.	Arrested.	Died in prison.	1889.	USA, NEW YORK.	135.
Early forensics.	Arrested.	Hanged.	1883.	Hungary, BUDAPEST.	114.
N/A.	Arrested.	Hanged.	1800–15.	Austria, VIENNA.	106–7.
Fingerprinting.	Arrested.	Hanged.	1905.	England, LONDON.	44–5.
Fingerprinting.	Arrested.	Hanged.	1905.	England, LONDON.	44–5.
Manhunt.	Uncaught.	N/A.	1871–73.	USA, KANSAS.	176–9.
Bertillonage.	Arrested.	Life imprisoned.	1902.	France, PARIS.	73.
N/A.	Arrested.	Life imprisoned.	1896.	France, PARIS.	71.
N/A.	Uncaught.	N/A.	1904.	England, LONDON.	43.
Bertillonage.	Uncaught.	N/A.	1902.	France, PARIS.	74.
N/A.	Uncaught.	N/A.	1886.	Germany, BAVARIA.	102.
N/A.	Uncaught.	N/A.	1870.	USA, NEW YORK.	140.
N/A.	Uncaught.	N/A.	1893.	USA, SAN FRANCISCO.	185.
Lacassagne.	Arrested.	Guillotined.	1894–97.	France, AUVERGNE.	84–9.
Bertillonage.	Arrested.	N/A.	1903.	France, PARIS.	75.
Early forensics.	Arrested.	Hanged.	1879.	England, LONDON.	24–5.
Parish Watch.	Arrested.	Suicide.	1811.	England, LONDON.	20–1.
N/A.	Arrested.	N/A.	1883	USA, NEW YORK.	135

FURTHER READING.

WRITER.	TITLE.	PUBLISHER.
ASBURY, HERBERT.	THE GANGS OF NEW YORK: AN INFORMAL HISTORY OF THE UNDERWORLD.	NEW YORK, NY: GARDEN CITY PUBLISHING CO., 1927.
BEGG, PAUL.	JACK THE RIPPER: THE DEFINITIVE HISTORY.	LONDON: LONGMAN, 2003.
CANTOR, DAVID.	CRIMINAL SHADOWS: INSIDE THE MIND OF THE SERIAL KILLER.	LONDON: HARPERCOLLINS, 1994.
COLE, SIMON A.	SUSPECT IDENTITIES: A HISTORY OF FINGERPRINTING AND CRIMINAL IDENTIFICATION.	CAMBRIDGE, MA: HARVARD UNIVERSITY PRESS, 2001.
CRONE, ROSALIND.	VIOLENT VICTORIANS: POPULAR ENTERTAINMENT IN NINETEENTH-CENTURY LONDON.	MANCHESTER: MANCHESTER UNIVERSITY PRESS, 2012.
EMSLEY, CLIVE.	THE ENGLISH POLICE: A POLITICAL AND SOCIAL HISTORY.	HEMEL HEMPSTEAD: HARVESTER WHEATSHEAF, 1991.
FLANDERS, JUDITH.	THE INVENTION OF MURDER: HOW THE VICTORIANS REVELLED IN DEATH AND DETECTION AND CREATED MODERN CRIME.	LONDON: HARPER PRESS, 2011.
GATRELL, V. A. C.	THE HANGING TREE: EXECUTION AND THE ENGLISH PEOPLE 1770–1868.	OXFORD: OXFORD UNIVERSITY PRESS, 1994.
GRAY, DREW.	LONDON'S SHADOWS: THE DARK SIDE OF THE VICTORIAN CAPITAL.	LONDON; NEW YORK, NY: BLOOMSBURY, 2010.
HARLEY LEWIS, ROY.	VICTORIAN MURDERS.	NEWTON ABBOTT: DAVID & CHARLES, 1988.
HOBSBAWM, ERIC.	BANDITS.	LONDON: WEIDENFELD & NICOLSON, 1969.
JAMES, P. D. & CRITCHLEY, T. A.	THE MAUL AND THE PEAR TREE: THE RATCLIFFE HIGHWAY MURDERS, 1811.	BATH: CHIVERS, 1988.
KRAFFT-EBING, RICHARD VON, BARON.	PSYCHOPATHIA SEXUALIS WITH ESPECIAL REFERENCE TO CONTRARY SEXUAL INSTINCT: A MEDICO-LEGAL STUDY. (TRANS. C. G. CHADDOCK)	PHILADELPHIA; LONDON: F. A. DAVIS CO., 1892.
LOMBROSO, CESARE.	THE CRIMINAL MAN. (TRANS. MARY GIBSON AND NICOLE HAHN RAFTER)	DURHAM, NC: DUKE UNIVERSITY PRESS, 2006.
SHPAYER-MAKOV, HAIA.	THE ASCENT OF THE DETECTIVE: POLICE SLEUTHS IN VICTORIAN AND EDWARDIAN ENGLAND.	OXFORD: OXFORD UNIVERSITY PRESS, 2011.
SPIERENBURG, PIETER.	A HISTORY OF MURDER: PERSONAL VIOLENCE IN EUROPE FROM THE MIDDLE AGES TO THE PRESENT.	CAMBRIDGE: POLITY, 2008.
STARR, DOUGLAS.	THE KILLER OF LITTLE SHEPHERDS: THE CASE OF THE FRENCH RIPPER & THE BIRTH OF FORENSIC SCIENCE.	LONDON: SIMON & SCHUSTER, 2011.
WATSON, KATHERINE D.	FORENSIC MEDICINE IN WESTERN SOCIETY: A HISTORY.	ABINGDON, OXON; NEW YORK, NY: ROUTLEDGE, 2011.
WATSON, KATHERINE.	POISONED LIVES: ENGLISH POISONERS AND THEIR VICTIMS.	LONDON; NEW YORK, NY: HAMBLEDON AND LONDON, 2004.
WIENER, MARTIN J.	MEN OF BLOOD: VIOLENCE, MANLINESS AND CRIMINAL JUSTICE IN VICTORIAN ENGLAND.	CAMBRIDGE: CAMBRIDGE UNIVERSITY PRESS, 2004.

SOURCES OF ILLUSTRATIONS.

Every effort has been made to locate and credit copyright holders of the material reproduced in this book. The author and publisher apologize for any omissions or errors, which can be corrected in future editions.

Unless otherwise indicated, all maps are David Rumsey Map Collection, www.davidrumsey.com.

a= above, c= centre, b= below, l= left, r=right, m= map

2 Frank P. Geyer, *The Holmes-Pitezel case; a history of the greatest crime of the century and of the search for the missing Pitezel children* (1896); **4** State Library Victoria; **6–11** Wellcome Collection; **12–15** Alphonse Bertillon, *Album of Paris Crime Scenes* (1901–08); **16** *Trial of Oscar Slater* (1910); **17** Alphonse Bertillon, *Album of Paris crime scenes* (1901–08); **18a** © The British Library Board. All rights reserved. With thanks to The British Newspaper Archive (www.britishnewspaperarchive.co.uk); **18b** *Full report, extracted from the "Times", of the extraordinary and interesting trial of Miss Madeleine Smith* (1857); **18l** *Das Interessante Blatt* (1884), Austrian National Library; **18r** Collection particulière de Pierre Piazza; **19b** Budapest City Archives; **20a** John Theodore Tussaud, *The romance of Madame Tussaud's* (1920); **20c, b** *London Chronicle* (1811); **21** *London Chronicle* (1811); **22** Robert Huish, *The progress of a crime, or the authentic memoirs of Maria Manning* (1849); **23a** Harvard Law School Library, Historical & Special Collections; **23c** Wellcome Collection; **23b 1, 2, 3, 5, 6** Robert Huish, *The progress of a crime, or the authentic memoirs of Maria Manning* (1849); **23b 4** Alamy Stock Photo; **24a** © The British Library Board. All rights reserved. With thanks to The British Newspaper Archive (www.britishnewspaperarchive.co.uk); **24c** Laundry copper at Christchurch Mansion, Ipswich, Prioryman, 2012; **24b** SWNS; **24m** Alamy Stock Photo; **25** © The British Library Board. All rights reserved. With thanks to The British Newspaper Archive (www.britishnewspaperarchive.co.uk); **28a** © The British Library Board. All rights reserved. With thanks to The British Newspaper Archive (www.britishnewspaperarchive.co.uk); **28l** Harvard Law School Library, Historical & Special Collections; **28r** Getty Images; **30–31** © The British Library Board. All rights reserved. With thanks to The British Newspaper Archive (www.britishnewspaperarchive.co.uk); **32a** © The British Library Board. All rights reserved. With thanks to The British Newspaper Archive (www.britishnewspaperarchive.co.uk); **32c, b** Metropolitan Police Service; **33** © The British Library Board. All rights reserved. With thanks to The British Newspaper Archive (www.britishnewspaperarchive.co.uk); **34a 1–5** Getty Images; **34b 1–5** Records of the Metropolitan Police Office, 1888; **35a a** Jack the Ripper Tour, **b** Casebook: Jack the Ripper, **c** Public domain, **d** Paul Smith, Attribution-ShareAlike 2.0 license, **e** Casebook: Jack the Ripper; **35b a–e** Records of the Metropolitan Police Office, 1888; **38** © The British Library Board. All rights reserved. With thanks to The British Newspaper Archive (www.britishnewspaperarchive.co.uk); **39a** City of London Police archives, 9 November 1888; **39b** © The British Library Board. All rights reserved. With thanks to The British Newspaper Archive (www.britishnewspaperarchive.co.uk); **40–43** © The British Library Board. All rights reserved. With thanks to The British Newspaper Archive (www.bwritishnewspaperarchive.co.uk); **44–45** Metropolitan Police Service; **44br** © The British Library Board. All rights reserved. With thanks to The British Newspaper Archive (www.britishnewspaperarchive.co.uk); **46l** Mary Evans Picture Library; **46lc** Getty Images; **46rc** Getty Images; **46r** Bridgeman Images; **46b** akg-images; **47l, lc, rc** Getty Images; **47r** Alamy Stock Photo; **48** National Archives; **49** Bridgeman Images; **50m** Copyright The Francis Frith Collection; **50–51** *An authentic and faithful history of the mysterious murder of Maria Marten* (1828); **52–53** © The British Library Board. All rights reserved. With thanks to The British Newspaper Archive (www.britishnewspaperarchive.co.uk); **54** *The Graphic* (1889); **54m** Alamy Stock Photo; **55** © The British Library Board. All rights reserved. With thanks to The British Newspaper Archive (www.britishnewspaperarchive.co.uk); **58a** Madeleine Smith; **58c** *Glasgow poisoning case: unabridged report of the evidence in this extraordinary trial* (1857); **58b** *Full report, extracted from the "Times", of the extraordinary and interesting trial of Miss Madeleine Smith* (1857); **60a** *Trial of Dr Pritchard* (1906); **60b** *On the detection of aconite by its physiological action being notes of experiments made in connection with the trial of Dr. E.W. Pritchard* (1865); **61m** Reproduced with the permission of the National Library of Scotland; **61** *Trial of Dr Pritchard* (1906); **62–64** *Trial of Oscar Slater* (1910); **66** Criminocorpus, Collection Philippe Zoummeroff; **67** *Le Petit Journal* (20 December 1890); **70–71** Collection particulière de Pierre Piazza; **72–77** Alphonse Bertillon, *Album of Paris crime scenes* (1901–08); **78** *Almanach du Bonhomme Jacquemert* (1909); **79** Alphonse Bertillon, *Album of Paris crime scenes* (1901–08); **80–81** Archives de la Préfecture de police de Paris, FRAPP_YB12_061, FRAPP_YB12_059, FRAPP_YB12_057; **82a** Rémi Cuisinier, *Dumollard, L'assassin des bonnes* (2008); **82b** *Causes célèbres de tous les peoples* (1858–74); **83a** Rémi Cuisinier, Dumollard, *L'assassin des bonnes* (2008); **83b** *Causes célèbres de tous les peoples* (1858–74); **84a** BmLyon | numelyo (Ms 4056, f ° 2); **84b 1–5** BmLyon | numelyo (*Le Progres Illustré* 362); **84b 6** Getty Images; **85a** BmLyon | numelyo (Ms 7056, f ° 8); **85b 7, 8, 9, 11** BmLyon | numelyo (*Le Progres Illustré* 362); **85b 10** *Le Petit Parisien* (31 October 1897); **87** Alexandre Lacassagne, *Vacher l'éventreur et les crimes sadiques* (1899); **88** BmLyon | numelyo (Ms 7056, f ° 13); **89** BmLyon | numelyo (Ms 4056, f ° 2); **92–93** BmLyon | numelyo (*Le Progres Illustré* 123, 183, 296, 475); **92–93m** Alamy Stock Photo; **94a** La Veuve Guillotine; **94b** La Veuve Guillotine; **94m** Alamy Stock Photo; **95** Alphonse Bertillon, *Album of Paris crime scenes* (1901–08); **95m** Alamy Stock Photo; **96a** Romans Historique; **96b** Execution of Liottard and Berruyer and David, 1909; **97** Execution of Liottard and Berruyer and David, 1909; **98–99** *Le Petit Journal* (1908); **100** Bayerisches Hauptstaatsarchiv; **101** Staatsarchiv München; **102a** King Ludwig II of Bavaria, c. 1874; **102c** Joseph Albert, *Bayerische Königsschlösser, Schloss Berg am Starnberger See* (c. 1886); **102b** Getty Images; **103** Staatsarchiv München; **104a** Bayerisches Hauptstaatsarchiv; **104b** Matthias Kniessl, 1901; **105l, r** Matthias Kniessl, 1901; **105c** Staatsarchiv München; **106a** Adolph Friedrich Kunike, *Die Räuber Grasel, Fähding und Stangel in Ketten*; **106b** Digitalen Bibliothek der Wienbibliothek; **108–10** *Das Interessante Blatt* (1884), Austrian National Library; **111** Alamy Stock Photo; **112** *Das Interessante Blatt* (1889), Austrian National Library; **113l** Max Edelbacher and Harald Seyr, *Wiener Kriminalchronik* (1993); **113r** *Wiener Bilder* (1899), Austrian National Library; **114a** *Vasárnapi Ujsá* (3 June 1883); **114bl** Alamy Stock Photo; **114blc** Fortepan/3286; **114bc** Newspaper image © The British Library Board. All rights reserved. With thanks to The British Newspaper Archive (www.britishnewspaperarchive.co.uk); **114brc** Budapest City Archives; **114br** Adolf Dauthage, *Georg von Majalth junior* (1869); **114m** Budapest City Archives; **115a** Murderpedia; **115bl, blc** Alamy Stock Photo; **115bc, brc, br** Murderpedia; **115m** Budapest City Archives; **116–117m** Budapest City Archives; **118** The Moravian Library in Brno; **118m** Alamy Stock Photo; **119a** Leopold Hilsner, before 1928, Erichs Kriminalarchiv; **119b** Jan Prchal; **120a** Getty Images; **120b** Fototeca Gilardi / agefotostock; **121a** Museo Civico del Risorgimento, Bologna; **121b** Serafino Baraldi – The bandit Spirito – Municipality of Monghidoro (BO); **124** Biblioteca Communale dell'Archiginnasio; **125m** Alamy Stock Photo; **126** 'Il Caso Murri Bonmartini', *Enciclopedia del crimine*, ed. F.lli Fabbri (1974); **126m** Alamy Stock Photo; **127** Getty Images; **128–129** Criminalia; **130a** © The British Library Board. All rights reserved. With thanks to The British Newspaper Archive (www.britishnewspaperarchive.co.uk); **130b, l** Murder by Gaslight; **130r** *Frank Leslie's Illustrated Newspaper* (21 February 1857); **132a** From The New York Public Library, retrieved from http://digitalcollections.nypl.org/items/510d47da-229c-a3d9-e040-e00a18064a99; **132c, b** *Frank Leslie's Illustrated Newspaper* (21 February 1857); **133** *Frank Leslie's Illustrated Newspaper* (21 February 1857); **134–135** Murder by Gaslight; **136a** *New York World* (23 January 1888); **136c** Herbert Asbury, *The Gangs of New York* (1926); **136b** Jacob A. Riis, *The Battle with the Slum* (1902); **137** Jacob A. Riis, *How the Other Half Lives* (1890); **140** © The British Library Board. All rights reserved. With thanks to The British Newspaper Archive (www.britishnewspaperarchive.co.uk); **141** Library of Congress; **142a** Library of Congress; **142c** Courtesy NYC Municipal Archives; **142b** Library of Congress; **143a** Alamy Stock Photo; **143b** Library of Congress; **144–145** Library of Congress; **146a** Portrait of Lizzie Borden, 1890; **146bl** Edwin H. Porter, *The Fall River Tragedy* (1893); **146blc** Getty Images; **146bc, brc** Collection of Fall River Historical Society; **146br** *Frank Leslie's Illustrated Newspaper* (29 June 1893); **147** 92 Second St, Fall River, MA, the home of Lizzie Borden at the time of the murders as it appeared in 1892; **149** Police forensic photographs, 1892, The Burns Archive; **150–152** La Porte County Historical Society; **154–155** Murder by Gaslight; **156a** McCord Museum; **156b** Newspaper image © The British Library Board. All rights reserved. With thanks to The British Newspaper Archive (www.britishnewspaperarchive.co.uk); **157** Newspaper image © The British Library Board. All rights reserved. With thanks to The British Newspaper Archive (www.britishnewspaperarchive.co.uk); **160a** Public domain; **160c** Murderpedia; **160b** *Chicago Tribune* (30 December 1893); **161al** *The Etiology of Osseous Deformities of the Head, Face, Jaws and Teeth* (1894); **160ar** Library of Congress; **160c** Murderpedia; **161b** *Chicago Journal* (13 September 1897), *Chicago Daily News* (4 September 1897); **164a** Dr Henry Howard Holmes, 1895; **164bl** Kilburn, B. W., *The surging sea of humanity at the opening of the Columbian Exposition* (1893); **164br** Frank P. Geyer, *The Holmes-Pitezel case; a history of the greatest crime of the century and of the search for the missing Pitezel children* (1896); **165a** Bentley Image Bank, Bentley Historical Library; **165bl, bc** Frank P. Geyer, *The Holmes-Pitezel case; a history of the greatest crime of the century and of the search for the missing Pitezel children* (1896); **165br** Library of Congress; **168–169b** Frank P. Geyer, *The Holmes-Pitezel case; a history of the greatest crime of the century and of the search for the missing Pitezel children* (1896); **169r** Library of Congress; **170a** Johann Otto Hoch, before 1906; **170c** DN-0003589, Chicago Sun-Times/Chicago Daily News collection, Chicago History Museum; **170b** DN-0001080, Chicago Sun-Times/Chicago Daily News collection, Chicago History Museum; **171l** Getty Images; **171c** DN-0050048, Chicago Sun-Times/Chicago Daily News collection, Chicago History Museum; **171r** Getty Images; **172a, r** Getty Images; **172l** *Chicago Examiner* (11 November 1910) courtesy Chicago Public Library; **174a** Kansas Historical Society; **174–175** Alamy Stock Photo; **175c** Alamy Stock Photo; **175m** Kansas Historical Society; **176–179** Heritage Auctions, HA.com; **180a** John Bender from *The five fiends; or, the Bender hotel horror in Kansas* (1874); **180a** Elvira, John Jr and Kate Bender from *The Benders of Kansas* (1913); **180b** Courtesy of the Historical Cherryvale Museum, Inc.; **181–182** Kansas Historical Society; **184a** Royal E. Towns papers, MS 26, African American Museum and Library at Oakland, Oakland Public Library. Oakland, California; **184c, b** Courtesy of the Society of Californian Pioneers; **185** Library of Congress; **188–189** *Report of the trial of William Henry Theodore Durrant* (1899); **190a** Library of Congress; **190b** Collection at the Campbell Museums; **191** San Jose Public Library, California Room; **192–193** Library of Congress; **194a** © The British Library Board. All rights reserved. With thanks to The British Newspaper Archive (www.britishnewspaperarchive.co.uk); **194b** *The Criminal of the century* (1892); **194l, r** State Library Victoria; **195b, r** National Library of Australia; **195l** State Library Victoria; **196–197** © State of New South Wales through the State Archives and Records Authority of NSW 2016; **196lm** State Library of New South Wales; **196rm** National Library of Australia; **198** © State of New South Wales through the State Archives and Records Authority of NSW 2016; **199m** City of Sydney & Suburbs, 1887 [City of Sydney Archives, CRS1177]; **200** © State of New South Wales through the State Archives and Records Authority of NSW 2016; **201l** Mawbey Family Australia; **201lc** State Library of New South Wales; **201rc** Dixson Library, State Library of New South Wales; **201r** Mitchell Library, State Library of New South Wales; **202–203m** National Library of Australia; **204–5** State Library Victoria; **207** State Library Victoria; **208a** State Library Victoria; **208bl** *The criminal of the century* (1892); **208br** State Library Victoria; **209am** National Library of Australia; **209ar** *The criminal of the century* (1892); **209cm** Copyright The Francis Frith Collection; **209cr** *The criminal of the century* (1892); **209b** State Library Victoria; **210–211** © The British Library Board. All rights reserved. With thanks to The British Newspaper Archive (www.britishnewspaperarchive.co.uk); **212a** © State of New South Wales through the State Archives and Records Authority of NSW 2016; **12m** National Library of Australia; **212b** State Library Victoria; **213** State Library Victoria; **213m** National Library of Australia

INDEX. [A–L]

Illustrations are in **bold**.

A.
abortion 141, 156, 159, 196
acquitted 47, 50, 70, 73, 124, 144, 146, 184
Alaise, Aline **84**, **87**
Album of Paris Crime Scenes (Bertillon) **12–15**, **17**, **72–81**, **95**
Allain, Louis 92
Alubert, Olympe 82–3
Anastay, Louis 70
Anderson, George 151
Angel, Miriam 32
anthropology 10, 126, 161
anthropometrics 66
Archives d'anthropologie criminelle (journal) 13
armour **80**, **207**
artist's impressions 28
Asbury, Herbert 136
atavism 10
Attenborough, David 24
Australia 196–213
Austria 106–13
autopsies 13, 66
Auvergne, France 84–99
Ávila, Dolores 129
axe **146**, 190, 208

B.
baby farming 198, **202–3**, 212
Baday, Marie 82
Bal, Jeanne 78–9
ballads 7, **90–1**, 98–9
ballistics 11, 136
bandits 82, 104, 106, 120–1, **122–3**, 124
Barnum, P.T. 132
Barrowman, Mary 62
Bassot, Henri 95
Bauer, Hugo **110**
Bavaria, Germany 100–5
beating 20, 33, 35, 44, 53, 72, 82, 136
Beaupied, Claudius **85**, **87**
Beer, Marie 78
Ben Ali, Ameer 142–3
Bender family 176–9
Benedikt, Moritz 108
Berchtold, Johann 103
Berecz, János 114
Berruyer, Pierre-Augustin-Louis 96
Bertillonage **12–15**, **17**, **72–81**, **95**
Bertillon, Alphonse 9–10, **11**, **12–15**, **17**, 39, 72, 74, 78
Bicknese, Louisa 161
Biles, Elizabeth 42
Bleak House (Dickens) 22
Bliss, Evelina 144–5
blood types 16
bludgeon 140, 150–51, 154
Bohemia 118–19
Bompard, Gabrielle 66–7
Bond, Thomas 39
Bonetti, Rosina 126
Bonmartini, Count Francesco 126
Borcino, Luciana 129
Borden, Andrew & Abby 146–9
Borden, Lizzie 146–9
Bourgeois, Jeanne-Marie 82
Bow Street runners 50
Brienne, Berthe 76
Briscoe, Robert 190
Brooks, Flora 156
Brown, Carrie 142–3
Bruce, James 196
Budapest, Hungary 114–17
Budsberg, Ole 151
bullets, forensics 13
Burdell, Harvey 132–3
Byrne, John 204
Byrnes, Alonzo 33

C.
Cammarola, Paolo 42
Canter, David 7
Cardozo, Albert 140
Catinot, Augustine 93
Ceneri, Giacomo 124
Ceneri, Pietro 124–5
Chapman, Annie **34**, 35, **38**
Chapman, George 142
Charletty, Josephte 82
Chauffeurs of Drome 96–9
Chicago 154–73
Cigrande, Emeline 165
cities as centres of crime 8
civilization and reduction in crime levels 8
Clarence, Dora 154
Clover, Matilda 156–7
Codebo 72
Cody, Charles 192
Cognevaux, Louis 71
Coles, Frances **35**, 38
Collins, Charles Stockley 16
composite portrait **193**, **28**
Conner, Julia & Pearl 165
Corder, William **6**, 50–1
Cotton, Mary Ann 150
Cream, Thomas Neill 156–9
crime scene
  photography **12–14**, **39**, **64**, **74–7**, **79**, **94–5**, 100, **149**
  plans 16, **22**, **59**, **65**, **72–3**, **76–7**, **78**, 112, **129**, **133**, **147–8**, **166–7**, **173**, **179**, **189**, **199**
crime scene investigation (CSI) 12
criminal investigation, historical milestones 6–12
Criminal Investigation: A Practical Handbook (Gross) 12
Criminal Investigation Department (CID) 9
Criminal Man (Lombroso) 10
Crippen, Cora 16, 46–7
Crippen, Hawley Harvey 16, 46–9
Cripps, Thomas William 42
Crittenden, Alexander 184
Cross, Charles 34
Crozier, Temple Edgecumbe 43
Cunningham, Emma 132–3

D.
dagger 43
Darwin, Charles 10, 13
David, Octave-Louis 96
Davis, John 35
De Balaguer, Higinia Ostalé 129
de Valley, Baroness Herminie 71
death, time since 13
Deeming, Frederick Bailey 208–11
Delhomme, Eugénie 84, **87**
Dellard, Baronness 70
Delorme, Margueritte 93
Denis, M. 75
Depalle, Marie 92
Deray, Célestin 80
detective agencies and departments, development 9
Dew, Walter 46
Dickens, Charles 22
Doležal, Otakar 118
Donworth, Nellie 156
Doyle, Arthur Conan 12–13
Dragoun, František 118
Driscoll, Daniel 136–7
Dumollard, Martin 82–3
Dunham, Hattie 190
Dunham, James C. 190–1
Durrant, William H. T. 188–9
Dwyer, John J. 134

E.
early forensics 114, 188, 24
Eckel, John 132–3
Eddowes, Catherine 'Kate' **34**, 38, **39**

Ellis, John 47
emotion readings **145**
executions 6, **23**, **25**, **51**, **96–7**, **128**
Eyraud, Michel 66–7

F.
Fähding, Jakob 106–7
Fair, Laura 184
Fanning, Andrew 141
Farmer, Harriet 43
Farrow, Thomas and Ann 16, 44
Faulds, Henry 13
Feoli, Raffaele 124
Ferensi, Rosa 108, **109**, **110**
Finger Prints (Galton) 16
fingerprints 13–14, 44, **172**
Fitzpatrick, Kieran 200
Flannagan, Catherine 52
Flannagan, John 52
Fleming, Mary Livingston 144–5
forensics, development 9–10, 12–16, 103
Forquet, Emile 85
Foucherand, Thérèse 94
Fougère, Eugénie 95
France
  Auvergne 84–99
  Paris 9, 66–81
  policing and detection development 9
Franks, Wilfred Moritz 43
Fuller, Nora 192–3
Furuseth, Andrew 185

G.
Galletly, George 33
Galton, Francis 13–16
gangs 33, 96–9, 136–7, **138–9**, 180, 204–7
The Gangs of New York (Asbury) 136
Gänswürger, Eduard 100, **101**
Garrity, Bridget 136
garrote 128, 129
Gaumet, Annet 94
Gay, Anthelme 78–9
Geppert, George 180
Germany, Bavaria 100–5
Geyer, Frank P. 165
ghosts 50
Gilchrist, Marion **16**, 62
Giriat, Victorine 95
Glasgow, Scotland 58–65
Gold, Isaac Frederick 28
Goodwin, Annie 141
Goron, Marie-François 66
Gouffé, Toussaint-Augustin 66–7
Governor, Jimmy & Joe 200–1
Gowen, Hames 20
Gradl, Maria 103
Graham, Madge 192
graphology 192
Grant, Hugh 192
Grázl, Jan Jiří 106–7
Grenetier, Victor 92
Greuling, Frederick 77
Gross, Hans 12
Gruber, Franz-Xaver 100
Gudden, Bernhard von 102
Guérin, Mme. 75
guillotine 66, 70, 80, 82, 83, 85, 89, 94, 96–7, 121
Gump, Ferdinand 100–1
gun 100, 104, 120–1, 124, 139, 190, 204
  pistol 22–3, 93, 108, 92, 50, 134–5, 136, 154–5, 184, 172
  revolver 70, 77, 160, 180, **181**
  shotgun **155**
Gunness, Belle 150–3
Gunness, Peter 150
gunpowder 185
guns, forensics 13
Gurholdt, Henry 151

H.
Hadley, Charles B. 192–3
Hamard, M. 95
hammer 62, **63**, **176**
handprints **144**
hanging 6, 7, 16, 20, 22, 23, 24, 25, 28, 32, 40, 44, 47, 50, 52, 54, 58, 62, 106, 208, 112, 113, 114, 136, 146, 155, 157, 159, 160, 165, 166, 172, 180, 196, 200, 204, 208, 209, 213
Harrison, Carter Henry 160
Harrison, Gus 155
Hart, Steve 204
Helgelein, Andrew 151
Herschel, William 13
Hess, Susie 155
Higgins, Margaret 52
Higgins, Mary 52
Higgins, Thomas 52
Hiller, Clarence B. 172
Hilsner, Leopold 119
Hoch, Johann Otto 170–1
Hochsmann, Emilie **108**
Hofer, Franciska 112
Hogg, Frank 40
Hogg, Phoebe 40
Hogg, Tiggy 40
Holmes, Henry Howard 164–9
Hrůzová, Anežka 119
Hugo, Victor 82
Hungary 114–17
Hutton, Susannah 53

I.
identification
  artist's impressions 28
  early developments 9–10, **11**, **17**
  post-mortems 66
  identity parade 62
Illustrated Police News **25**, **30–1**, **38–9**, **40**, **52–3**, **55**
imprisoned 8, 33, 42, 53, 82, 93, 103, 104, 105, 124, 142, 156, 159, 165, 199, 208
informants 9
investigating officers (IOs) 12
Italy 120–7

J.
Jack the Ripper 7, 16, 34–9, 112, 142, 157, **208**
Jakubec, Mrs 115
James, Marie 208
Jaurès, Jean 80
Jennings, Margaret 52
Jennings, Thomas 172–3
Jewell, Margaret 20
Jones, Thomas H. 134
Juncken, Herman 213

K.
Kelly, Mary Jane **34**, 38, 39
Kelly, Ned 204–7
Kelly, William 140
Kerz, Helen 200
Ketterl, Theresia 108, **109**, **110**
Kiesgen 71
Kinsley, Patrick 154
Kiss, Béla 115
Klimová, Marie 119
Klosowski, Severin 142
Kniessl, Mathias 104–5
knife **1**, 33–4, 42, 44, 70–1, 73, **80**, 84, 88, 92–3, 112, 118–9, 126, 129, 132, **142**, 176, **177**, 188, 208
Knorr, Frances 212
Krafft-Ebing, Richard von 112
Kříž, Josef 118
Kufer, Margarethe 100

L.
Lacassagne, Alexandre 13, 66, 85–7, 93, 94
Ladermann, Cesar 95

INDEX. [M–Z]

Lafuente, José 128
Lagneny, Fernard 71
Lamarque, Jean 96
Lamont, Blanche 188–9
Lamphere, Ray 150
Lamprand, Lucie 92
L'Angelier, Emile 58–9
Lassimonne, Yvonne 70
Laurent, Pierre **85, 87**
Le Brun, Charles **8**
Le Neve, Ethel 46–7
Lebassac, Mme. 75
Lee, Elizabeth 33
Lee, Emily 33
Lenin, Vladimir 80
Les Misérables (Hugo) 82
Liabeuf, Jean-Jacques 80–1
Lidl, Jakob 102
Lindboe, Thomas 151
Lindbloom, Olaf 151
Liottard, Urban-Célestin 96
Lipski, Israel 32
'Lisson Grove Lads' 33
Liverpool, England 54–5
Lloyd, Eva 154
Locard, Edmond 12–13
Lombroso, Cesare 10, 126, **145**
London
    Bermondsey 22–3
    Camden 46–7
    Deptford 44
    Holborn 43
    maps **26–7, 56–7, 159**
    Marylebone 33
    Notting Hill 42
    policing and detection
        development 8–9
    Richmond 24–5
    Rotherhithe 42
    Swiss Cottage 40–1
    Vauxhall 52–3, **56–7**
    Wapping 20–1
    Whitechapel 32, 34–9, 43
Lonigan, Thomas 204
Lortet, Prof. 94
Ludwig II of Bavaria 100
Luetgert, Adolph 161
Luff, Arthur P. 47
Lusk, George 38
Lyons, Dan 136

M.
McCarthy, John 136
McGarry, Philip 53
McGlincy, Richard & Ada 190
McGonigal, Dr H. G. 141
McGrain, Elizabeth 60
McKay, Alexander 200
McKenzie, Alice **35**, 38
McLeod, Mary 60–1
Macnaghten, Melville 16, 44
Madame Tussauds 24, 33
Madrid, Spain 128–9
Mahnken, Diedrich 134
Maire, Lucie 95
Majláth, György von 114
Makin, John & Sarah 198–9
Malcolm, Sarah 24
manhunt 78, 94, 100, 104, 180–1,
    200
Manning, Frederick & Maria 22–3
Manouvrier, Léonce **10**
Mapleton, Percy Lefroy 28–31
maps
    Budapest **116–17**
    France **68–9, 90–1**
    Italy **122–3**
    London **26–7, 56–7, 159**
    USA **138–9, 159**
Marcel, Louise 84, **87**
Marina, Antonio & Clara 128
Mariotti, François 93
Mariotti, Mme. 93
Marr, Timothy and wife 20–1
Marsh, Alice 156

Marten, Maria 50–1
Martin, Paul Jules 76
Martinet, Marie-Anne 82–3
Marwood, William 28
Masaryk, Tomáš 119
mass killings 174–5, 185, 190, 200
Massot-Pellet, Pierre **85, 87**
Mather, Emily 208
maul **20**
Mawbey, John & Sarah 200–1
Maybrick, Florence 54–5
Maybrick, James 54–5
Mazzini, Maria 124
Meignen, Albert 75
Melville, Herman 22
Mercier, Hélène 74
Metropolitan Police Service
    8–9, 13
Minnoch, William 58
Minter, Mary 142
Moe, John 151
Morand, Mme. 84, **87**
Morrot, Jules 78–9
mortuary photography **142**, 39,
    72–3, 83
Mortureux, Adèle 84, **87**
Moussier, Marie **85, 87**
Mrva, Rudolf 118
mug shots 10, **17, 81, 118, 136, 189,**
    197–8
Murray, Horace 198
Murri, Linda 126
Murri, Tullio 126–7

N.
Naldi, Pio 126
Nathan, Benjamin 140
Needle, Martha 213
Neil, John 34
New York 9, 132–45
newspapers 7, 84
Newton Brown, Henry 180–3
Nicholls, Jessie Amelia 196
Nichols, Mary Ann 'Polly' 34–5, **38**
Nouguier, Evariste 94

O.
O'Brien, Daniel 196
O'Brien, Elizabeth 200
O'Brien, Isabella 196
O'Connor, Patrick 22–3

P.
Page, Ethel 200
Pagès, Victor 78–9
palmistry **144**
Papillon (Charrière) 96
parasitology 94
Paris 9, 66–81
parish watch 20
Parry, Lewis 53
pathology 47, 66, 93, 94
Paul, Robert 34
Payne, E.W. 180
Pearcey, Mary 40–1
Pelloni, Stefano 120
Pepper, Augustus Joseph 47
Perrin, Victorine 82
Peterson, John 20
Pettus, Stephen L. 135
photography 10
phrenology **9**
physiognomy **8**, 10, **11, 17, 23,** 126,
    145
Pichon, Marie 82
Pierson, Célestin-Nicolas 78–9
Piette, Marie 73
Pillot 72
'Pinchin Street Torso' **35**
Pitéli, Mihály Oláh 114
Pitezel, Benjamin 164–5, **169**
Podpera, Franz **110**
poison 6, 7, 9, 32, 46, 50, 52, 54,
    55, 58, 60, 115, 134, 146, 150–1,
    156–7, 167, 170, 204, 205, 213

antimony 60
antimony, effects of **60**
arsenic 7, 52, 144, 170, 54, 213,
    58
nitric acid **32**
poker 40
policing, early professional
    development 8–9
Popescu, Elene **15**, 77
Portalier, Victor 85, **87**
positivism 10
post-mortems 13, 66
Prague, Bohemia 118–19
Prainville, Mme. 78
Prendergast, Patrick E. 160
Pritchard, Edward W. 60–1
Pritchard, Mary Jane 60–1
profiling 12, 39
Prosperi, Gaetano 121
Psychopathia Sexualis
    (Krafft-Ebing) 112

Q.
Quantrill, William C. 174–5

R.
radiotelgraphy 46–7
Ratcliffe Highway murders 16,
    20–1
Reigh, Sadie 154
Reymond, Claire 70
Richetto, Luigi Giovanni 93
Riis, Jacob **137**
Robardet, M. 95
Rodier, Rosine **85, 87**
Rollet, Etienne 66
Roos, Julie von 103
Roos, Karoline von 103
Roughland, William 62
Rumbold, Joseph 33
Ruppert, Marie 71
rural areas, case resolution
    levels 8
Ryan, Charles 155

S.
Schaeble, George 190
Scheffer, Paul 75
Schenk, Hugo 108–11
Schenk, Karl 108
Schlossarek, Karl 108, **110**
Schosteritz, Simon 112–13
Scotti di Carlo, Andrea 42
Secchi, Carlo 126
Secor, George 134
Shaw, Fannie 141
Sheridan, Thomas Meredith
    196–7
Sherlock Holmes 12–13
Shesler, Minnie 190
Shippy, George 170
Shrivell, Emma 156
Siegler, Herman 155
Siels, Caroline 155
Slater, Oscar 62–5
Smith, Emma Elizabeth **35**
Smith, Henry 157
Smith, Madeleine 58–9
Smith, William 176
Sondaz, Giacomo 121
Sorensen, Mads 150
Southworth, Hannah Martin 135
souvenirs 6, 7, **23**, 50, **96–7**
Spain 128–9
Spanga, Pál 114
Spilka, Anna 112
Spilsbury, Bernard 47
Stangel, Ignaz 106–7
Stanton, Bridget 52
Stead, William 32
Stebbing, Walter 53
Steffens, Diedrich 134
Stephen, Fitzjames 54, **55**
Stott, Daniel 156
strangulation 24, 66, 67, **71**, 74–8,

87, 94–5, 102–3, 114–5, 119, 128,
    132, 142–43, 188, 192
Stratton, Albert & Alfred 16,
    44–5
Stride, Elizabeth **34**, 35–8, **39**
Styles, Phoebe 40
suffocation 43
Suffolk England 50–1
suicides 20, 84, 155, 184, 192, 204
Sutcliffe, Peter 7
Svenherud, Olaf 151
Swanson, Donald 28
sword 106

T.
Tabram, Martha 35, **35**
Taylor, Jane 60–1
Thiboef, Henri 73
Thomas, Julia Martha 24
Thompson, Jane 42
Timal, Josefine 108, **109, 110**
Timal, Katharina 108, **110**
Toth, Margaret **115**
tomahawk 20
'Tottenham Court Road Lads' 33
toxicology 32, 52, 54, 58, 60, 129,
    144, 170
trains 28
Traphagen, Sadie 141
Truel 71
Turner, John 20
Tusseau, Victoire 73
Tyrell, John 185

U.
Uhlenhuth, Paul 16
Underwood, Jack 200
unknown murderers 43, 74, 102,
    140, 185, **186–7**
unknown victims 72
USA
    Boston 9
    Chicago 154–5
    Indiana 150–3
    Kansas 174–83
    Massachusetts 146–9
    New York 132–45
    policing and detection
        development 9
    San Francisco 184–93

V.
Vacher, Joseph 13, 84–9
Van Noorweghe, Paul 75
Van Tassel, Edna 165
Varela, José Vázquez 129
Varga, Katherine **115**
Victor Emmanuel III 126
Vidocq, Eugène-François 9
Vienna, Austria 106–13

W.
Walcker, Marie 170–1
wanted posters **28**
Webster, Kate 24–5
Wells, James 190
Wheeler, Ben 176
Whittaker, Frank 155
Whyos gang 136–7
Willcox, William 47
Williams, John 20–1
Williams, Minnie 188–9
Williams, Minnie & Nannie 165
Williamson, John and Elizabeth
    20
wives murdered by husbands,
    Chicago **162–3**
women killed by women, London
    26–7
Wood, Thomas McKinnon 62

Y.
York, William Henry 176
Young, Mrs 135
Young, Thomas 135

ACKNOWLEDGMENTS.

This has been a collaborative project and so I would like to acknowledge and thank the team at Thames & Hudson for their creative input and their faith in me. Writing is often a lonely process but this has been enlivened by Tristan de Lancey and his team. Particular thanks are due to Isabel Jessop for her amazing ability to dig up long-forgotten murderers from across the globe! I would also like to thank my wife, Dru, who has had to listen to these grim stories of man's (and woman's) inhumanity over tea and biscuits at length. I hope it was worth it.

ABOUT THE AUTHOR.

Dr. Drew Gray is a social historian of the 18th and 19th centuries, specializing in the history of crime and punishment. He has written extensively on this subject, and is the author of 'The Police Magistrate', a daily blog deciphering Victorian crime. He is a member of the editorial board of *The London Journal* and a fellow of the Royal Historical Society. At the University of Northampton he teaches on both the History and Criminology programmes, and is subject lead for History.

Right. A DISMEMBERED CADAVER IS REASSEMBLED BEFORE IT IS PHOTOGRAPHED IN THE MORGUE; TAKEN FROM ALPHONSE BERTILLON'S *ALBUM OF PARIS CRIME SCENES* (1901–08).

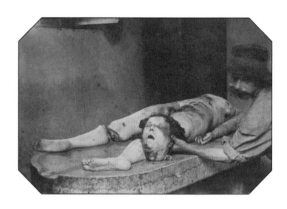

with 730 illustrations

Page 2. POLICE PHOTOGRAPH OF THE SHOVEL USED BY SERIAL KILLER H. H. HOLMES TO BURY THE BODIES OF ALICE AND NELLIE PITEZEL IN TORONTO.

Page 4. A PLASTER CAST OF FREDERICK BAILEY DEEMING'S RIGHT HAND, ON DISPLAY WITH HIS DEATH MASK IN THE OLD MELBOURNE GAOL, MELBOURNE.

Cover. THE CADAVER OF VICTOIRE TUSSEAU, FROM ALPHONSE BERTILLON, *ALBUM OF PARIS CRIME SCENES* (1901–08). © 2020. IMAGE COPYRIGHT THE METROPOLITAN MUSEUM OF ART/ ART RESOURCE/SCALA,FLORENCE.

Front. CENTRE TOWNSHIP MAP, LAPORTE COUNTY, INDIANA, MORGAN. DAVID RUMSEY MAP COLLECTION, WWW. DAVIDRUMSEY.COM.

Back, above left. THE CADAVER OF VICTOIRE TUSSEAU, FROM ALPHONSE BERTILLON, *ALBUM OF PARIS CRIME SCENES* (1901–08).
Back, above right. JOSEPH VACHER, BIBLIOTHEQUE DE LA VILLE DE LYON.
Back, below. THE CADAVER OF WIDOW BAL, FROM ALPHONSE BERTILLON, *ALBUM OF PARIS CRIME SCENES* (1901–08).

First published in the United Kingdom in 2020 by Thames & Hudson Ltd, 181A High Holborn, London WC1V 7QX

First published in the United States of America in 2020 by Thames & Hudson Inc. 500 Fifth Avenue, New York, New York, 10110

Murder Maps © 2020 Thames & Hudson Ltd, London

Text © 2020 Drew Gray

For image copyright information, see p.221

Designed by Anıl Aykan at Barnbrook

Map and floor plan illustrations by Adrian Cartwright at Planet Illustration

British Library Cataloguing-in-Publication Data
A catalogue record for this book is available from the British Library

Library of Congress Control Number 2020933570

ISBN 978-0-500-25245-1

Printed and bound in China by C&C Offset Printing Co. Ltd